PATHWAYS IN TIME

PHOTO JOURNEYS

Pathways in Time: Photo Journeys
ISBN-10: 1-941184-14-6
ISBN-13: 978-1-941184-14-1

© February 2017 Fletcher & Co. Publishers LLC.
All photography © Noël Fletcher (unless otherwise attributed).

Cover and graphic design by Zita Steele.
Front and back cover photo by Noël Fletcher.

All rights reserved. No part of this publication may be reproduced, distributed, or transmitted in any form or by any means, including photocopying, recording, or other electronic or mechanical methods, without the prior written permission of the publisher, except in the case of brief quotations embodied in critical reviews and certain other noncommercial uses permitted by copyright law. For permission requests,
see: www.fletcherpublishers.com.

Cataloging-in-Publication data for this book is available from the Library of Congress.

Library of Congress Catalog Number: 2017901970

Fletcher & Co. Publishers LLC
www.fletcherpublishers.com

First Edition
Printed in the United States of America

PATHWAYS IN TIME

PHOTO JOURNEYS

by

Noël Fletcher

Fletcher & Co. Publishers
www.fletcherpublishers.com

Inside:

My pathways →→▷→ 8

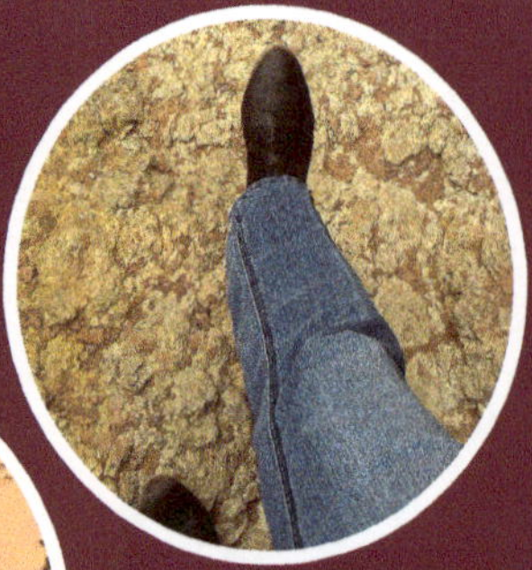

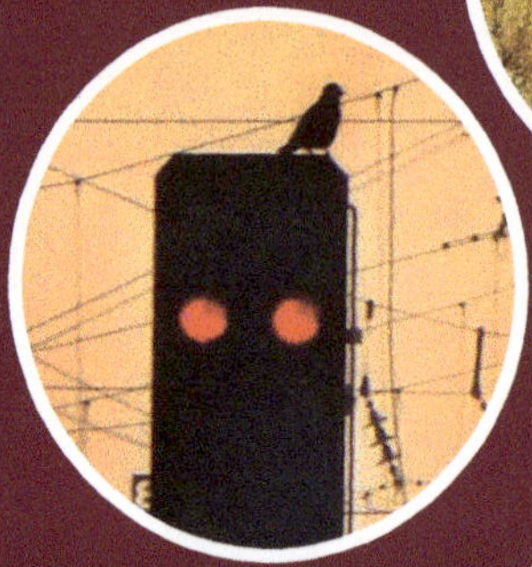

Chapter 1: City birds → 9

Chapter 2: Architecture ▷→▷→ 41

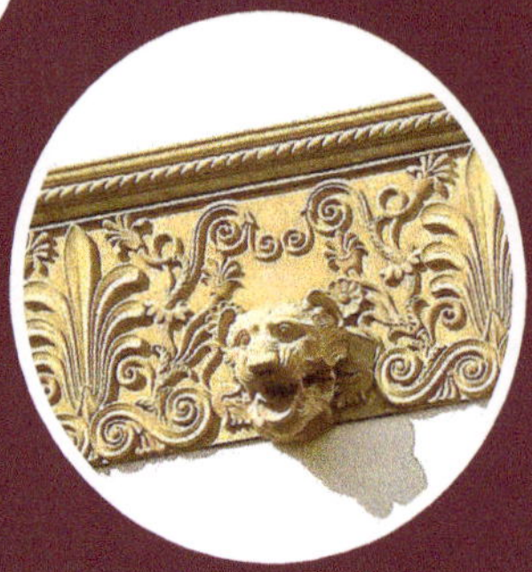

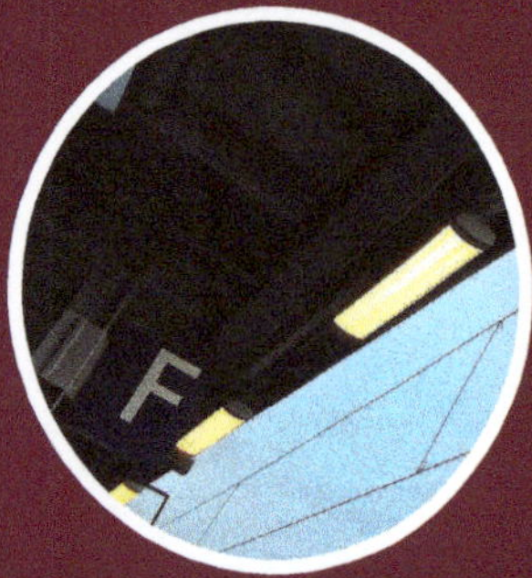

52 ◁←Chapter 3: Urban places

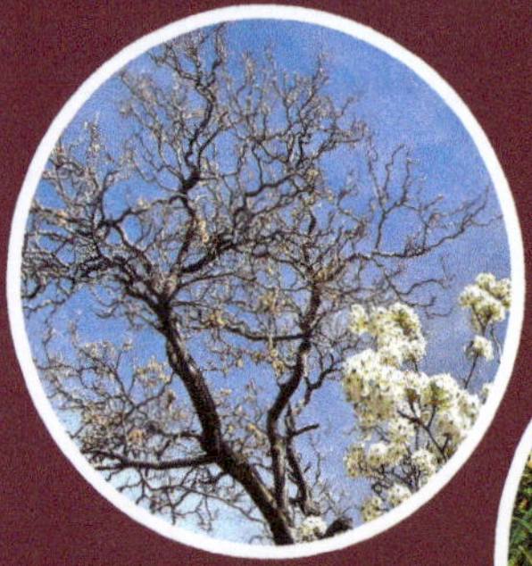

61 ←←←◁← Chapter 4: Trees

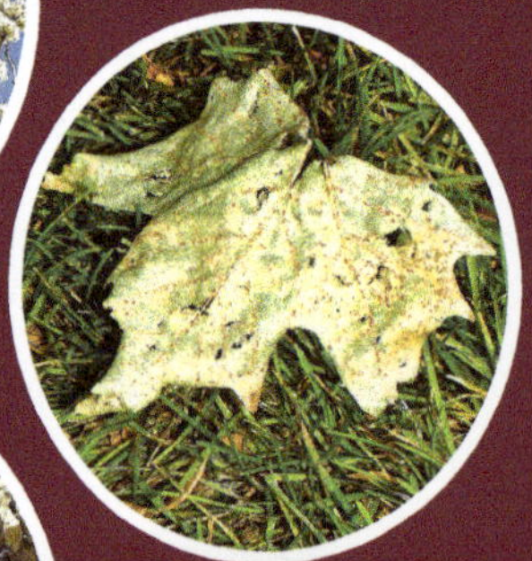

72 ←Chapter 5: Leaves

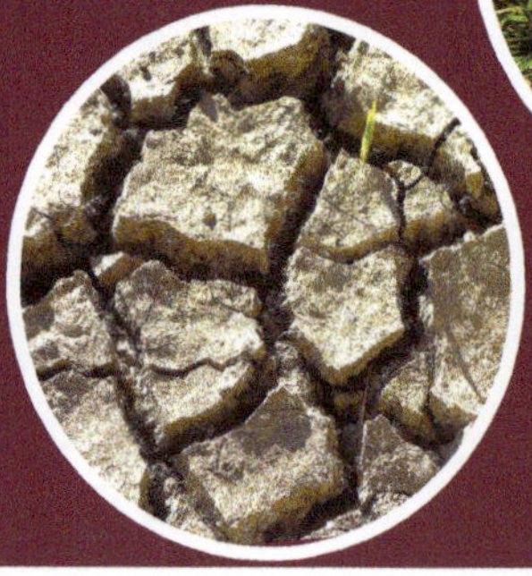

78 ←←◁←◁←← Chapter 6: Earth

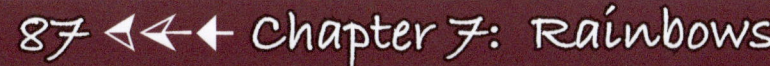
87 ◄◄← Chapter 7: Rainbows

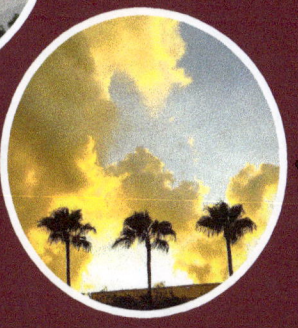
92 ◄ Chapter 8: Sunsets

Chapter 9: Night ➢➢➤ 103
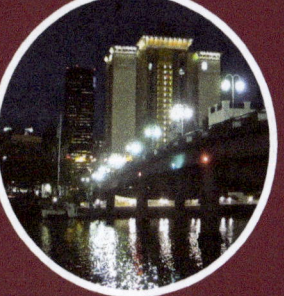

Chapter 10: Patterns ➤➤ 116
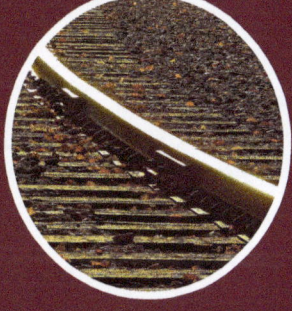

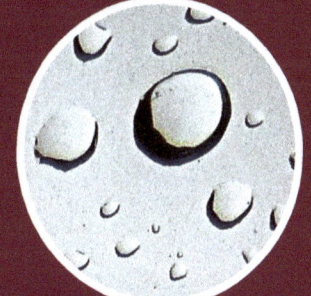
132 ◅◅◅← Chapter 11: Rain

Me ➢➤➢ 148
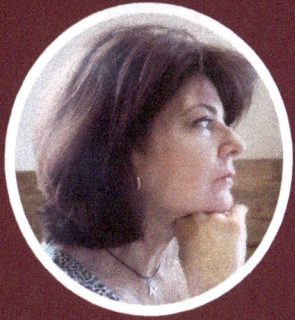

Foreword by Zita Steele

As both an author and a daughter, I am grateful to have the opportunity to write this Foreword to "*Pathways in Time: Photo Journeys*" by my mother Noël Fletcher.

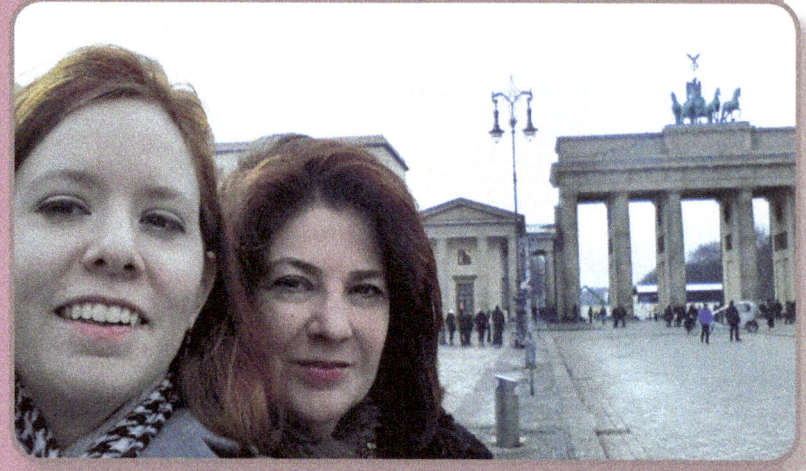

Zita and Noël in Berlin in 2017.

I was present when many of these photographs were taken. These photographs exemplify my mother's artistic eye and her ability to appreciate beauty in all forms of life, and also to compose abstract expressions from seemingly ordinary subject matter.

The photos contained here are but a small portion of my mother's work as a photographer.

Over many years, she has created diverse arrays of unique and thought-provoking pictures.

Although the subject matter of her images varies,

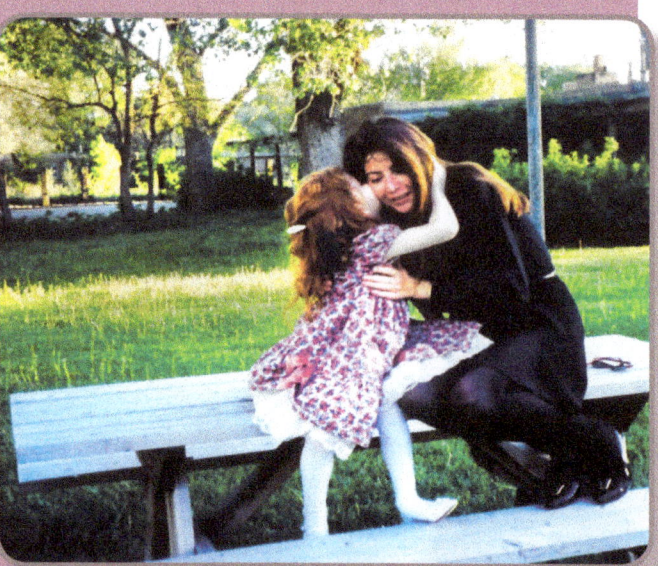

Zita at 4 years old with Noël.

the common characteristics that define my mother's photography are her sincerity, skill and creative spirit.

I am also grateful to my mother for sharing her photography with me. Her vast knowledge of visual art, and her willingness to teach me about diverse types and techniques, have enabled me to improve my own artistic abilities and develop my own style.

More importantly, her optimism and her never-failing gift to perceive goodness and beauty in the world helped me to grow not only as an artist, but as a person.

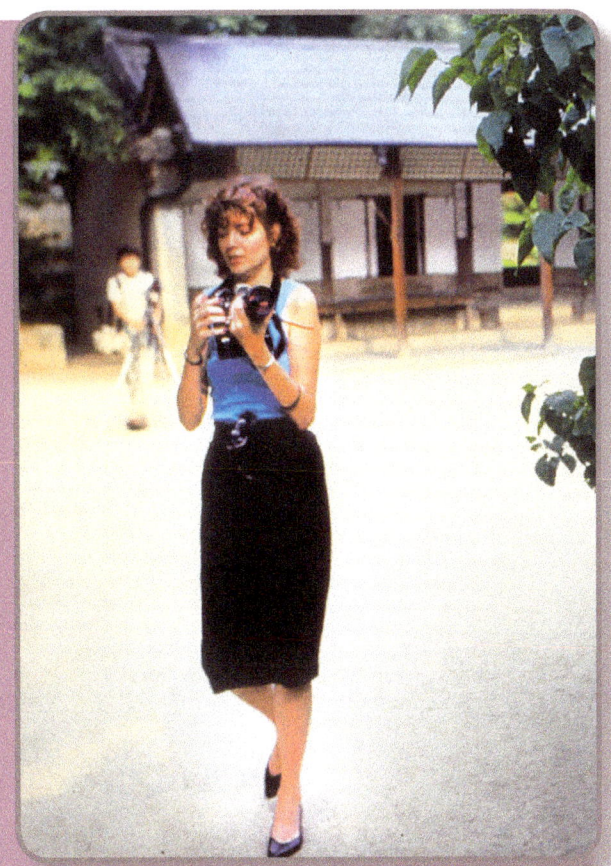

Noël, working as a journalist in Asia, takes photos in Jeju-do, South Korea.

My pathways

What sets my photos in this book apart from other similar works is that all these images were taken during my daily life. No big glitzy photo shoots. No big camera. No heavy bag with lots of lenses. No tripod.

Just me with my camera in my purse or in my pocket. My camera came with me on walks, shopping for groceries, driving around town, taking the dog for a stroll, waiting in the car, running errands, and venturing out to restaurants, events, museums, or historical sites.

I photographed things I thought were beautiful, funny, ironic, spectacular, sad, interesting...

I suppose you could say these images present a glimpse of the world around me during the last 5 years as well as moments in time for the creatures and nature sharing the same space as me. So I invite you in the following pages to journey into my recent world and along my pathways.

Looking out a window of a former Catholic church in Corrales, New Mexico. The church had a special place in the hearts of my Perea family for generations. One relative was buried under the floor in the 1800s and still rests there although the ground is no longer consecrated.

Pathways in Time: Photo Journeys

Chapter 1: City birds

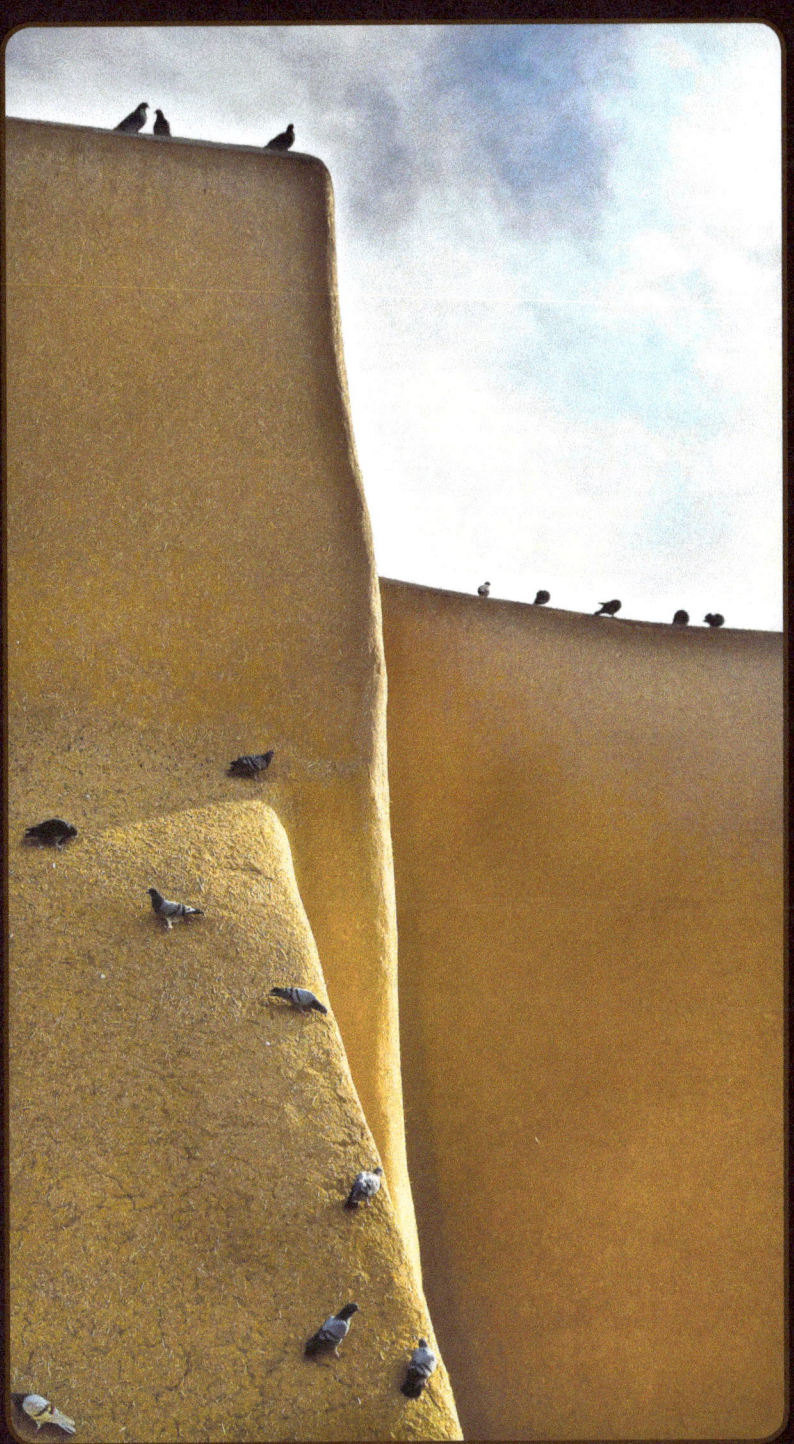

Pigeons search for straw to pluck out of the adobe plaster on a church in New Mexico.

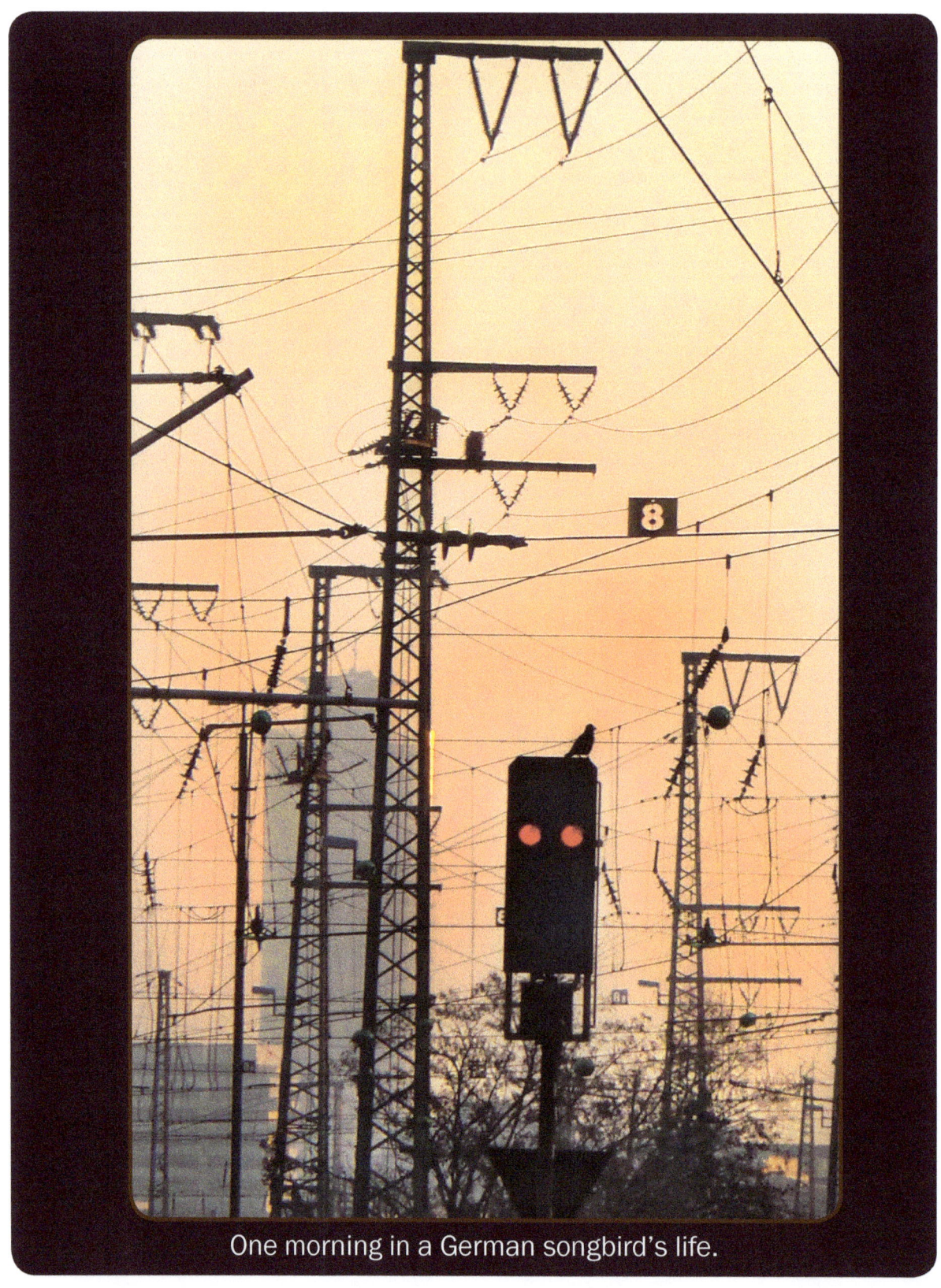

One morning in a German songbird's life.

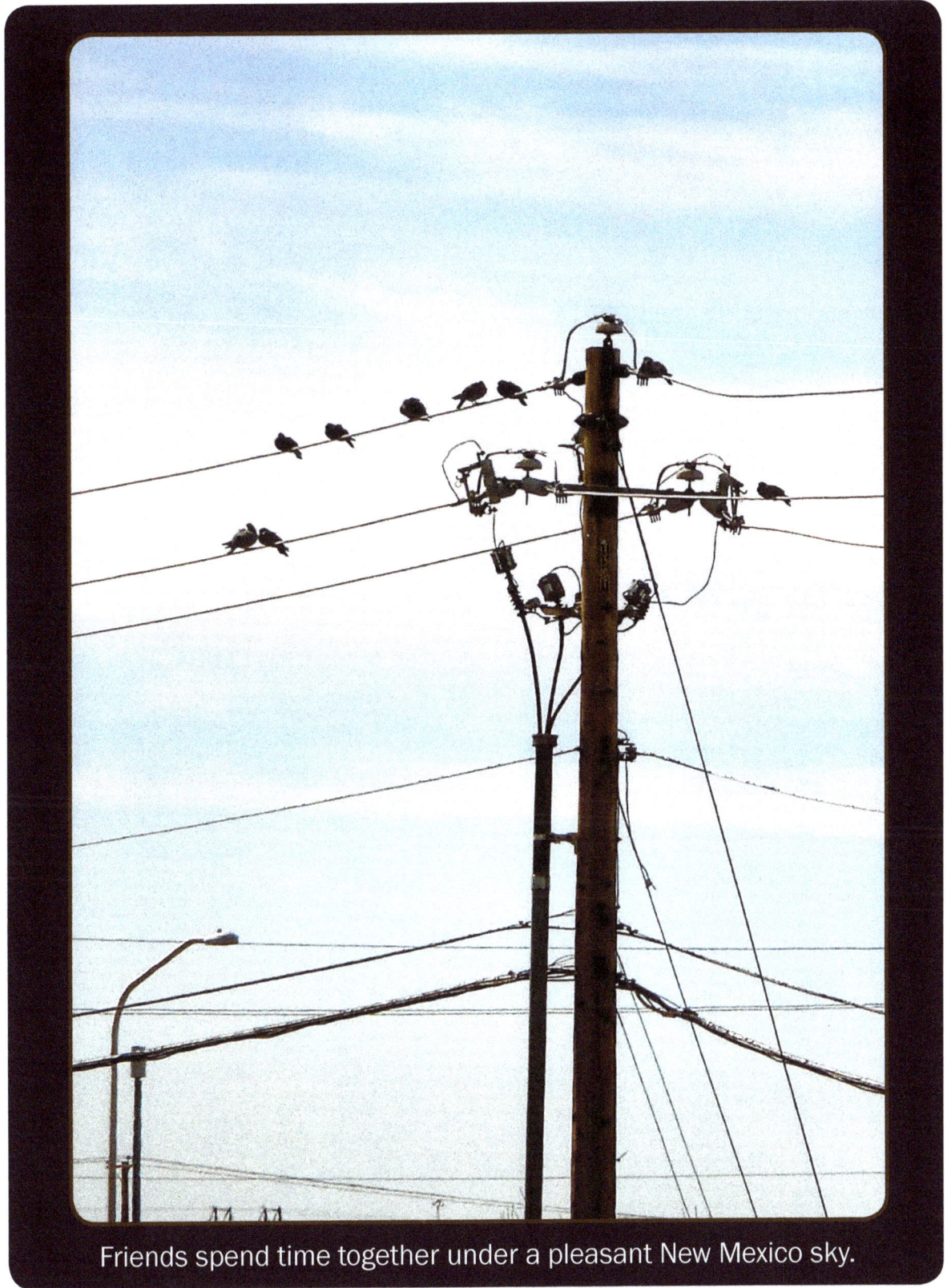
Friends spend time together under a pleasant New Mexico sky.

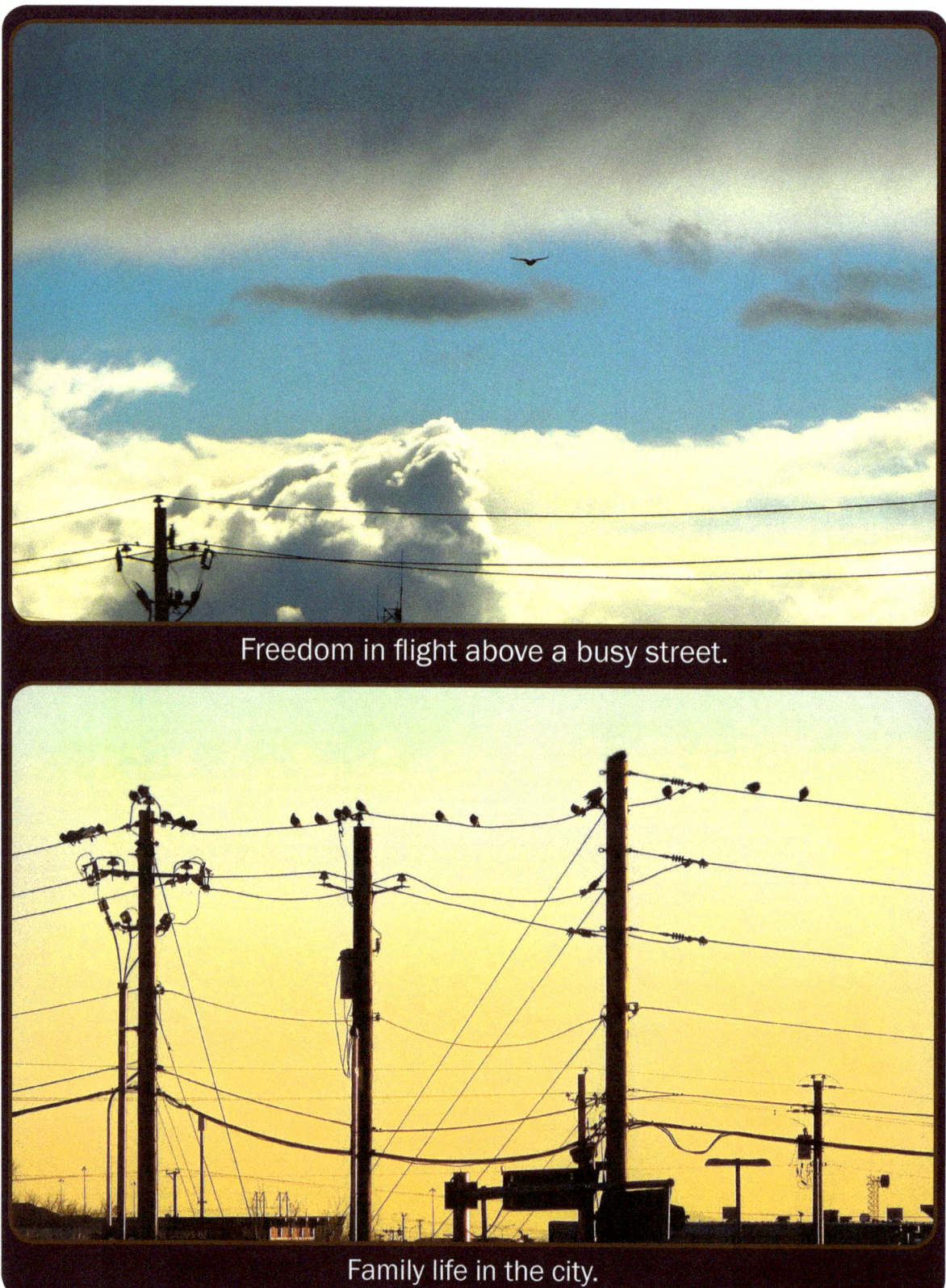

Freedom in flight above a busy street.

Family life in the city.

• Pathways in Time: Photo Journeys • 13

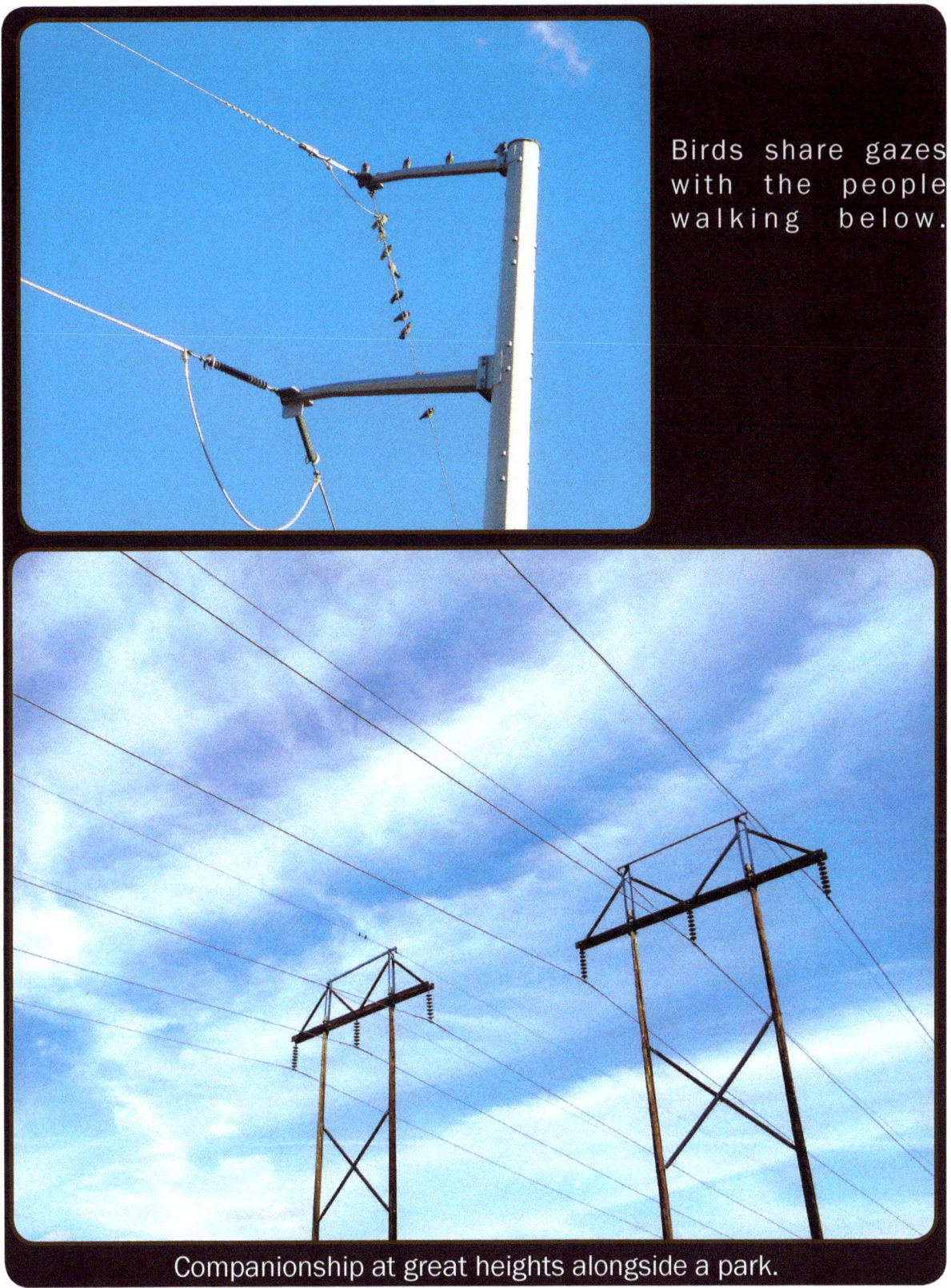

Birds share gazes with the people walking below.

Companionship at great heights alongside a park.

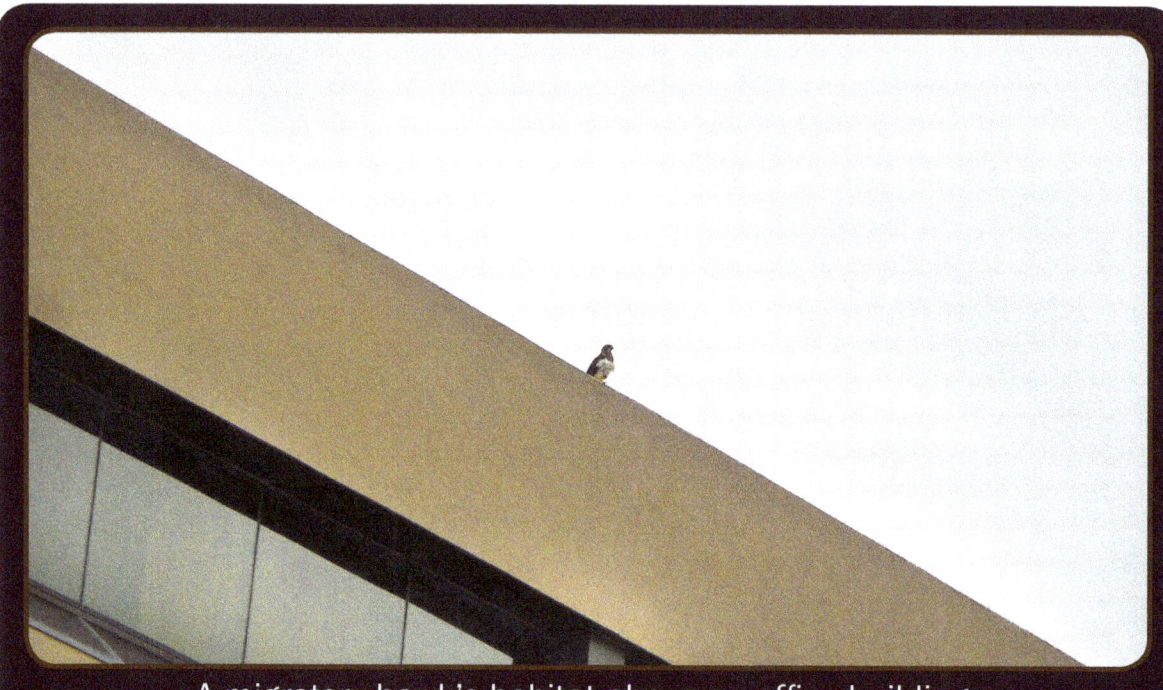
A migratory hawk's habitat above an office building.

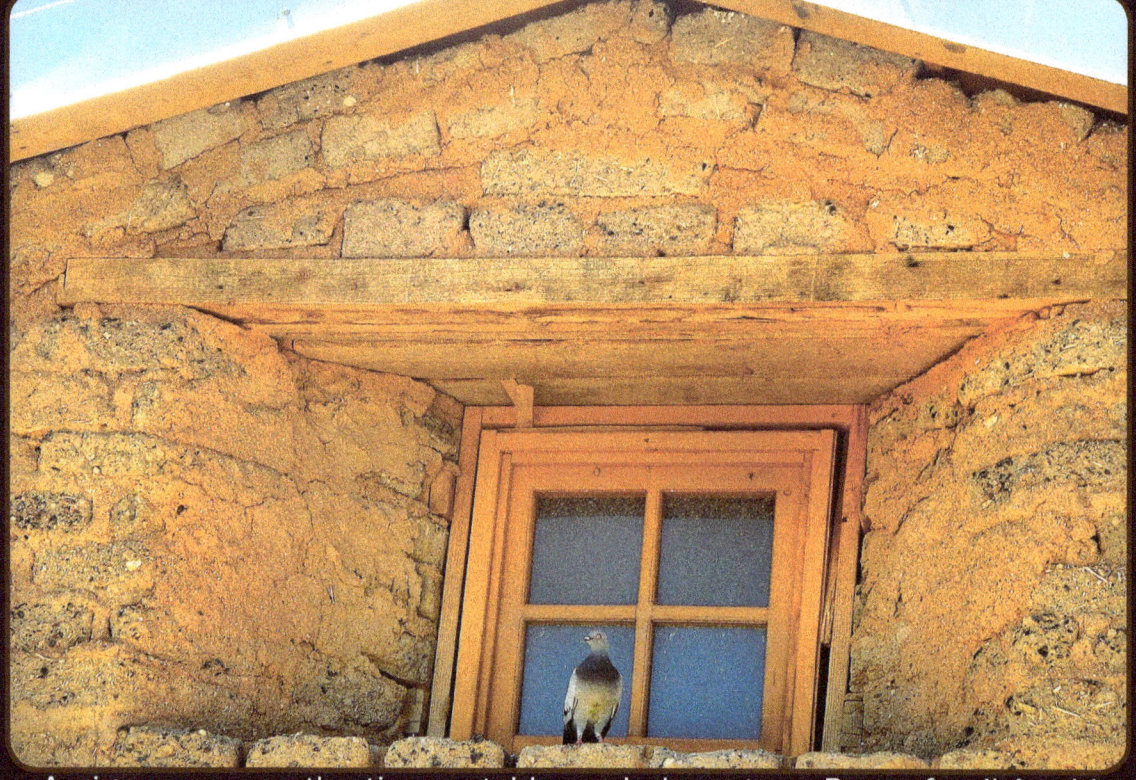
A pigeon passes the time outside a window at my Perea family's old flour mill in Bernalillo, New Mexico.

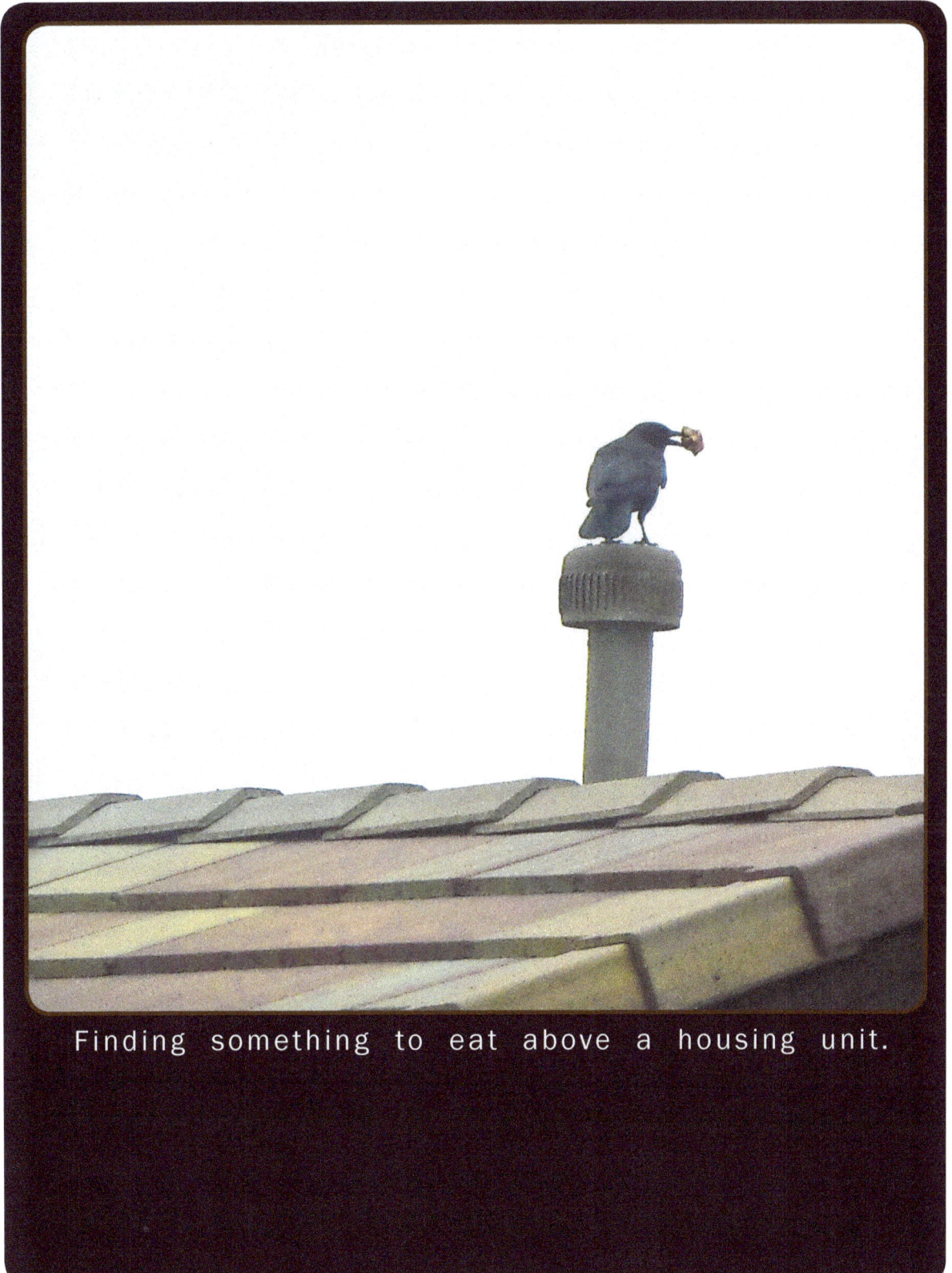
Finding something to eat above a housing unit.

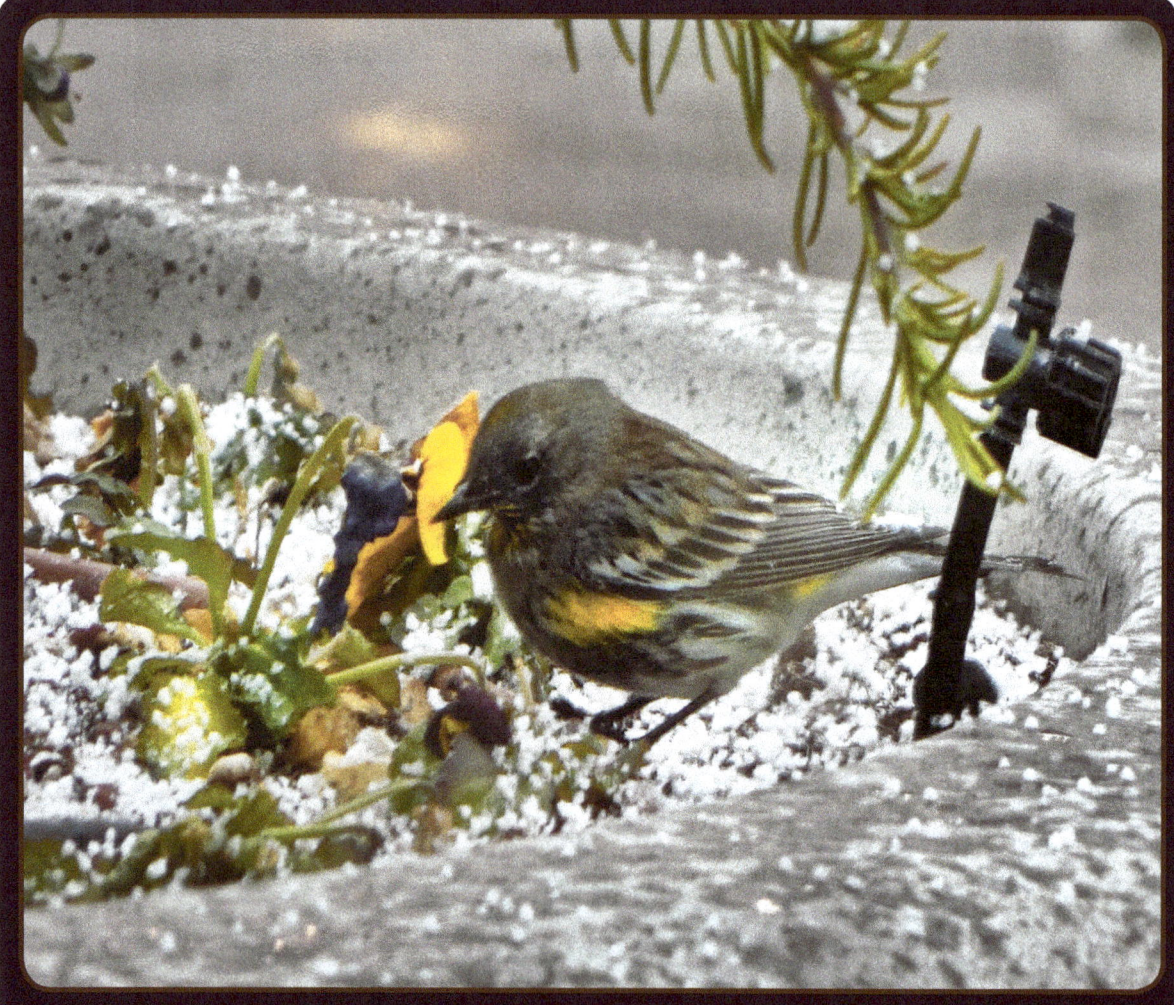

A songbird perches on a cold flower planter in a shopping center after a January snowstorm.

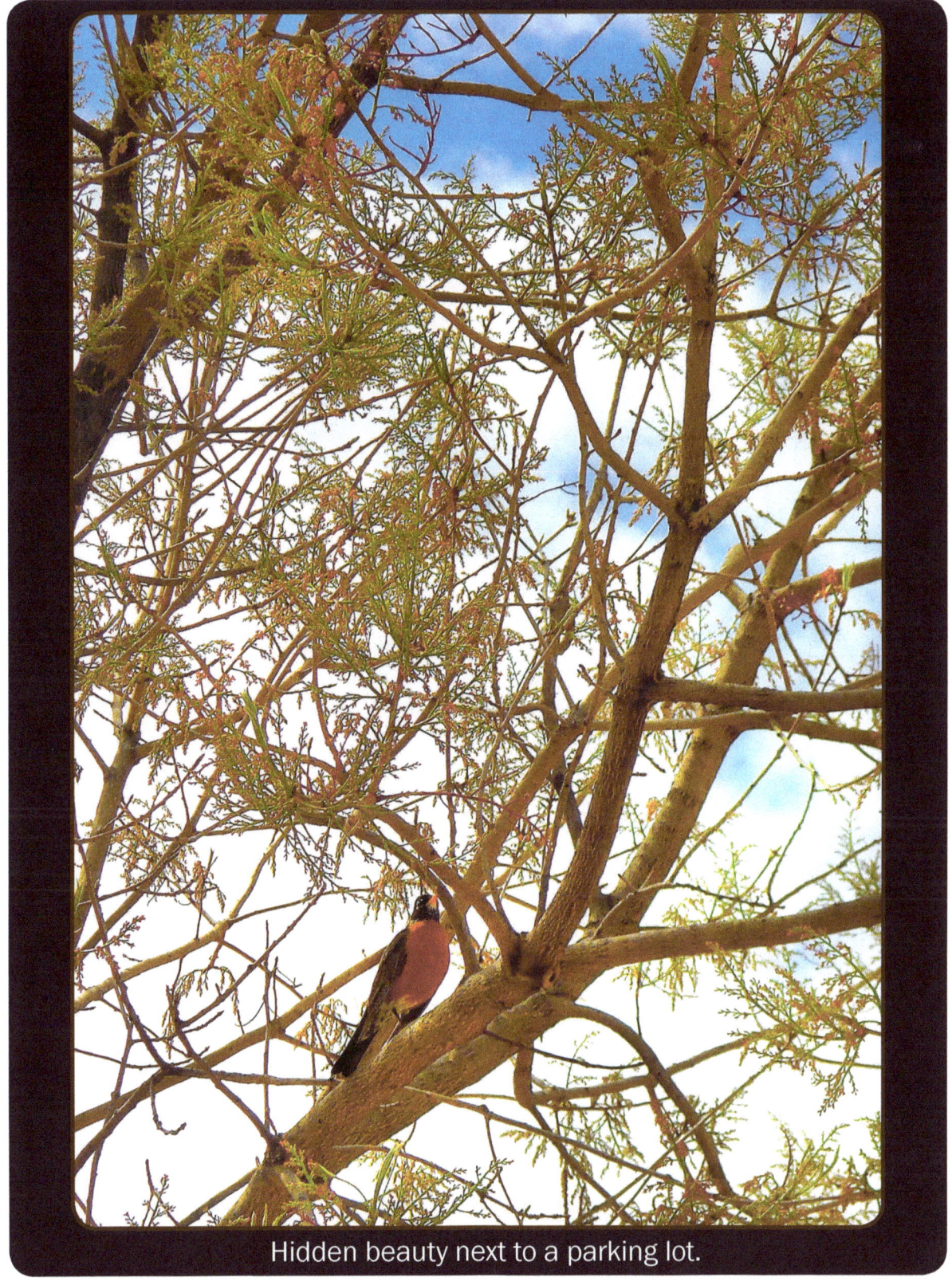

Hidden beauty next to a parking lot.

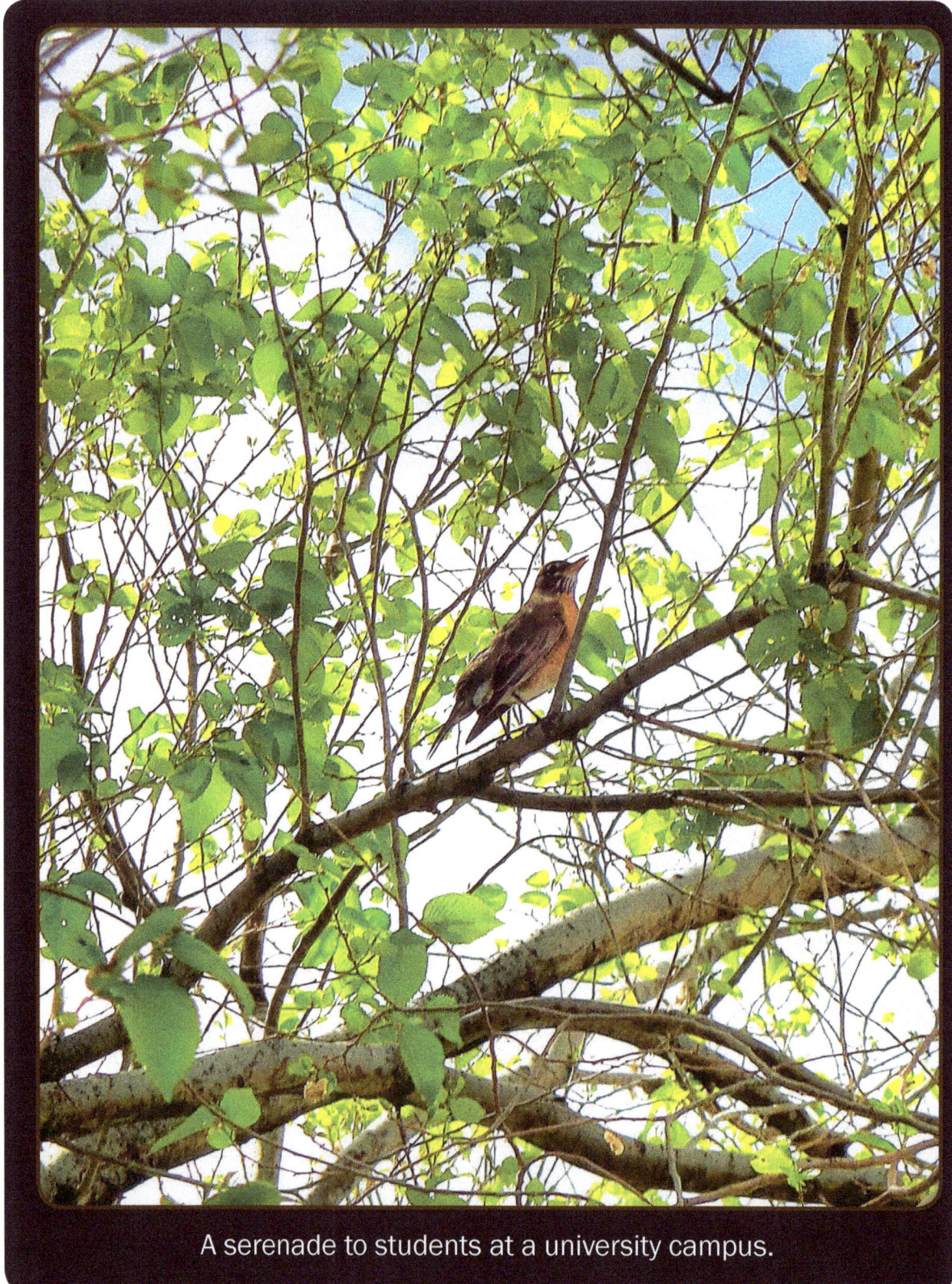

A serenade to students at a university campus.

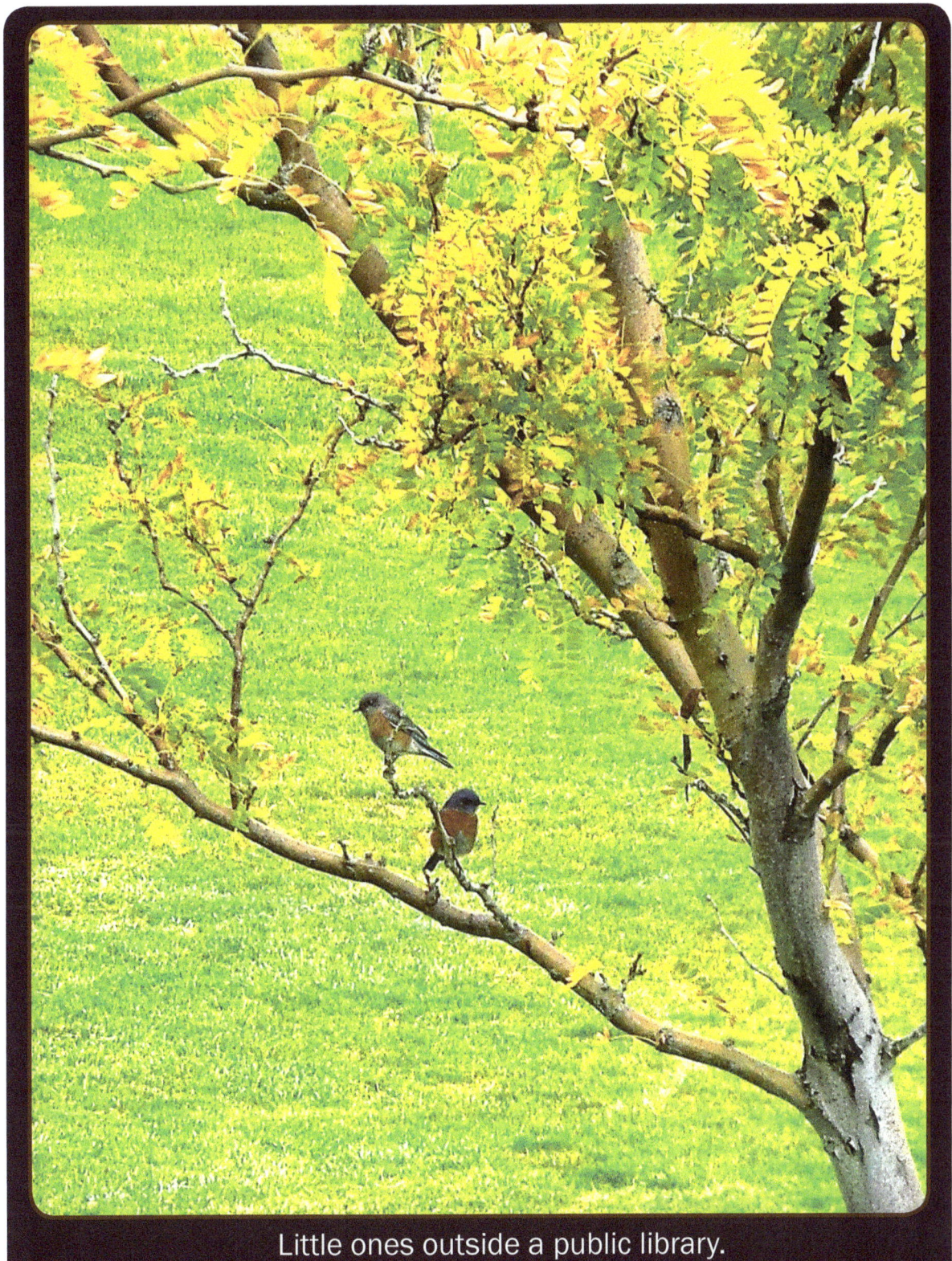
Little ones outside a public library.

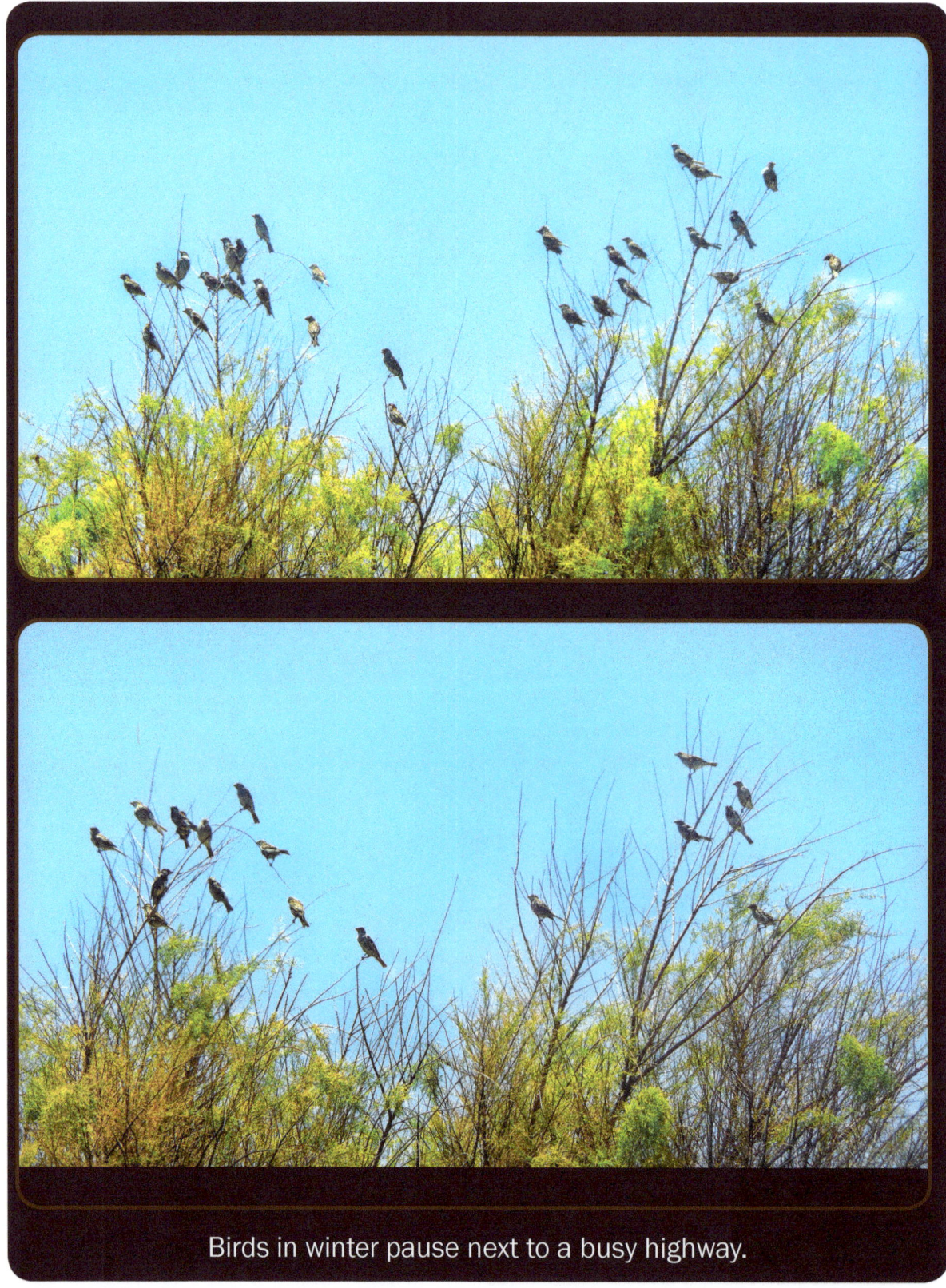
Birds in winter pause next to a busy highway.

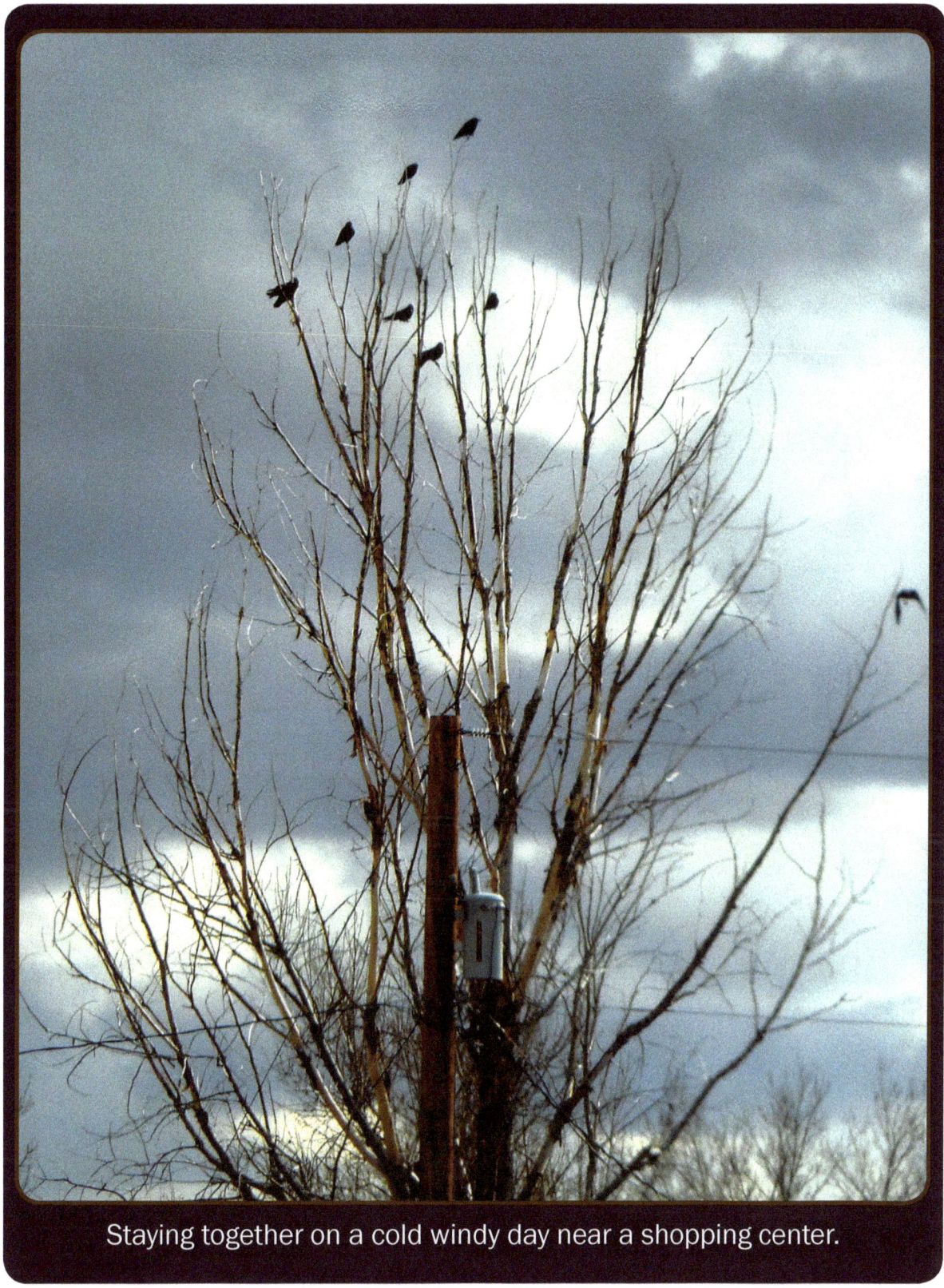
Staying together on a cold windy day near a shopping center.

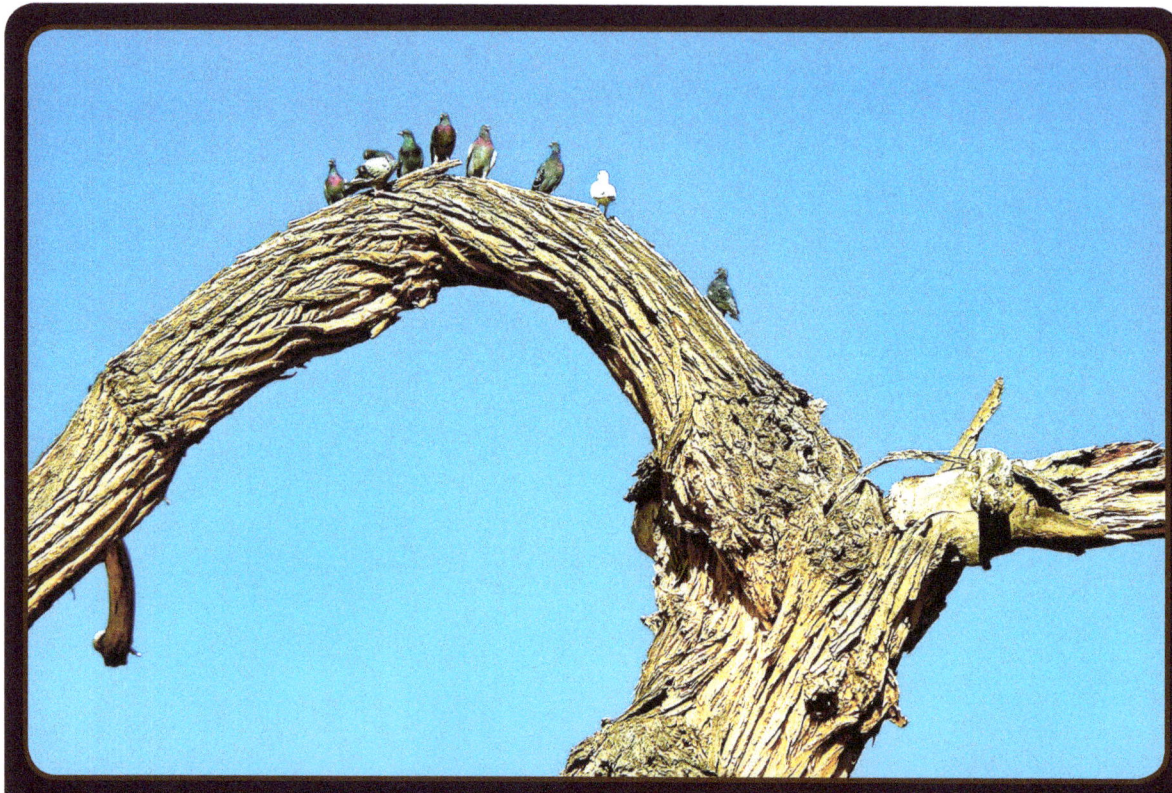

Togetherness on a lazy autumn afternoon.

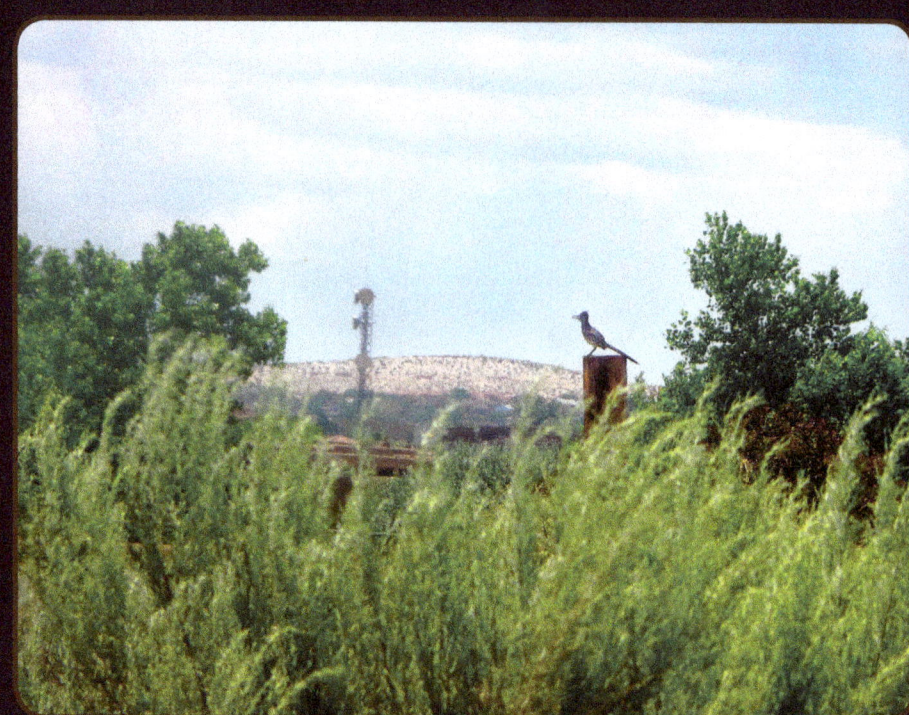

A roadrunner perches on a post in a neighborhood.

• Pathways in Time: Photo Journeys • 23

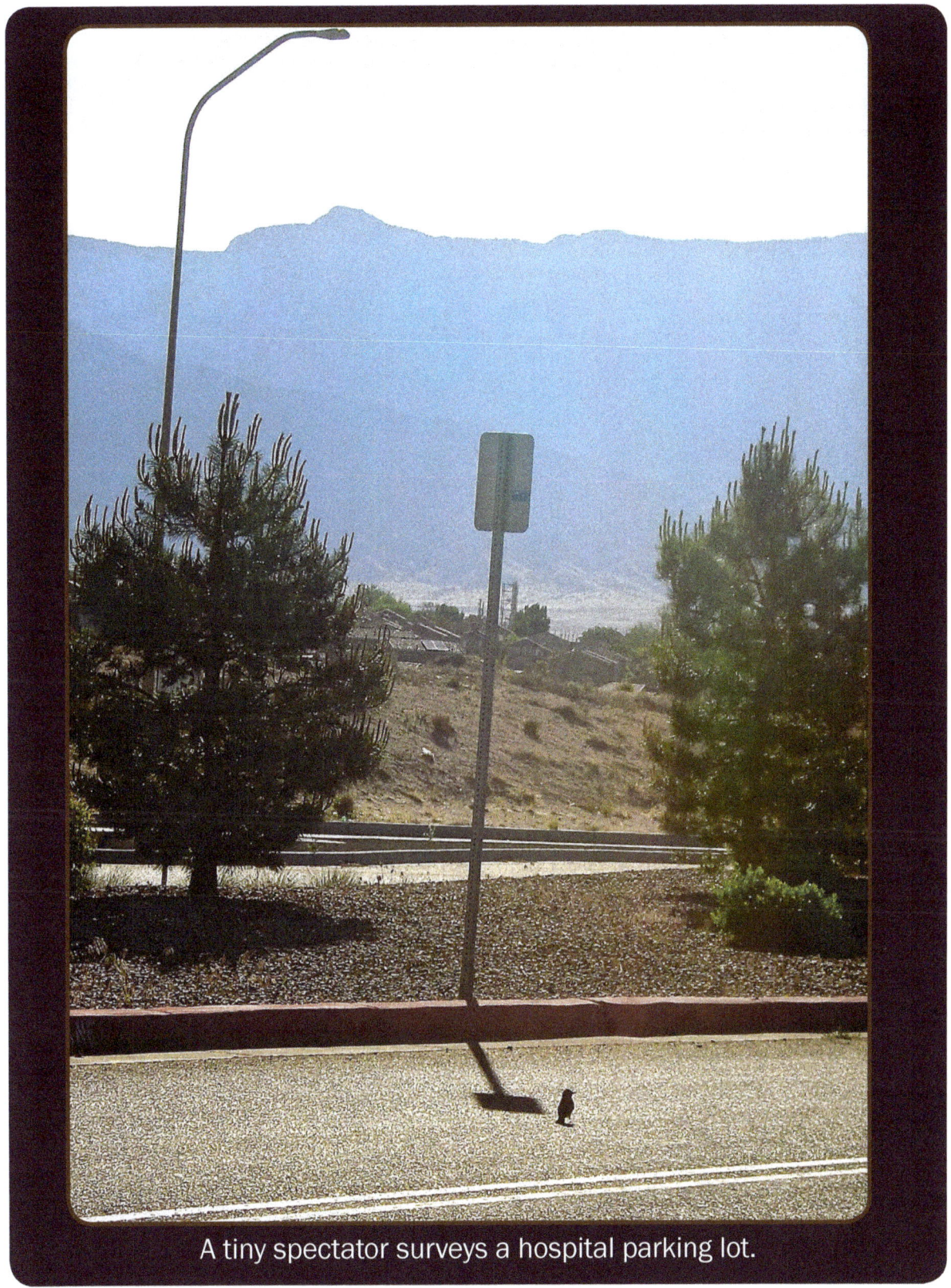

A tiny spectator surveys a hospital parking lot.

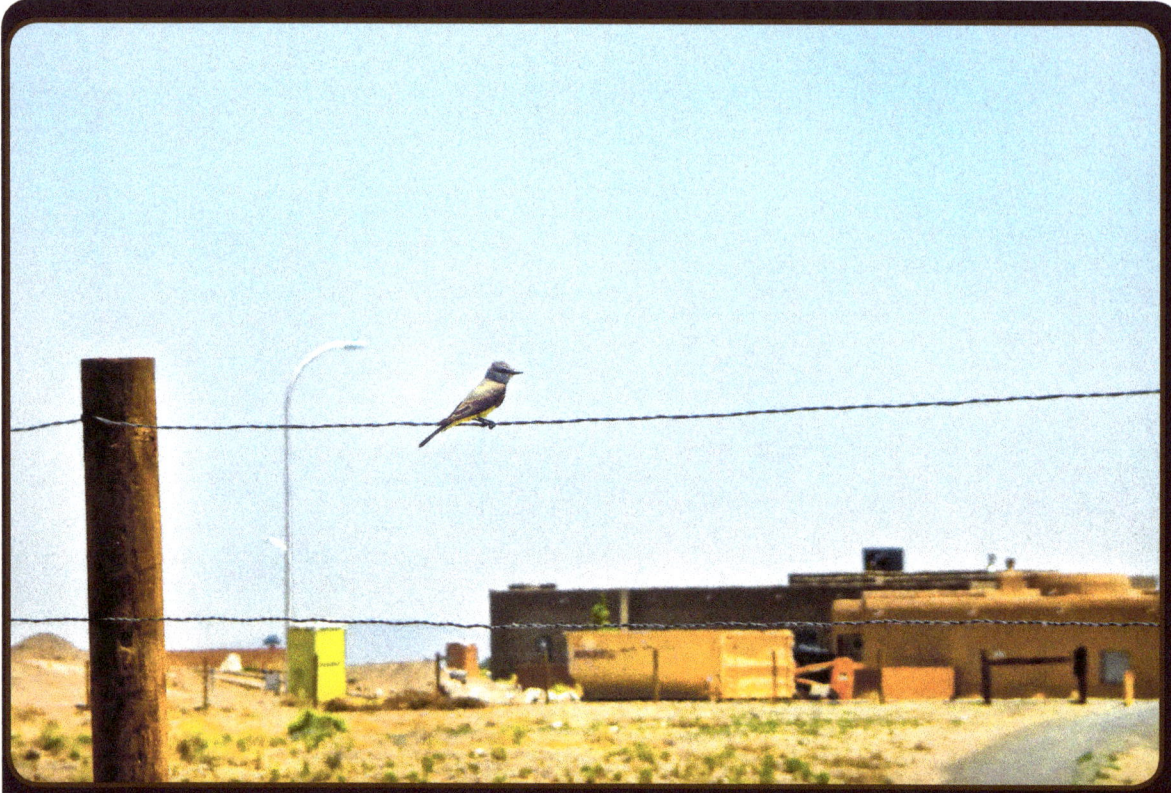

Songbird watches a home being built as open land becomes community for the rich.

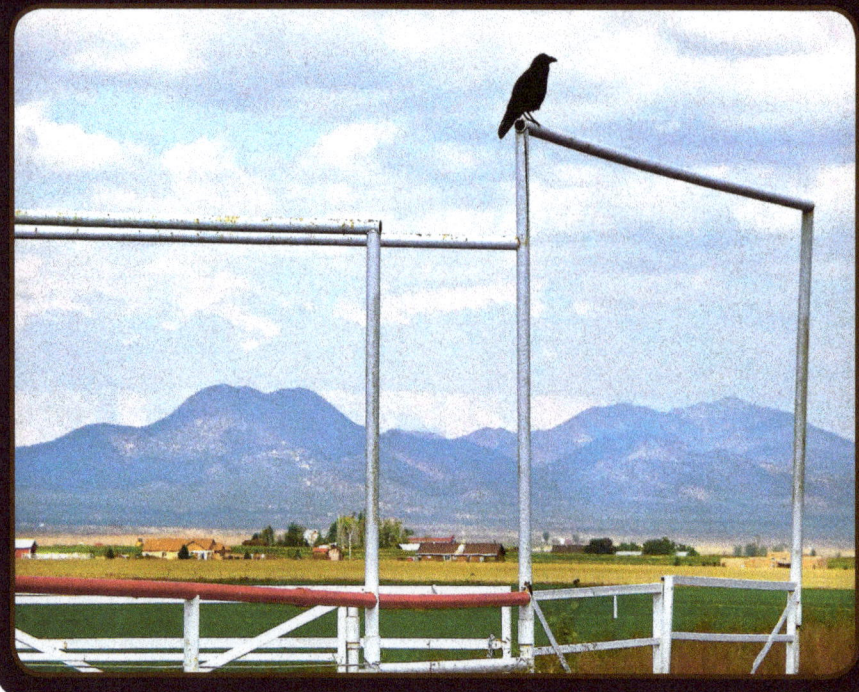

A crow rests on empty livestock pen.

• Pathways in Time: Photo Journeys • 25

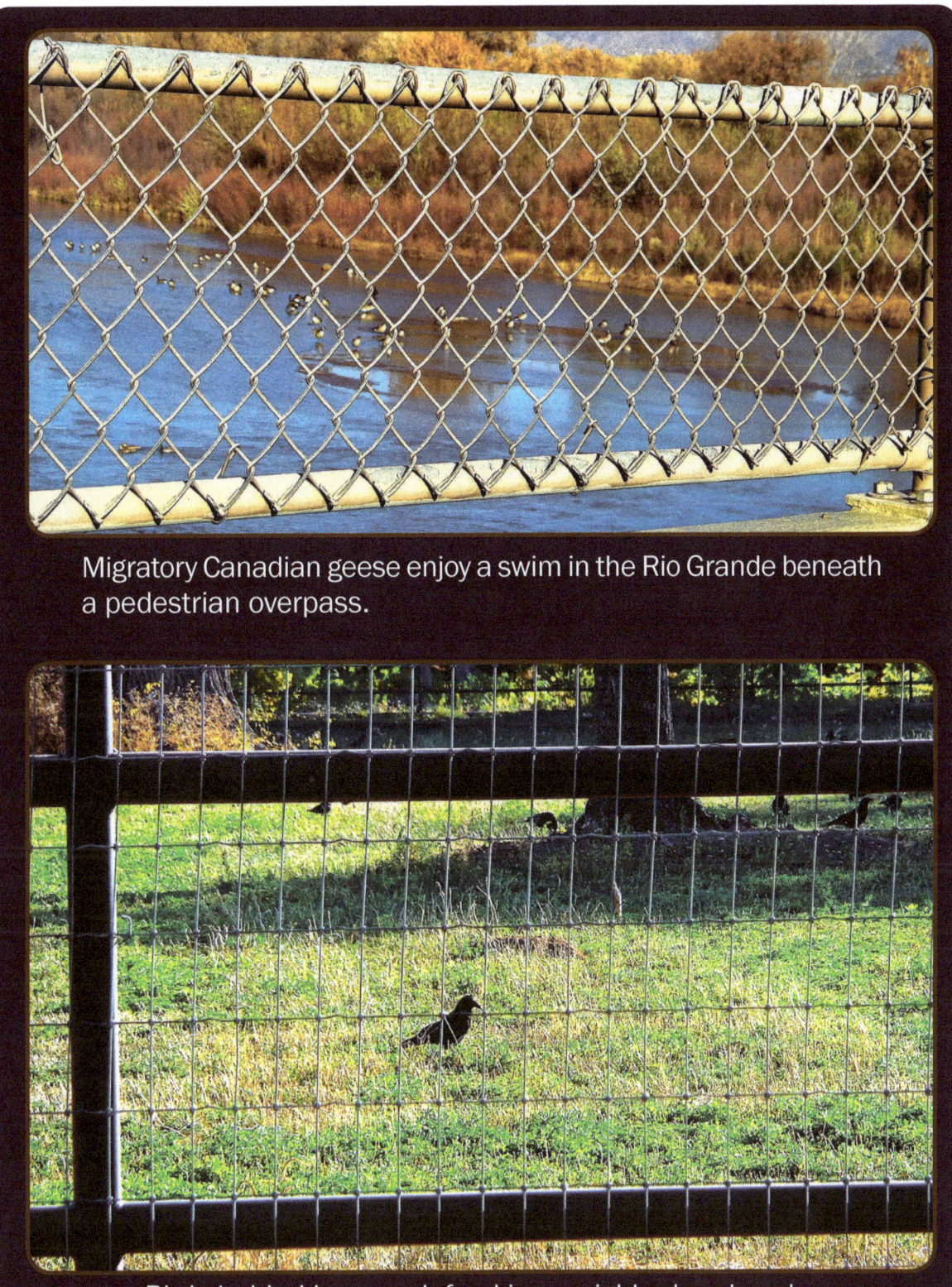

Migratory Canadian geese enjoy a swim in the Rio Grande beneath a pedestrian overpass.

Birds behind bars seek food in a neighborhood yard.

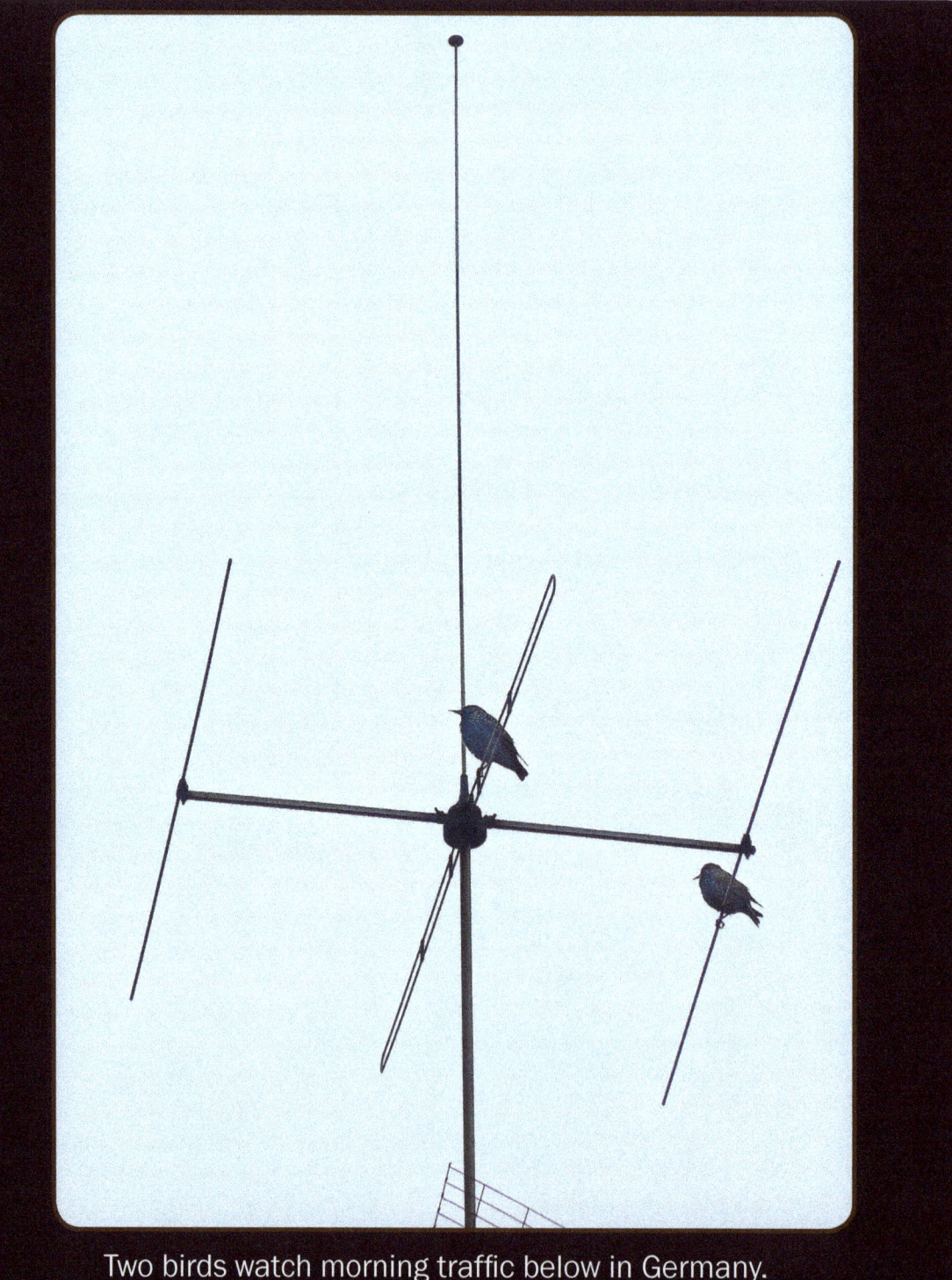
Two birds watch morning traffic below in Germany.

• Pathways in Time: Photo Journeys • 27

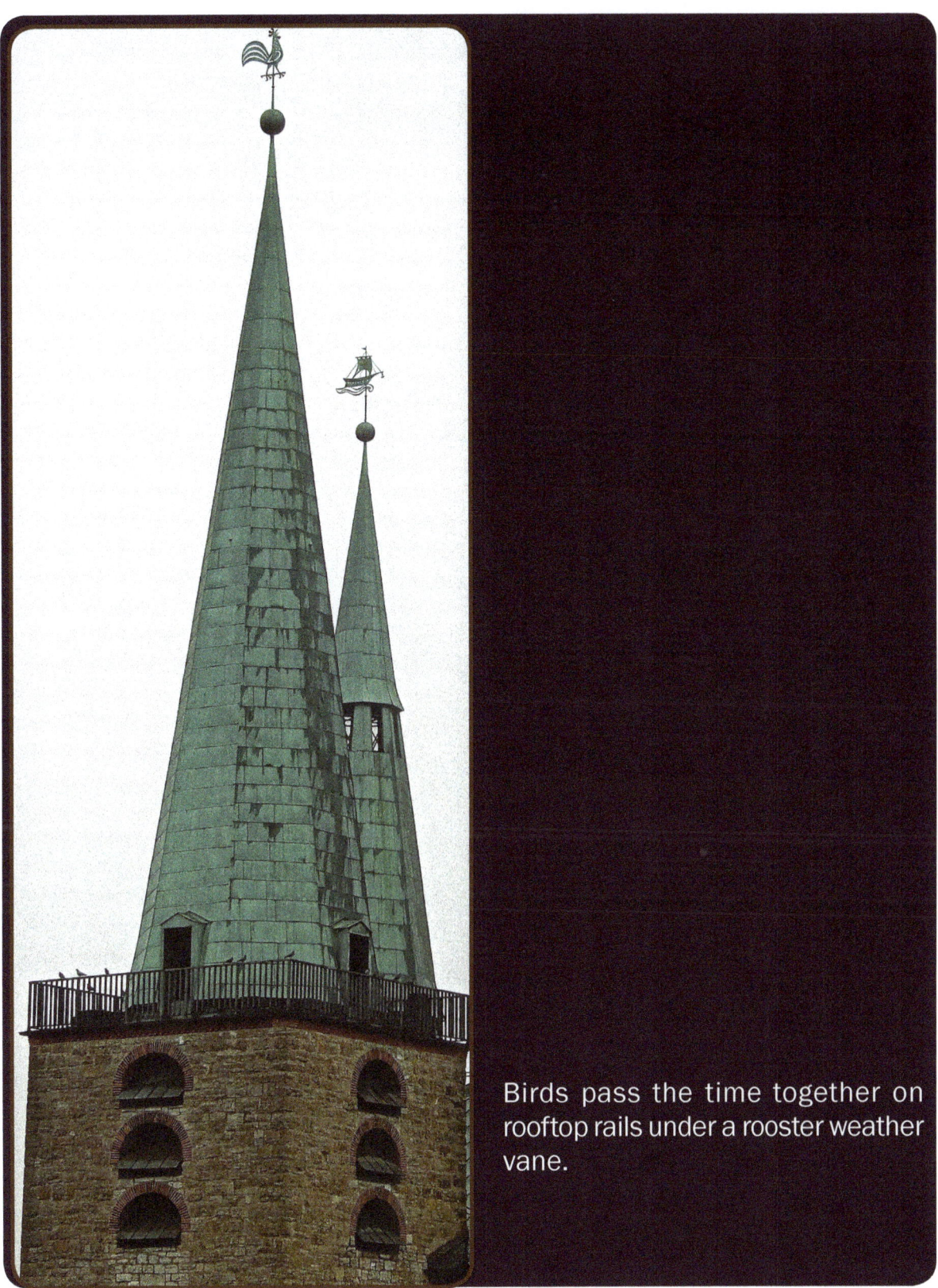

Birds pass the time together on rooftop rails under a rooster weather vane.

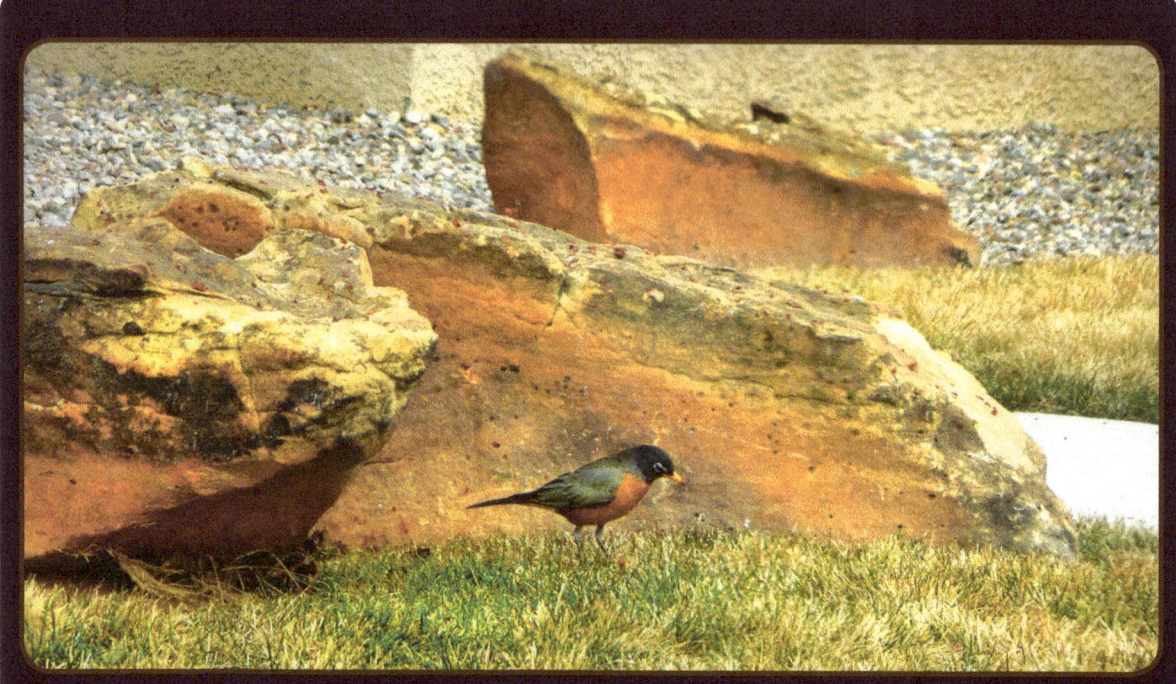
Songbird hunts for food along a busy community pathway.

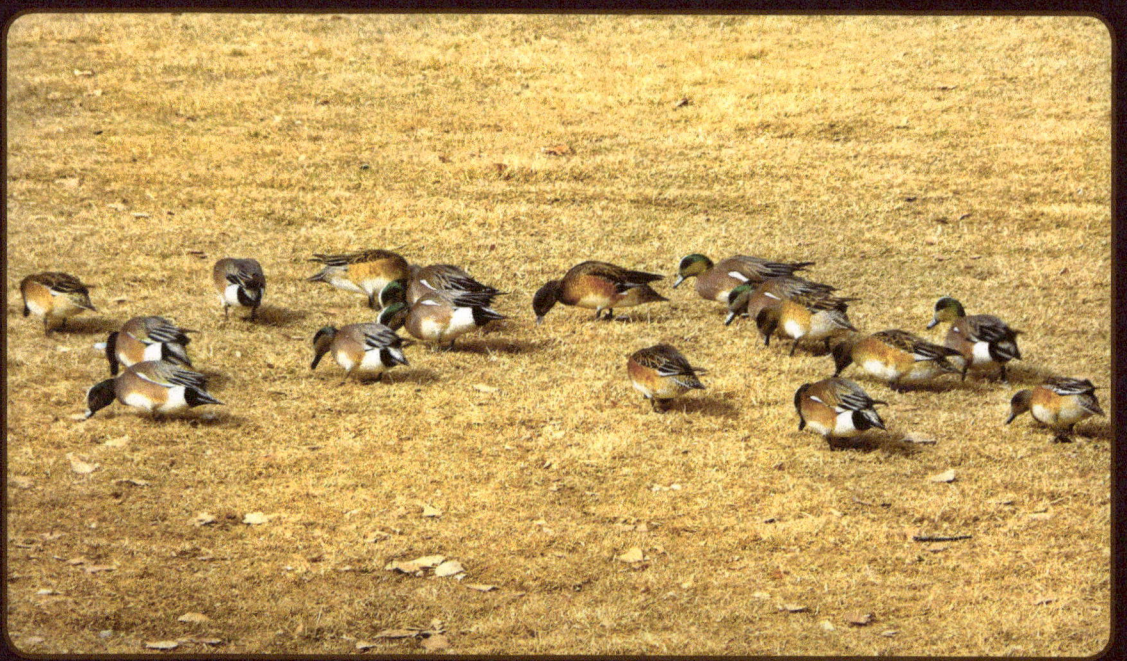
Ducks look for lunch on grass outside a fire station.

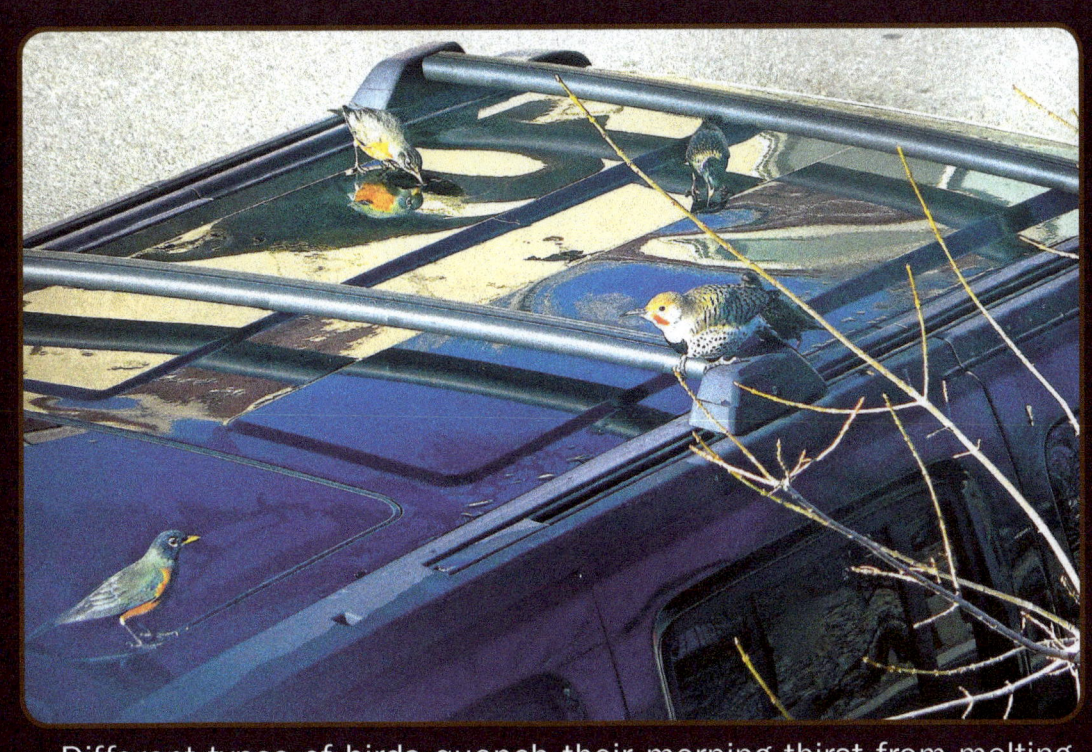
Different types of birds quench their morning thirst from melting frost on top of a car.

Geese watch people in a park.

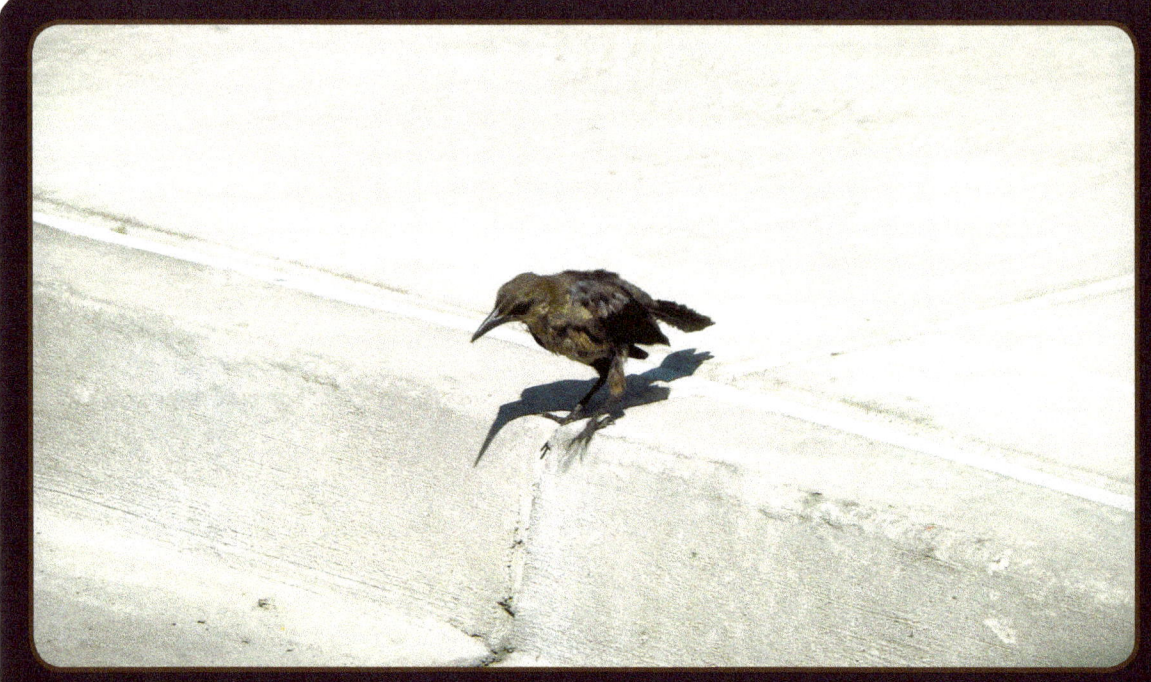
A bedraggled bird tries his luck in a crowded fast-food parking lot.

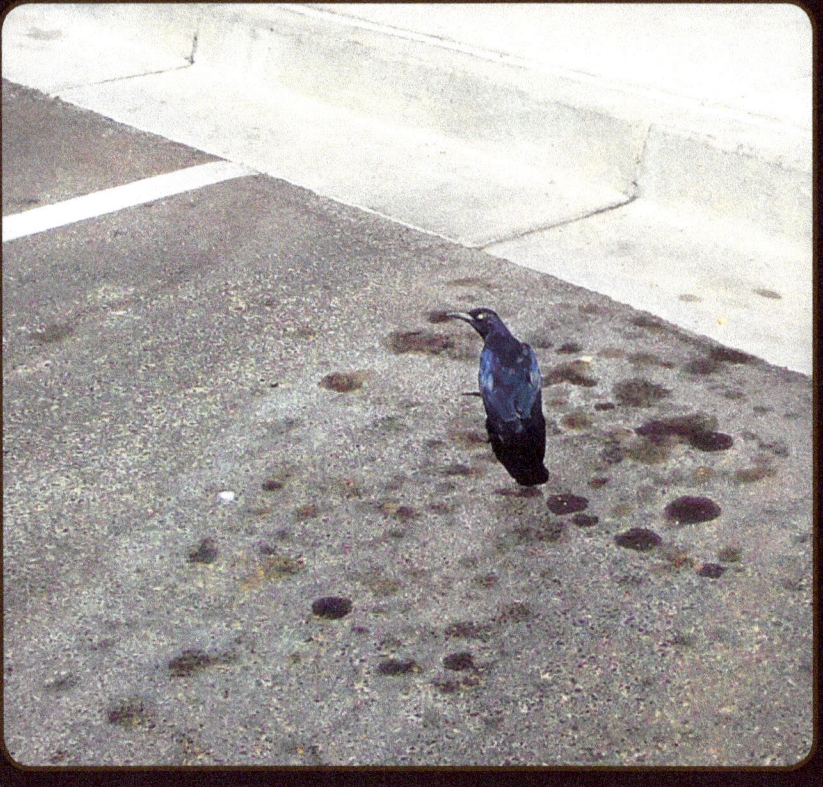
A brave bird stands on oil-stained pavement while seeking discarded fast-food near a restaurant entrance during a lunch hour rush.

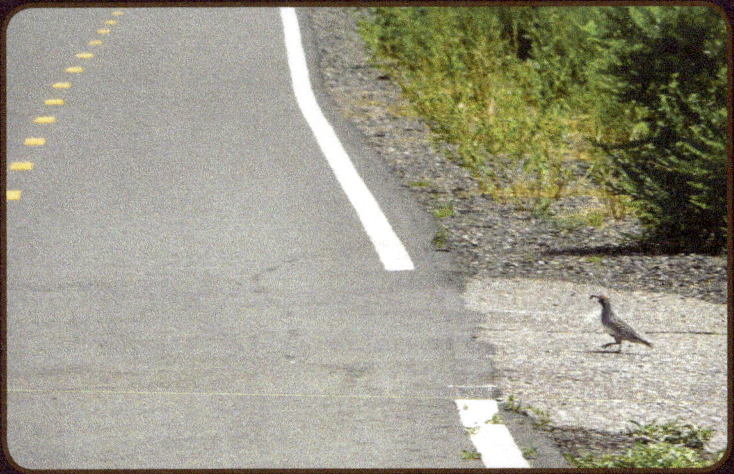

Pathways in Time: Photo Journeys · 31

A quail speeds across a bike path and jogging trail.

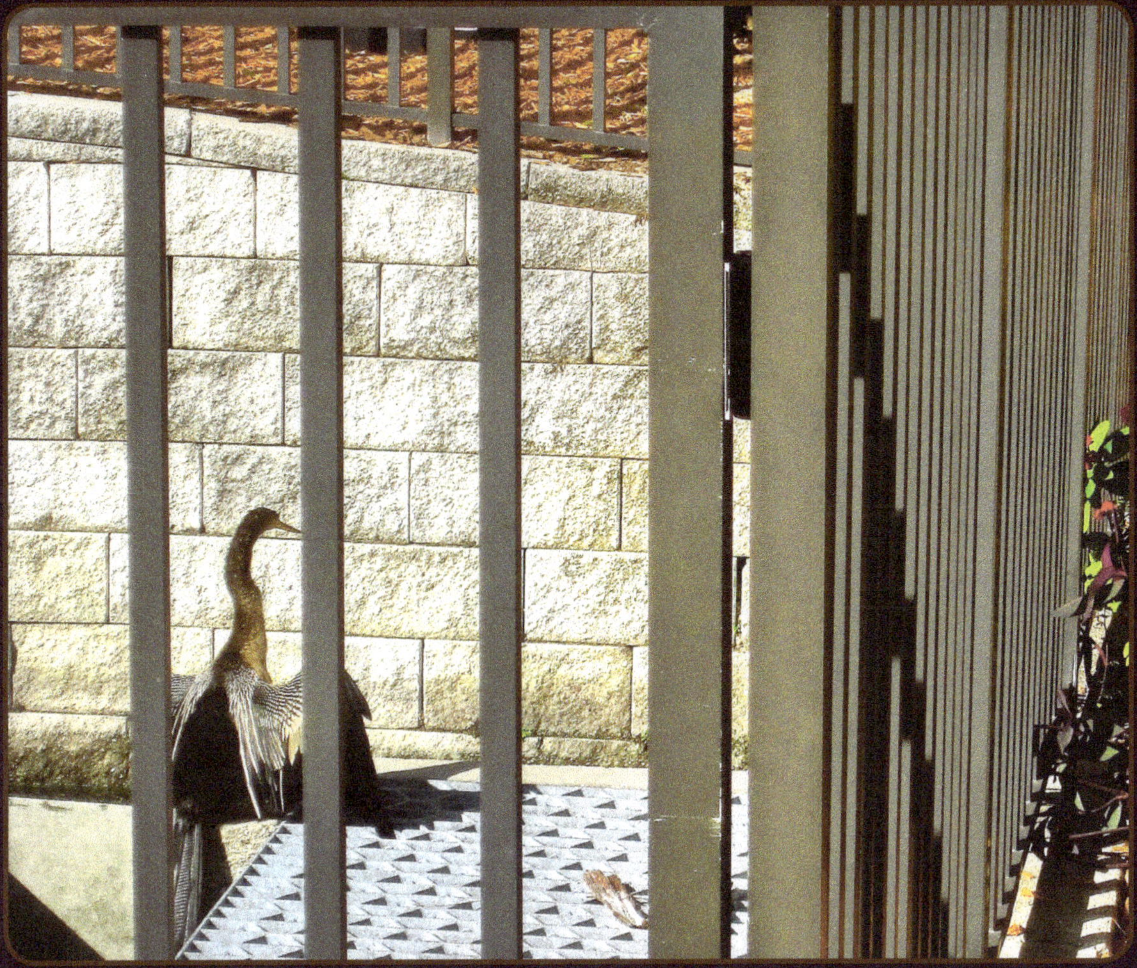

A bird opens its wings to enjoy the sun's warm rays in a residential utility enclosure.

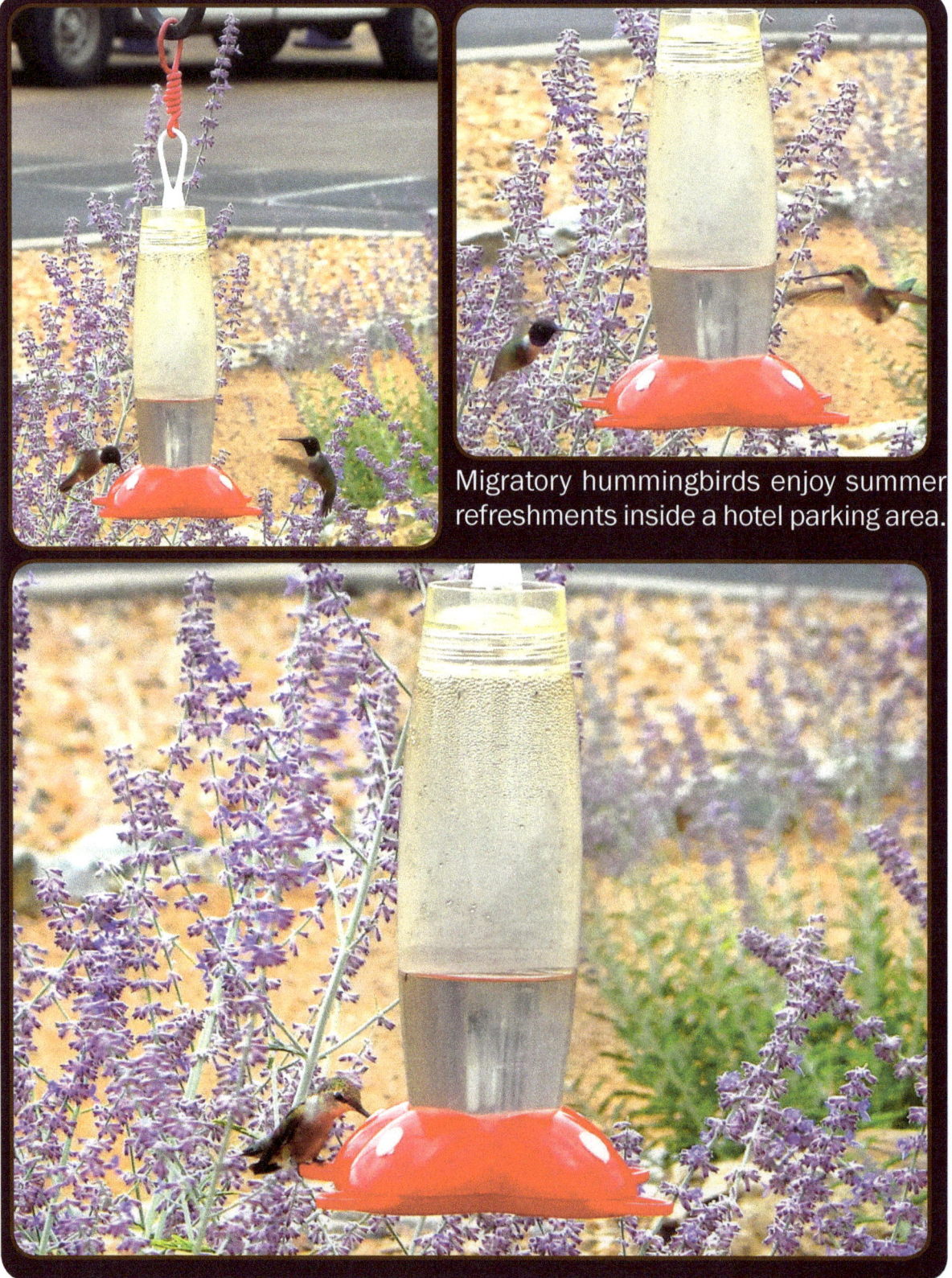

Migratory hummingbirds enjoy summer refreshments inside a hotel parking area.

• Pathways in Time: Photo Journeys • 33

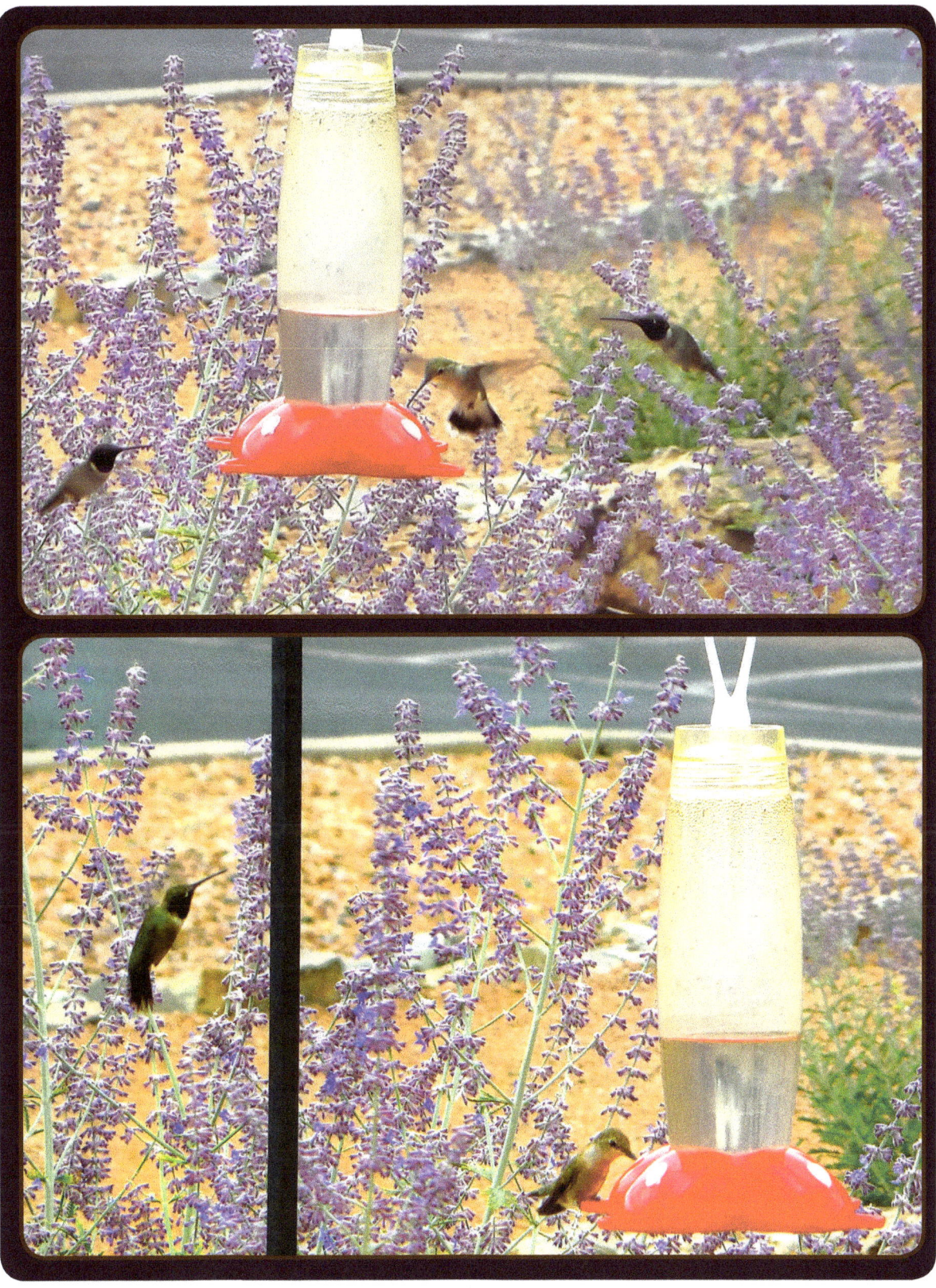

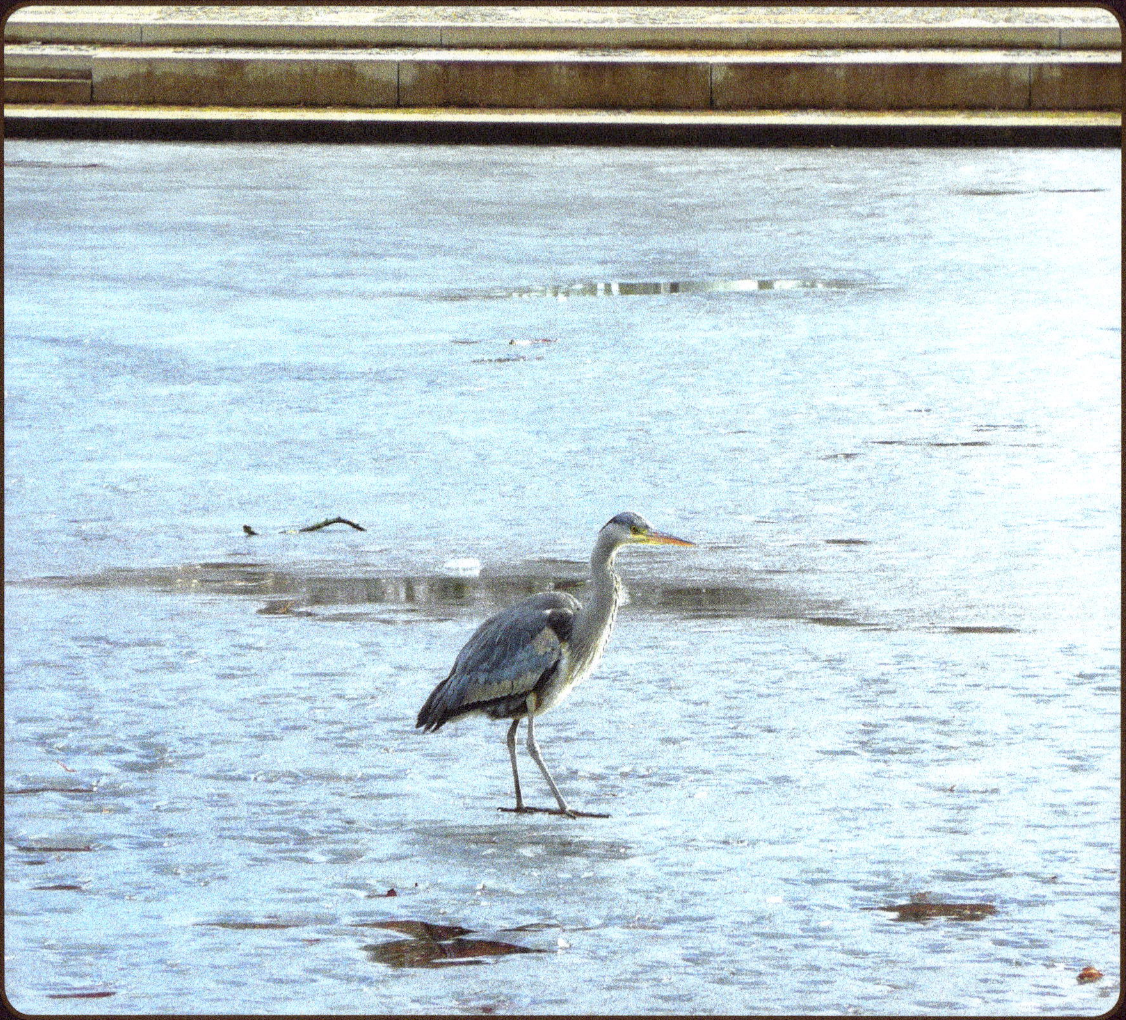

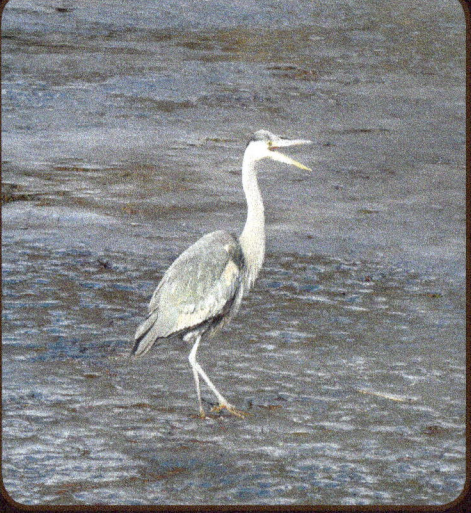

A crane looks for lunch through melting ice in a park in Germany.

• Pathways in Time: Photo Journeys • 35

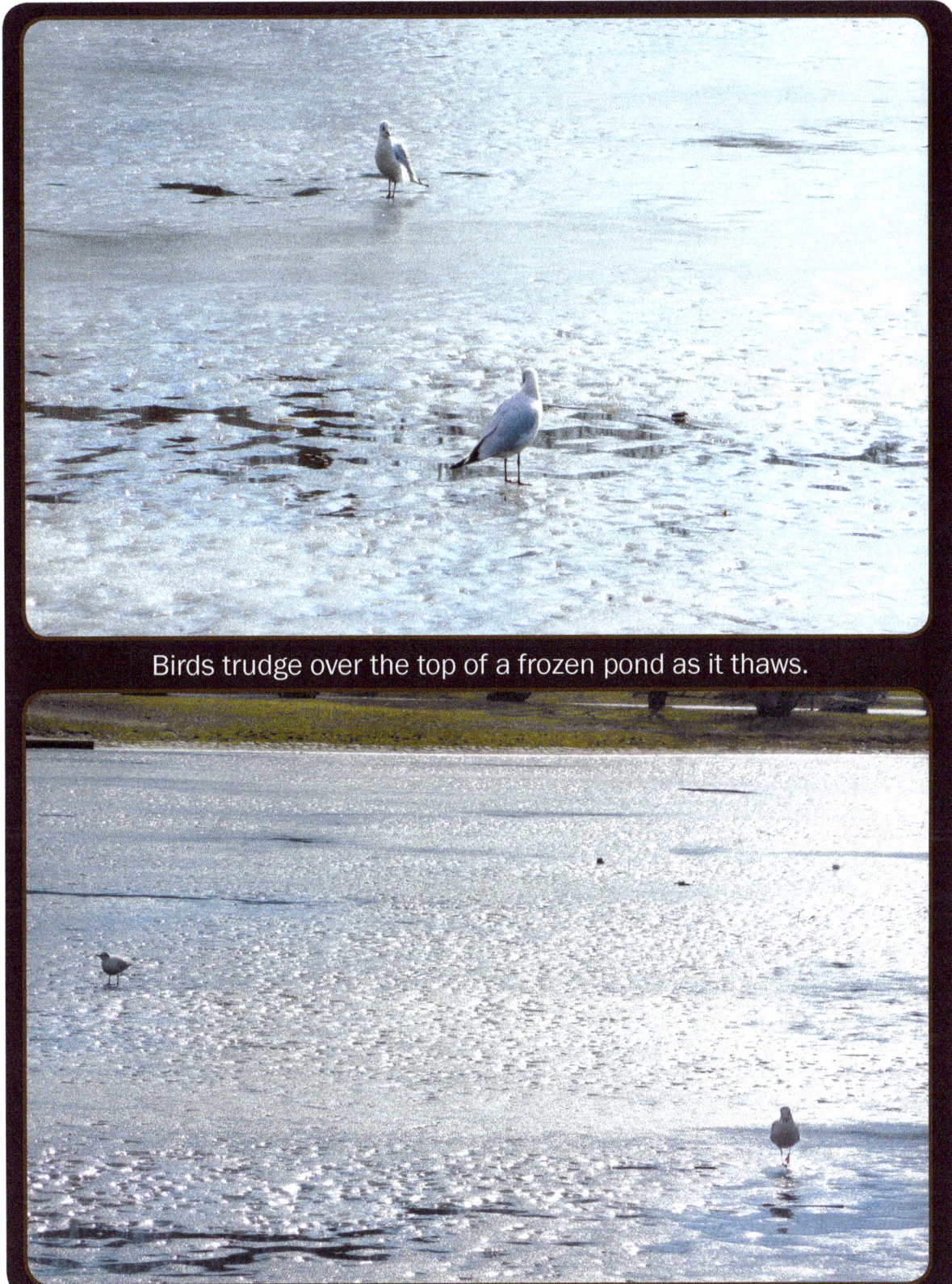

Birds trudge over the top of a frozen pond as it thaws.

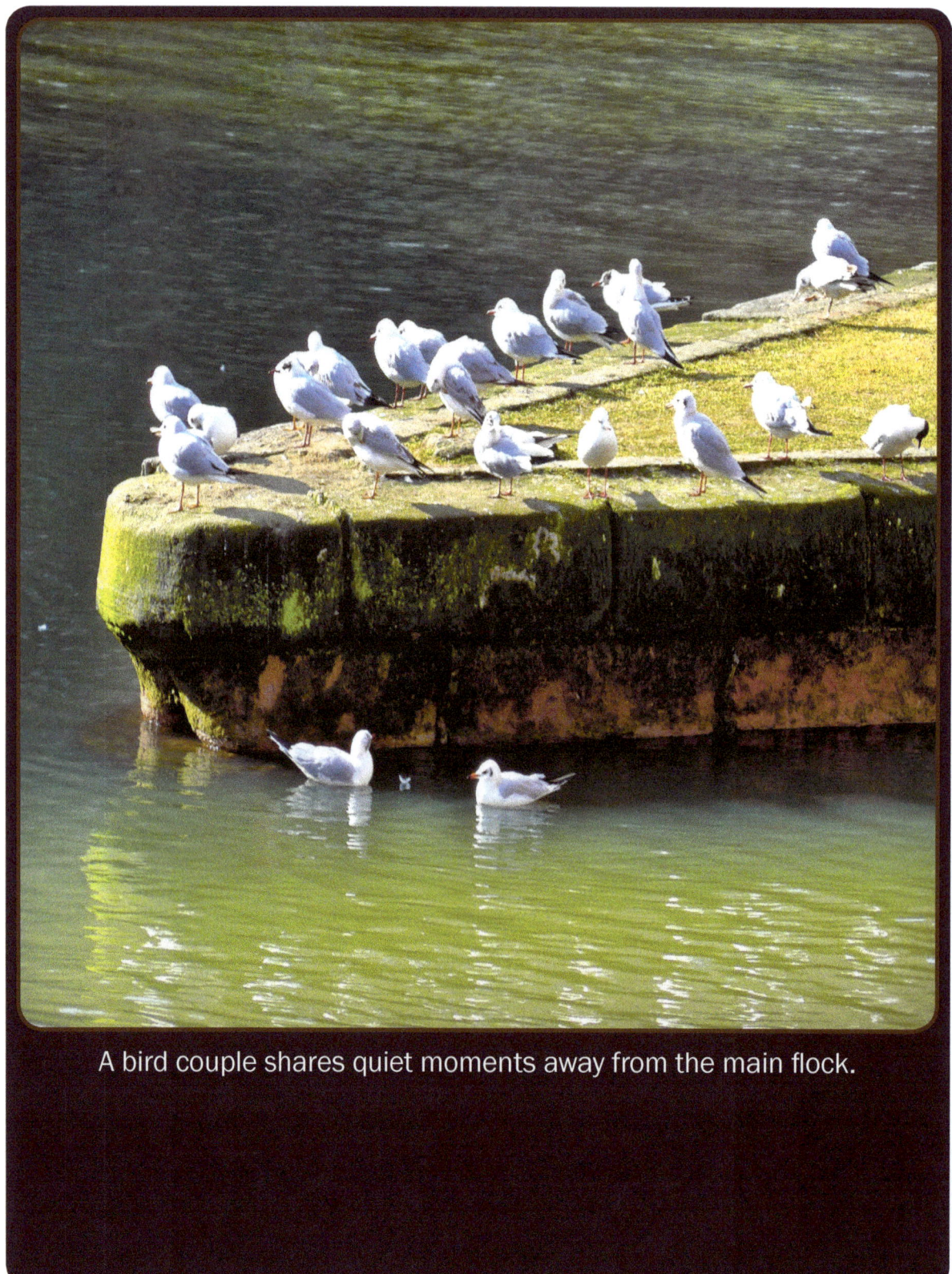

A bird couple shares quiet moments away from the main flock.

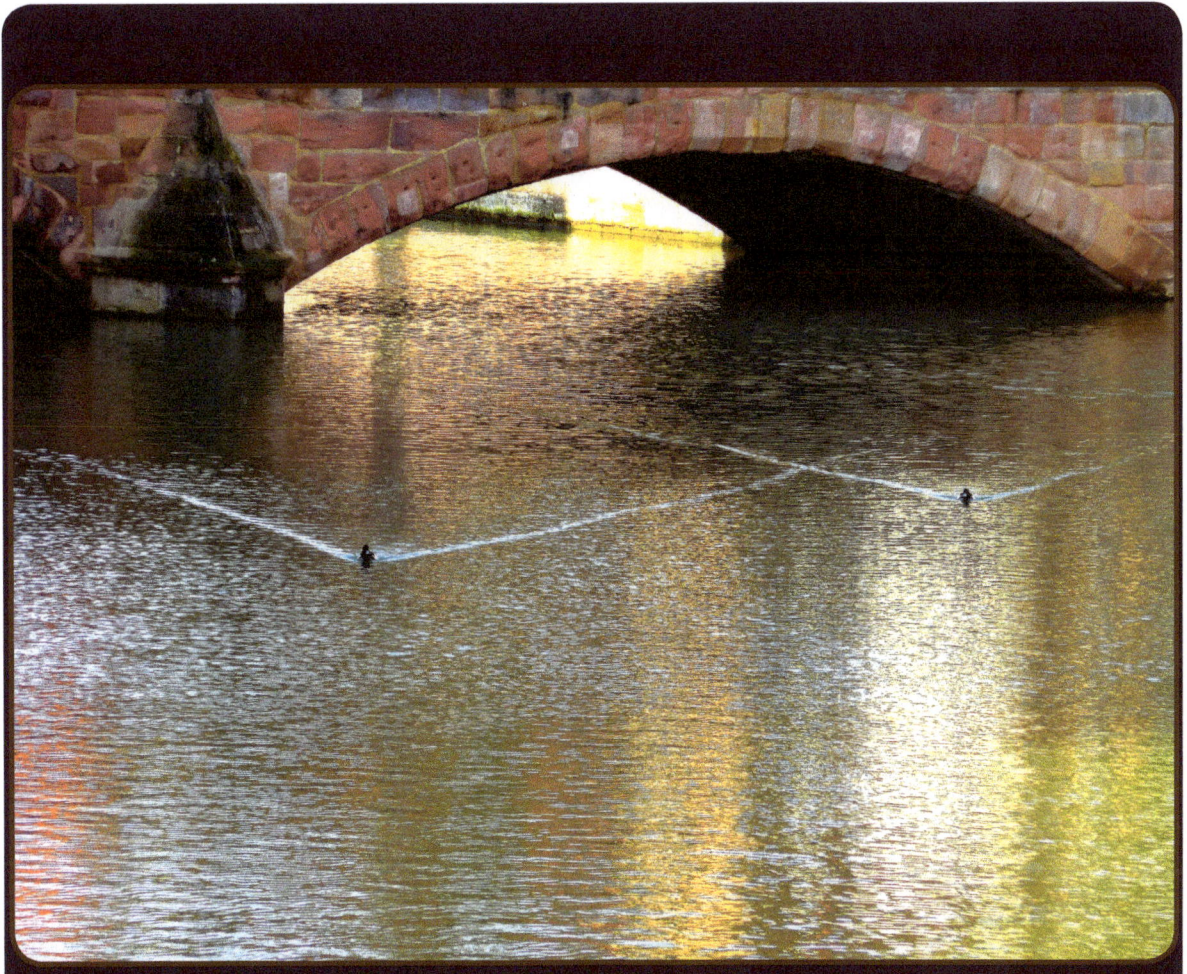

A pair of ducks race through a river in Franconia and together they leave behind a giant "W" in the water.

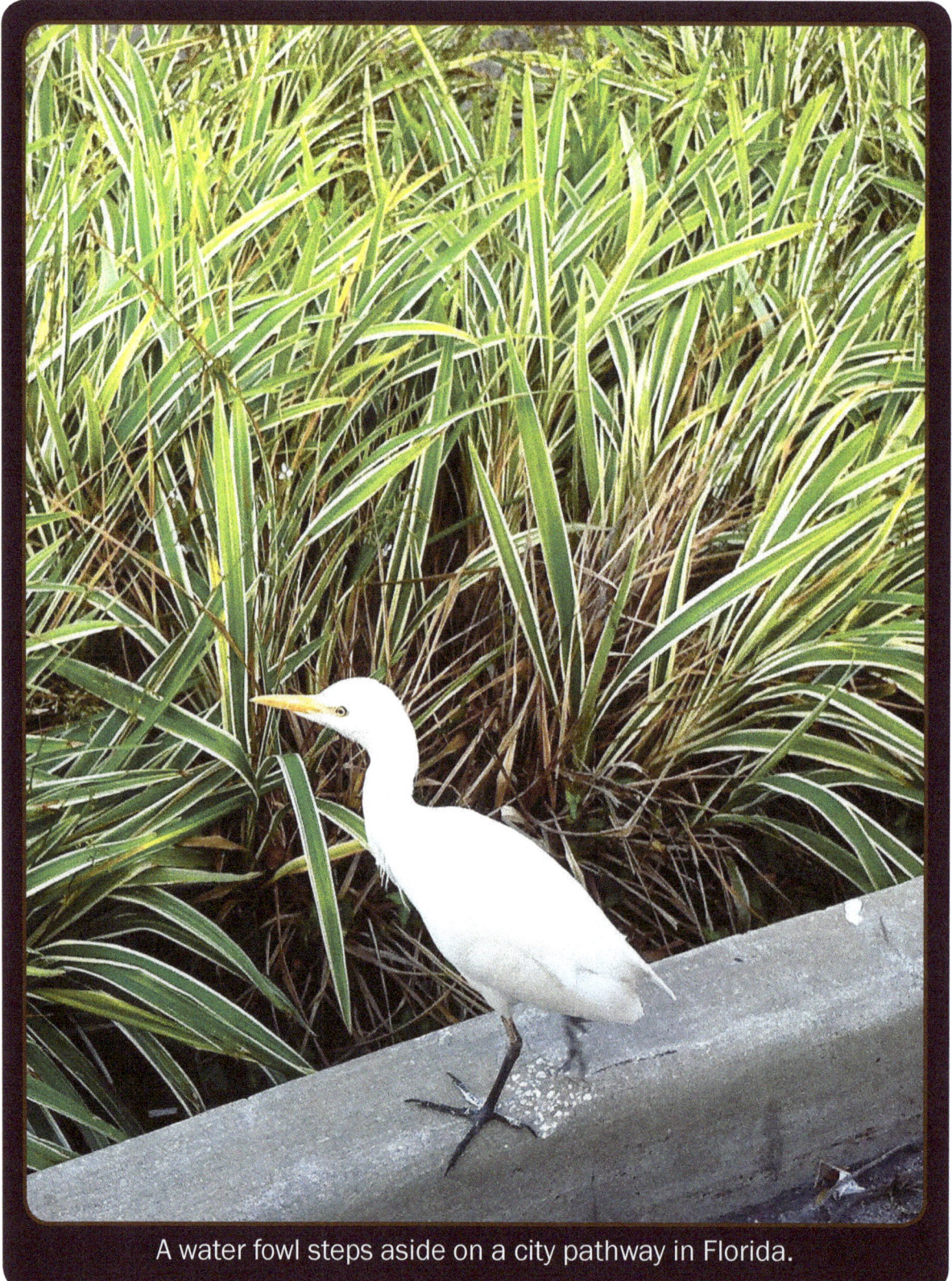
A water fowl steps aside on a city pathway in Florida.

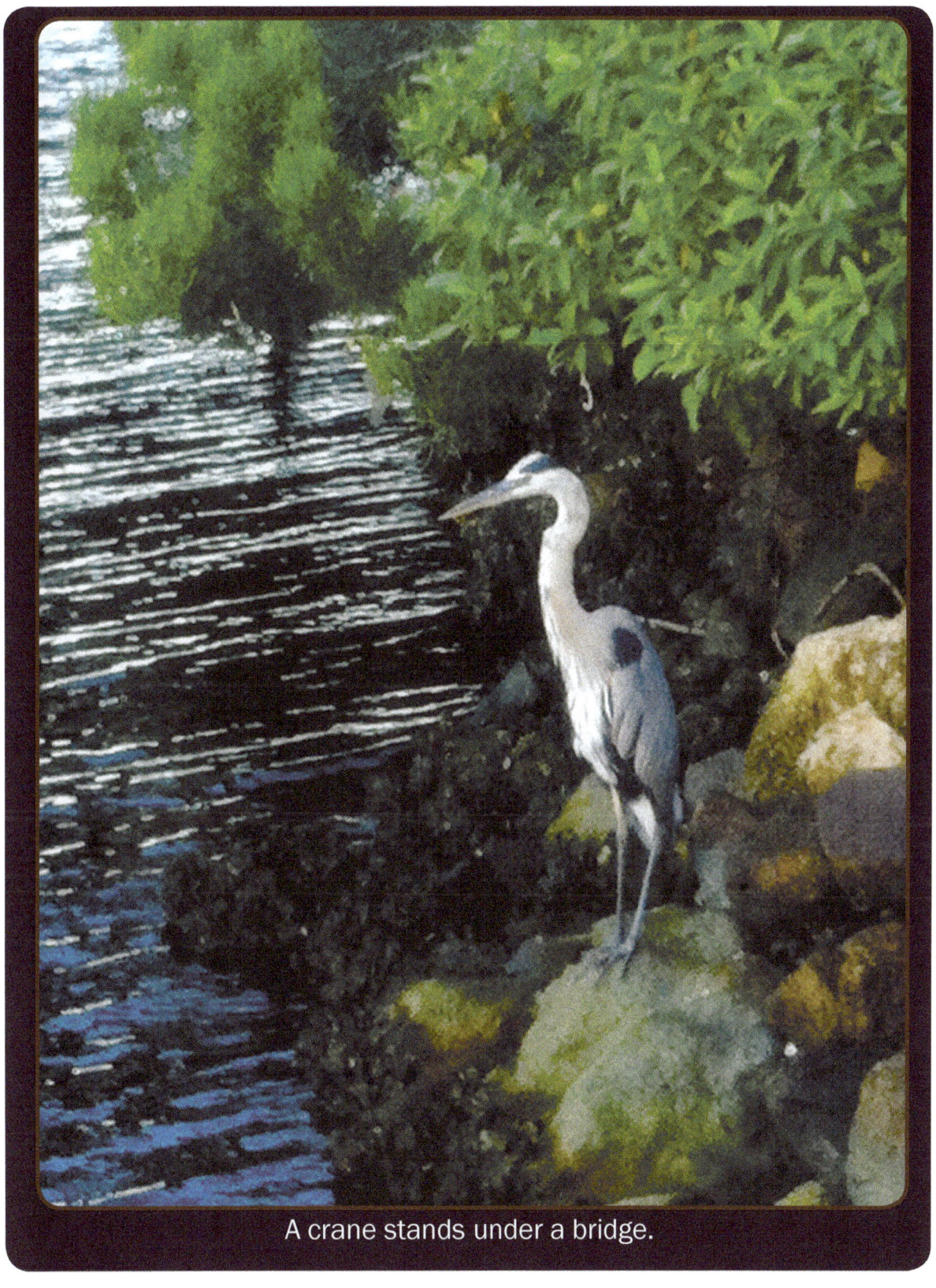

A crane stands under a bridge.

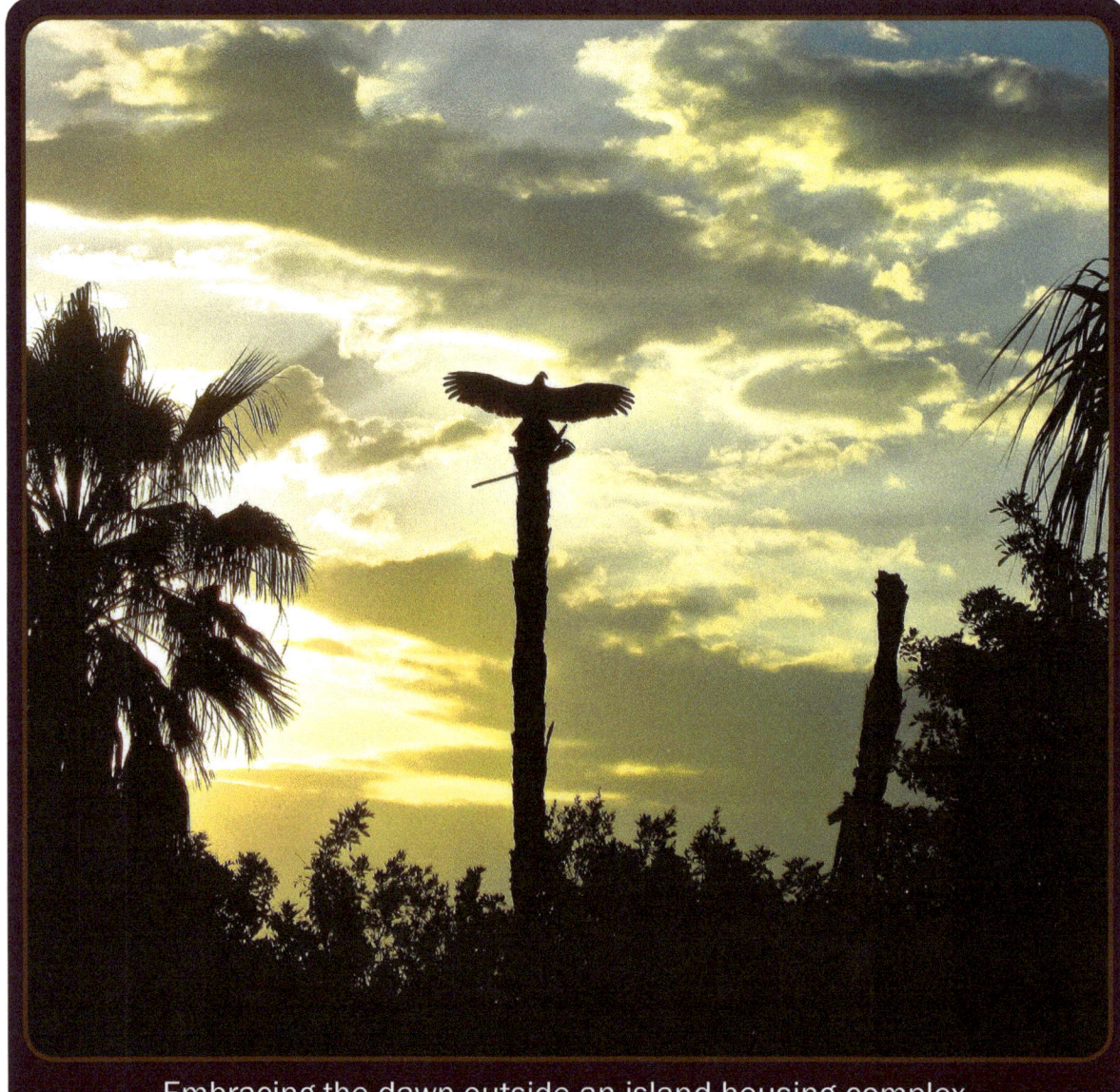

Embracing the dawn outside an island housing complex.

Chapter 2: Architecture

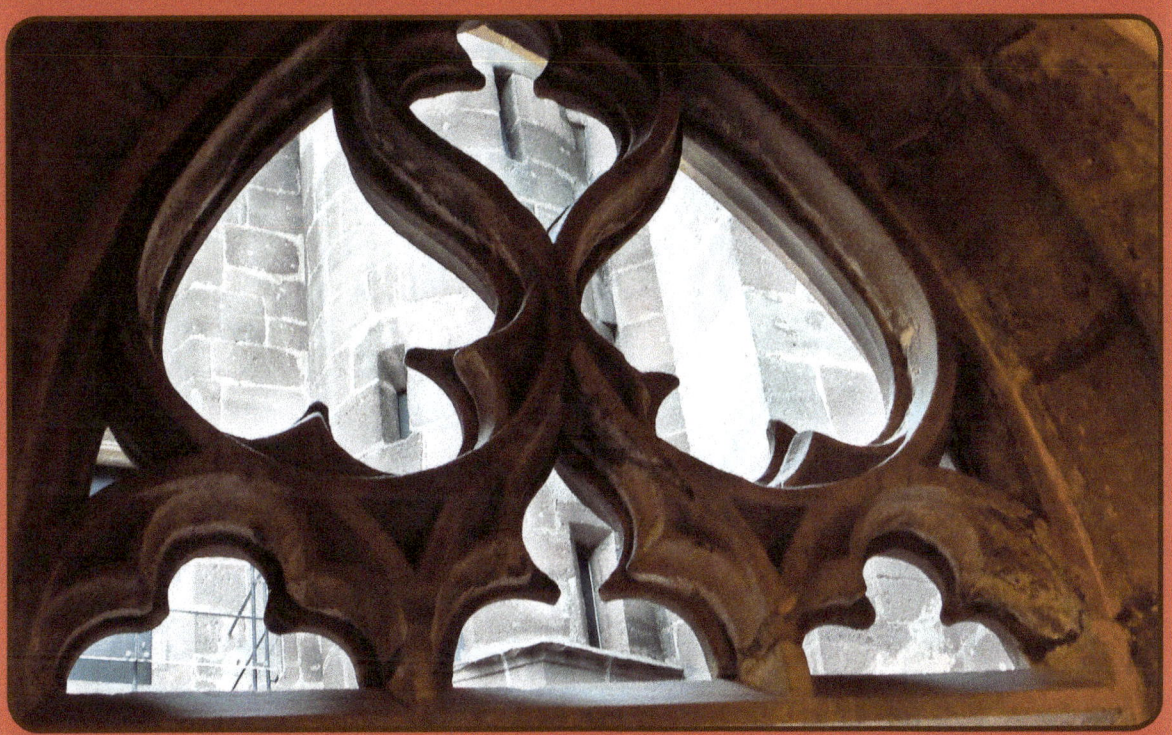

Window looking outside of a former Carthusian monastery built in 1380s.

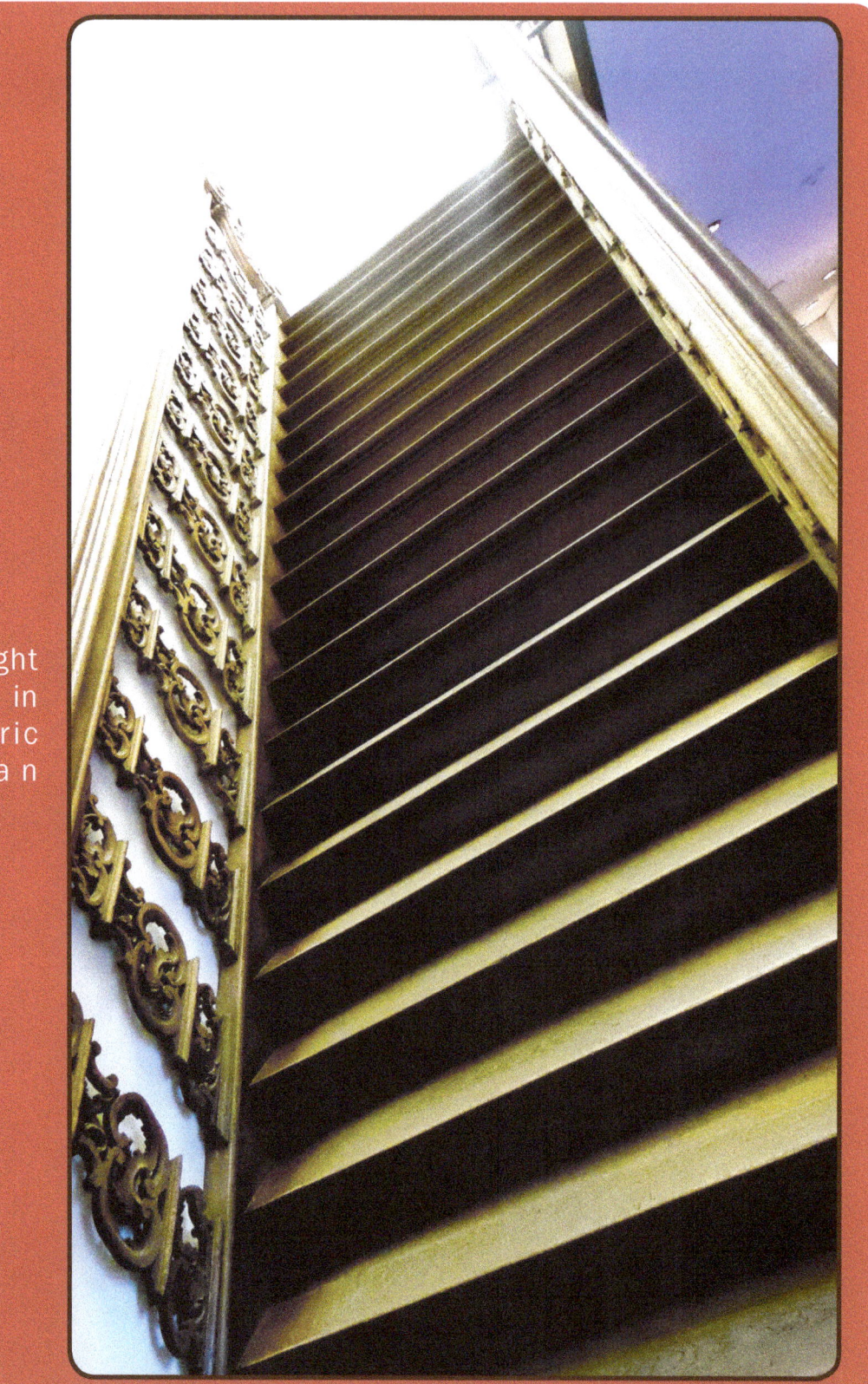

Up a flight of stairs in a historic German museum.

Pathways in Time: Photo Journeys • 43

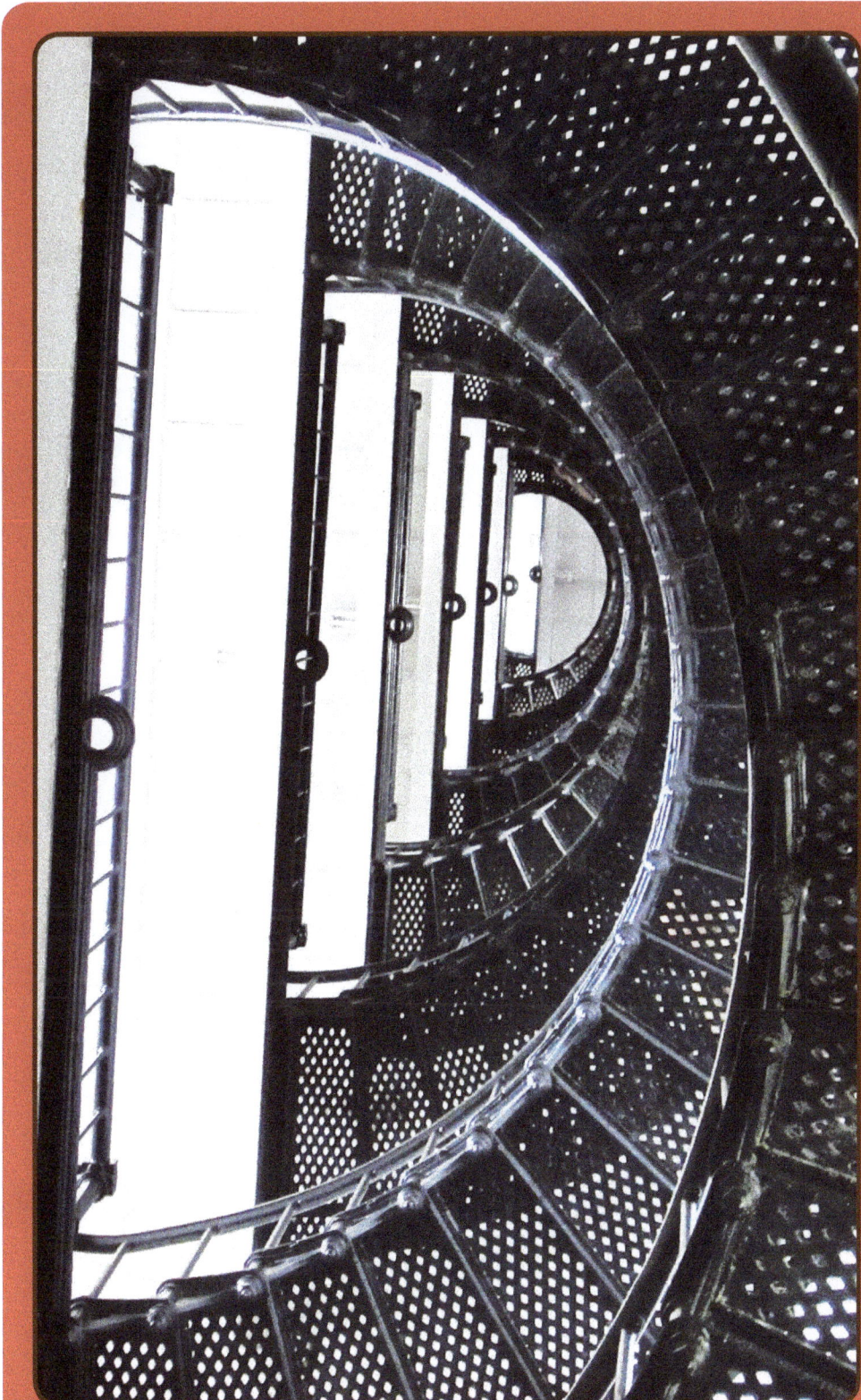

Inside an East Coast lighthouse.

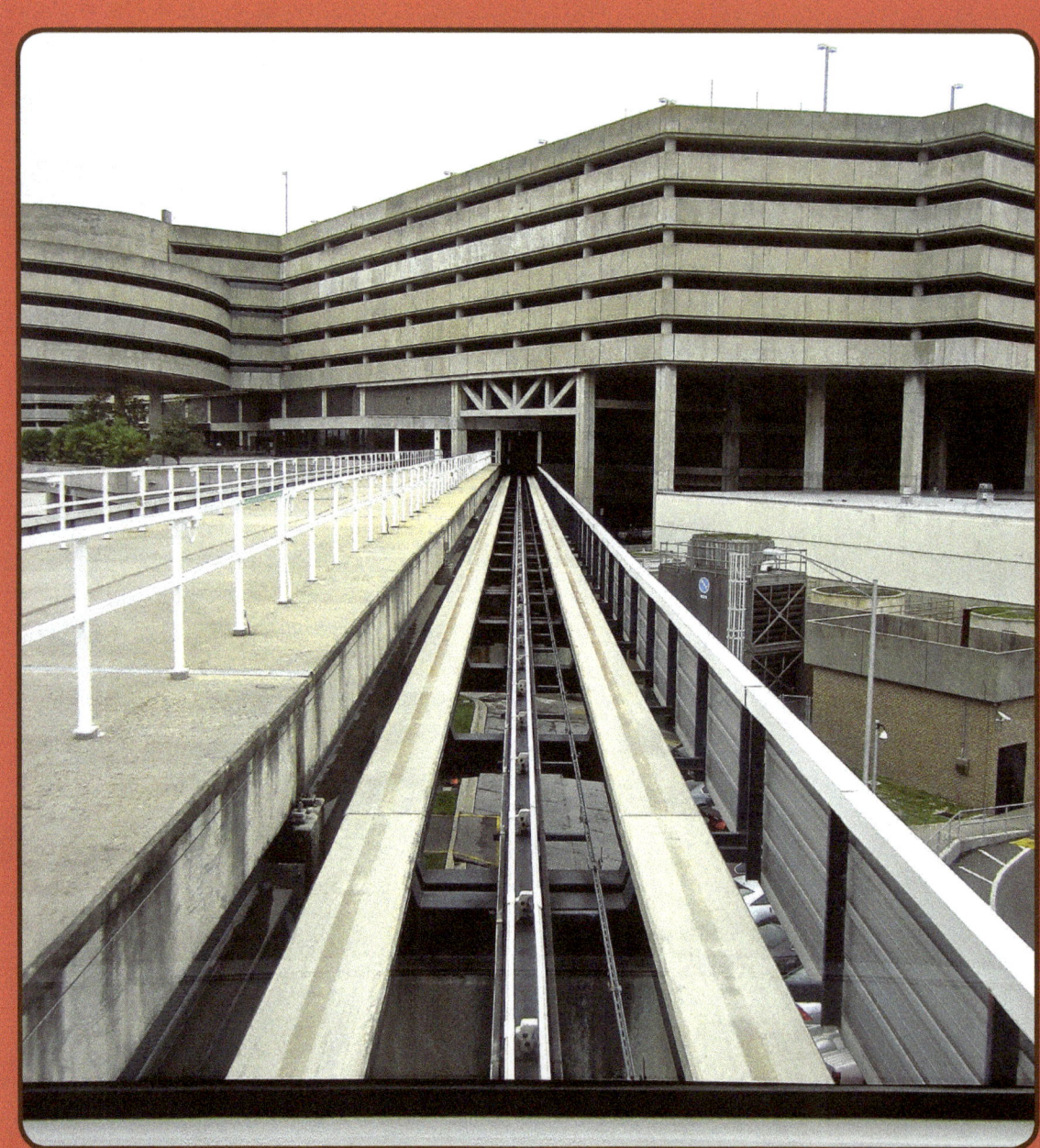
Airport passenger railcar tracks.

• Pathways in Time: Photo Journeys • 45

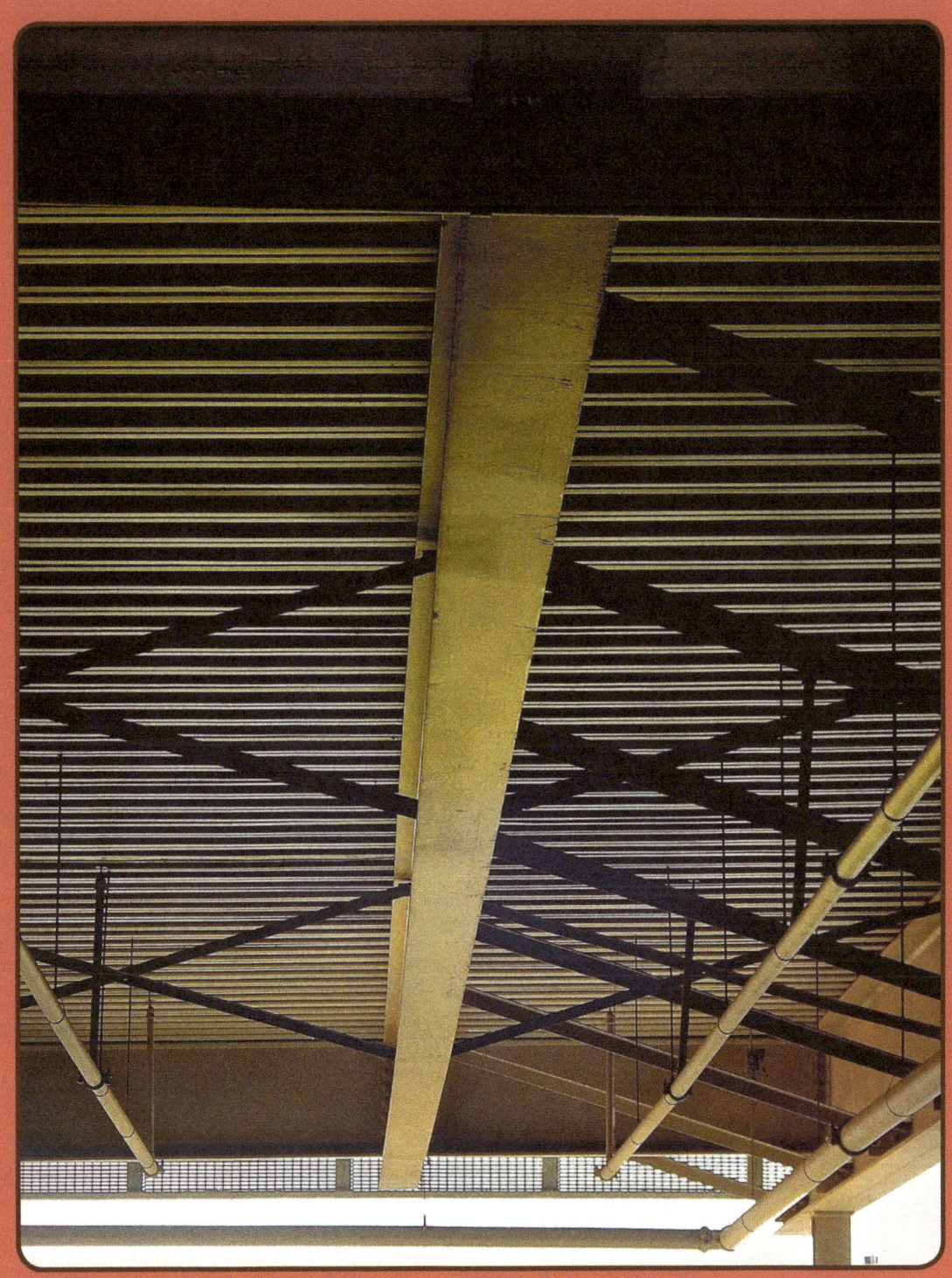

Interior rooftop in a multi-story parking garage.

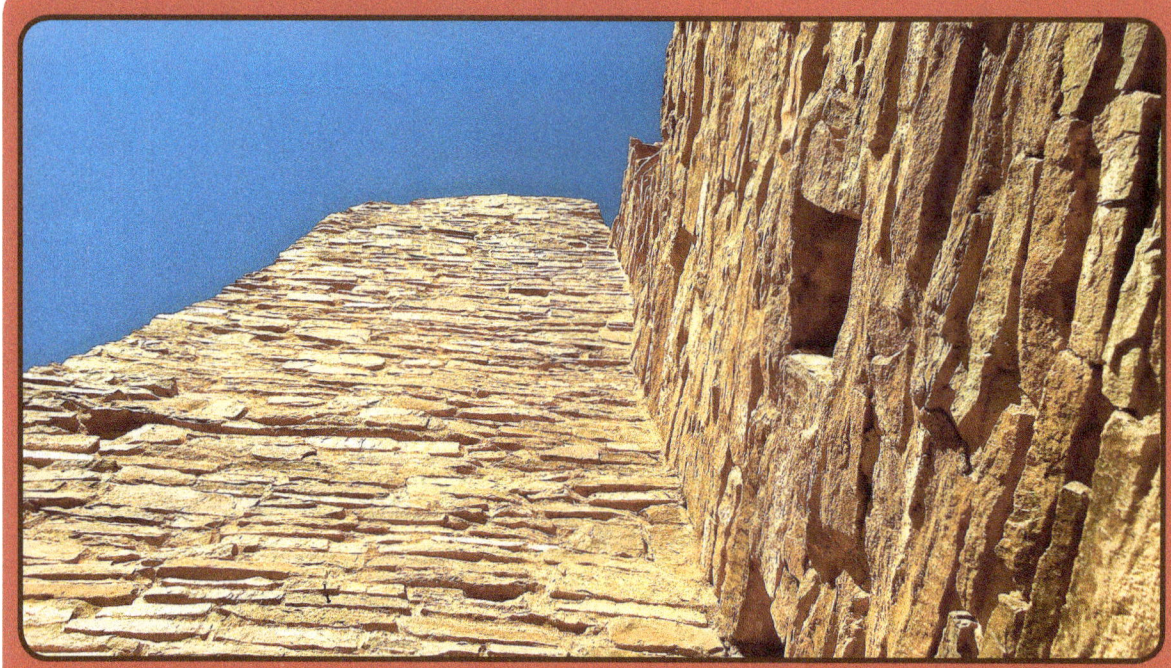

Brick walls and windows built by craftsmen in the early 1600s arise from a hilltop in New Mexico. Franciscan missionaries from Spain and Pueblo Indians lived in these buildings during the days of the Conquistadors when colonies were established in the New World.

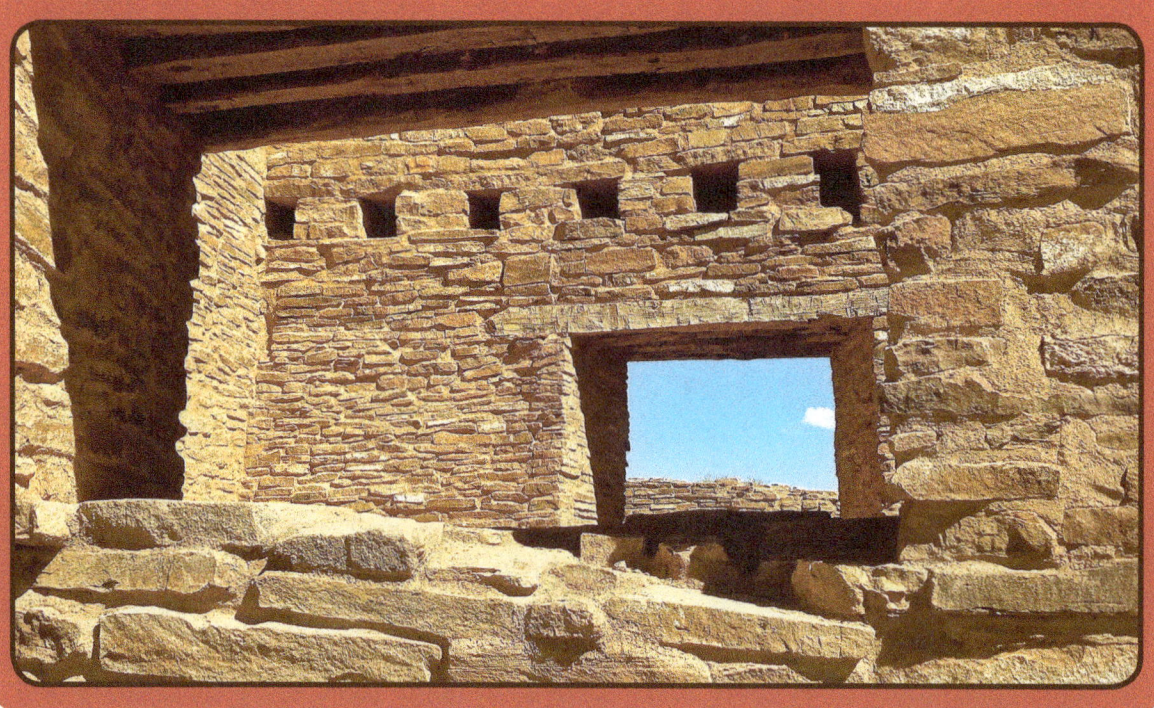

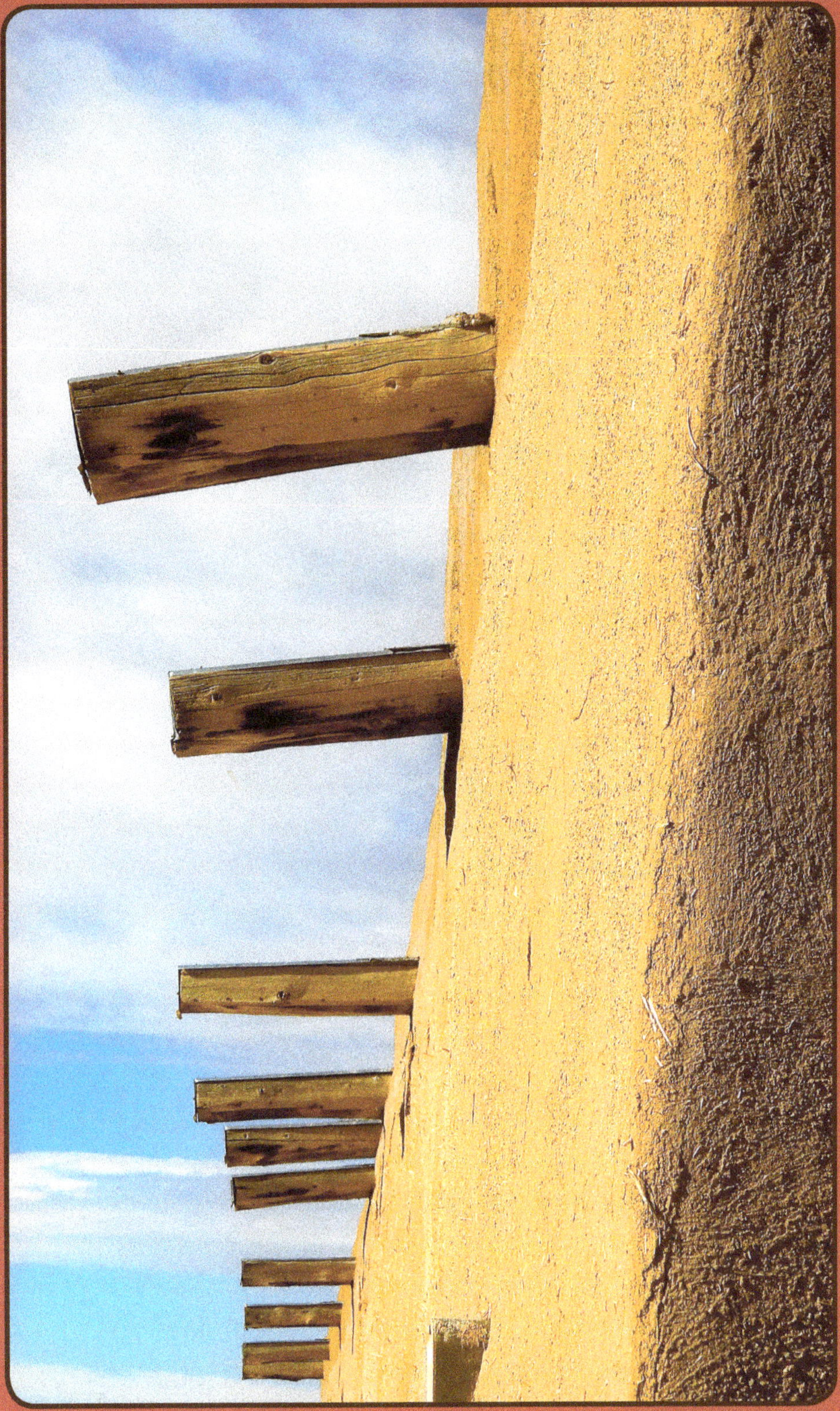

Pathways in Time: Photo Journeys • 47

Wooden roof beams called vigas reach beyond the walls of an old adobe building hacienda built in 1804 in northern New Mexico.

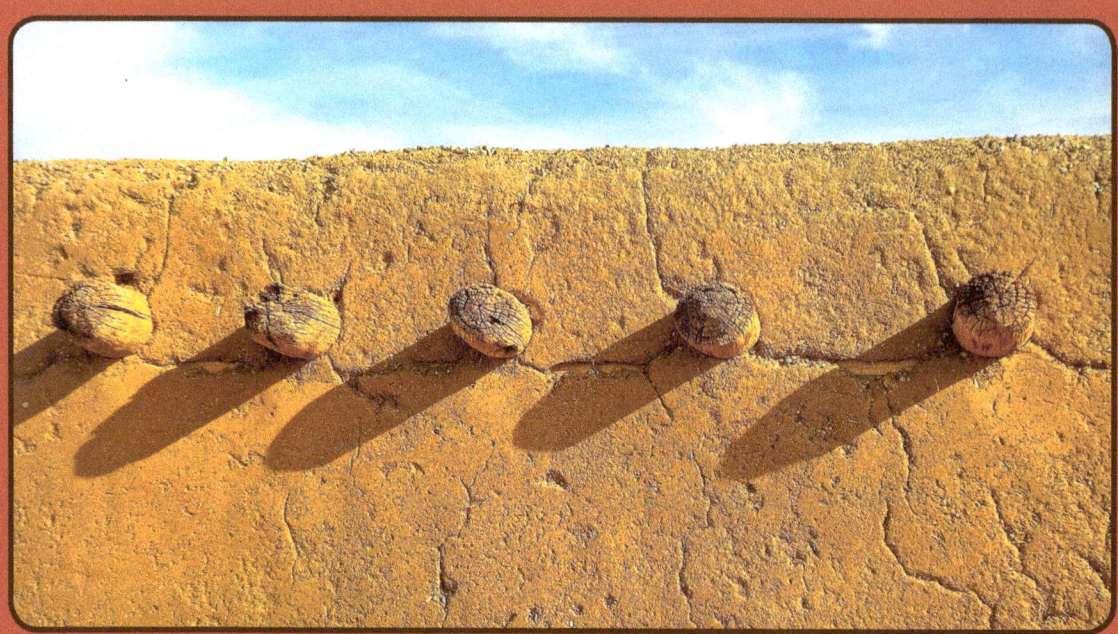

Vigas rise above the site of a village in New Mexico where Spanish explorer Francisco Vásquez de Coronado walked in 1540 when he wintered there with his soldiers.

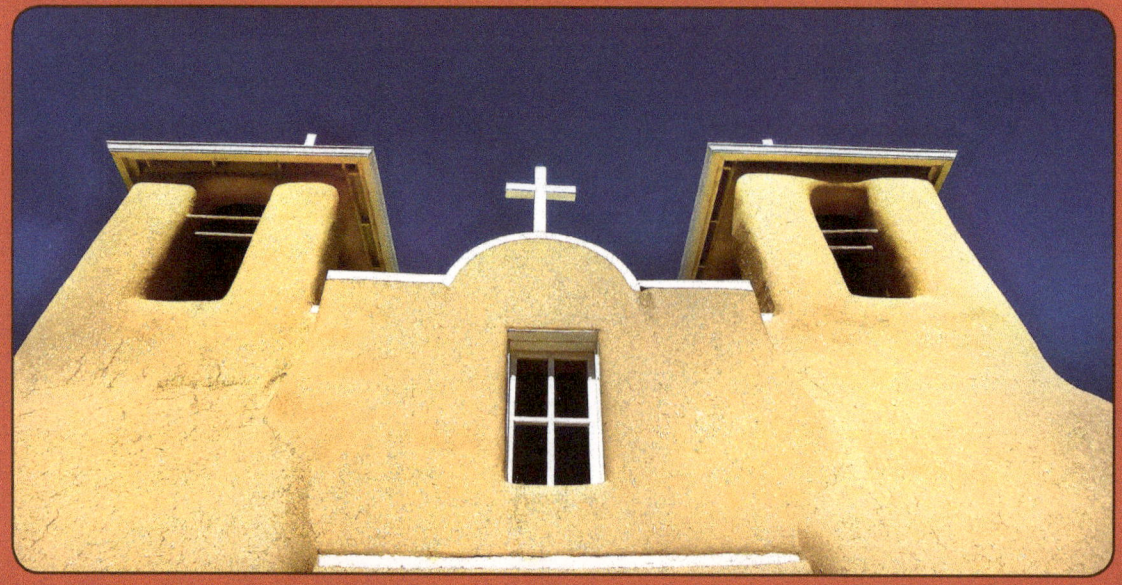

San Francisco de Asis Church in Taos remains an religious and historic landmark since it was built in northern New Mexico around the late 1700s.

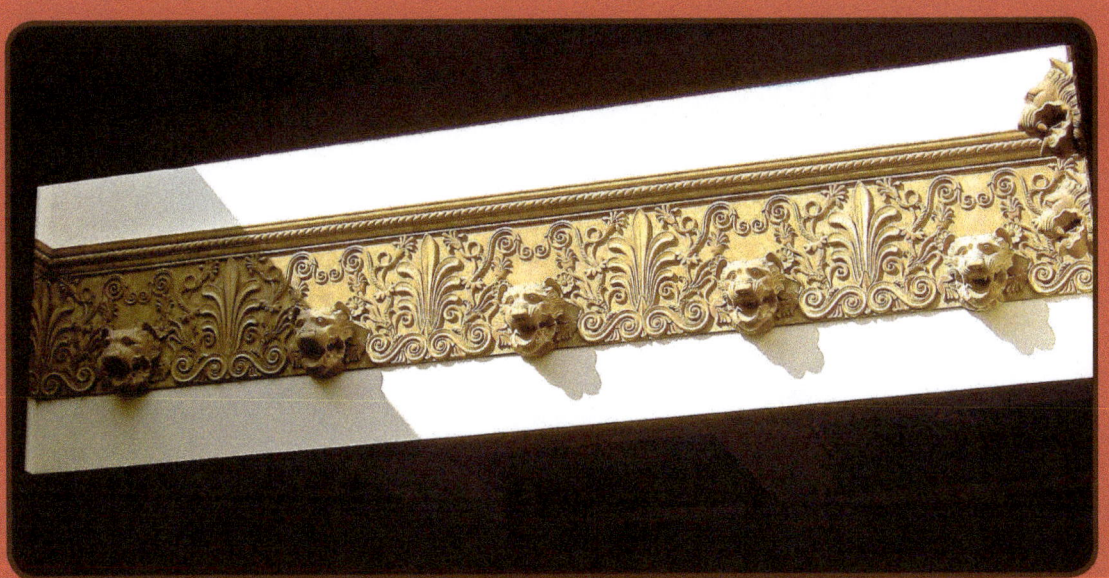

Roman motifs imported by a wealthy patron now adorn a building in a museum.

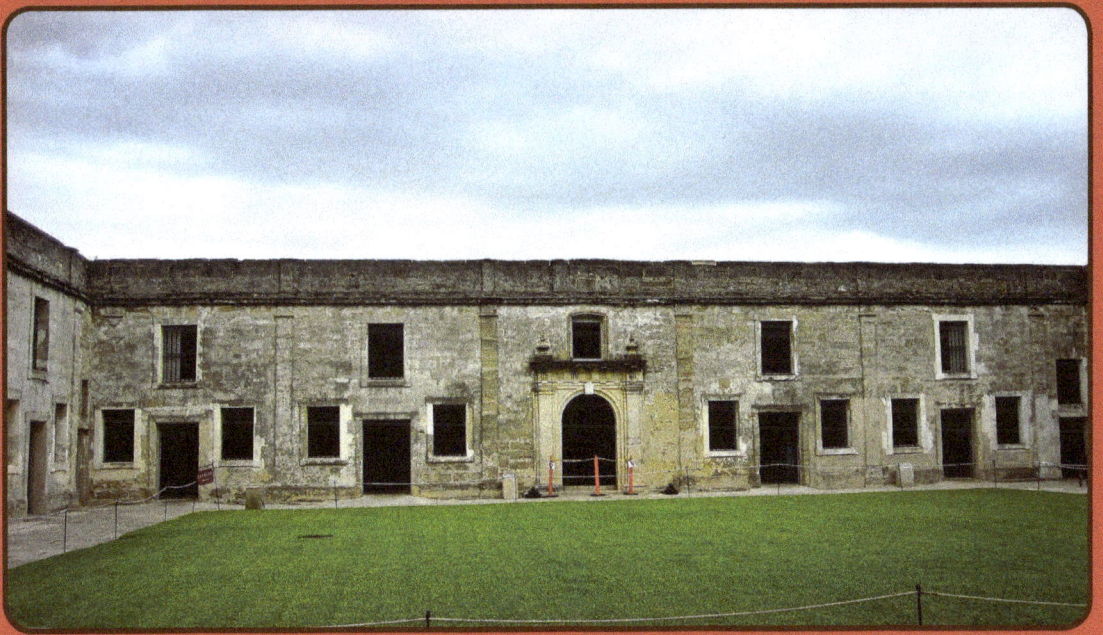

An old Spanish fort in St. Augustine, Florida was built by the Spanish in 1672. In the late 1880s, it became a military prison where Apache men, women and children (as young as 7 years old) were shipped from desert regions of New Mexico and Arizona to be held as prisoners of war. The fort was a site of suffering for the nomadic people to be incarcerated in such a distant and unfamiliar seaside environment.

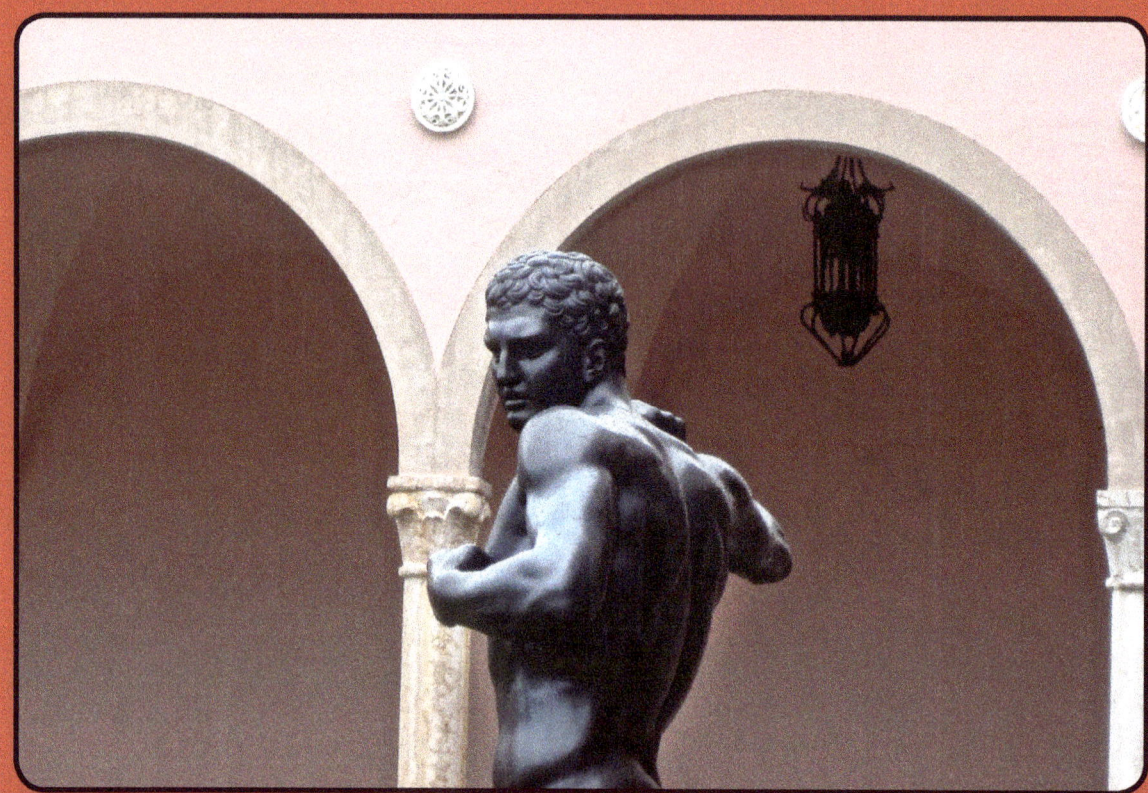

A bronze sculpture enlivens a quiet courtyard in an art museum in Florida.

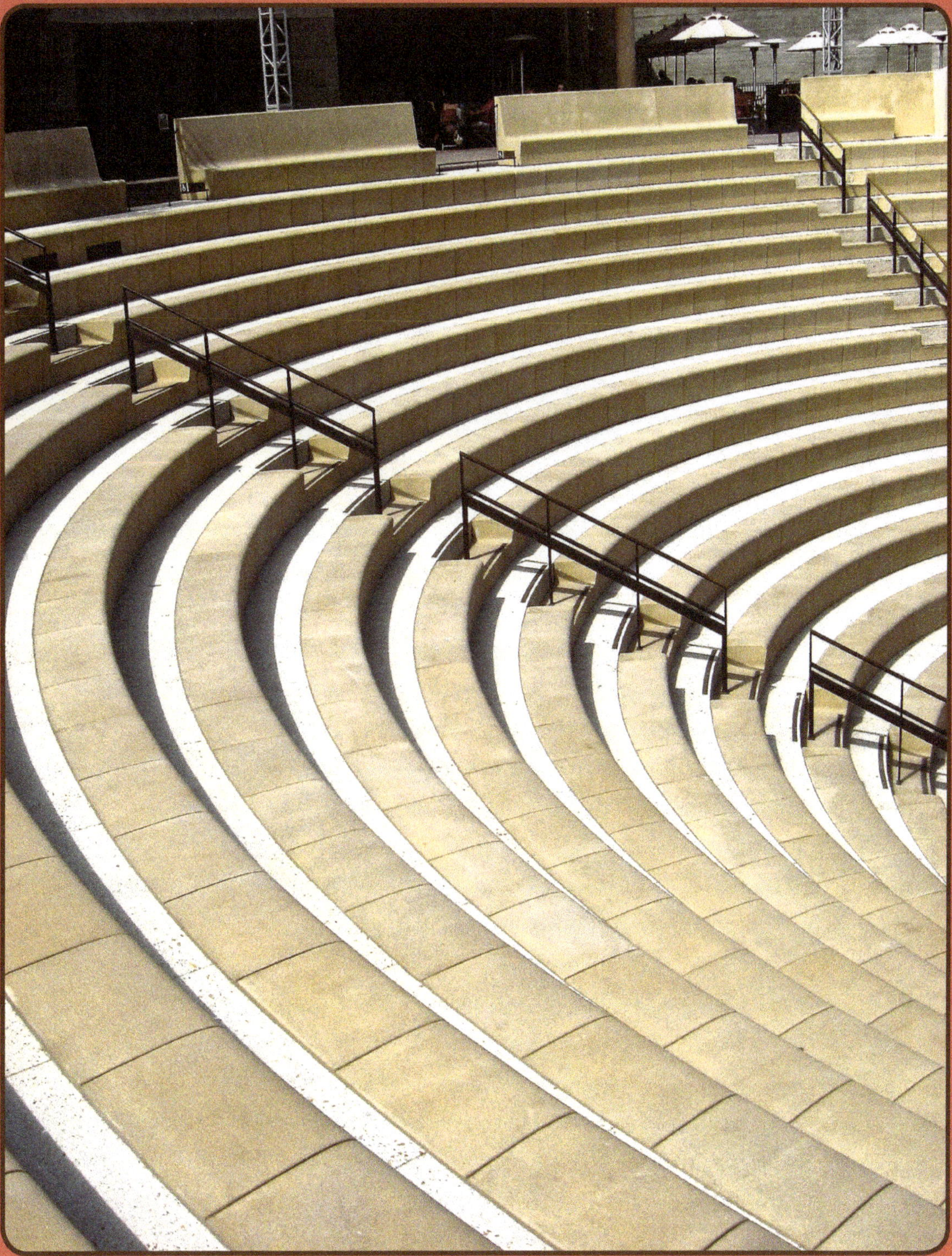

Sunshine highlights an amphitheater in an art museum in California.

Urban Places

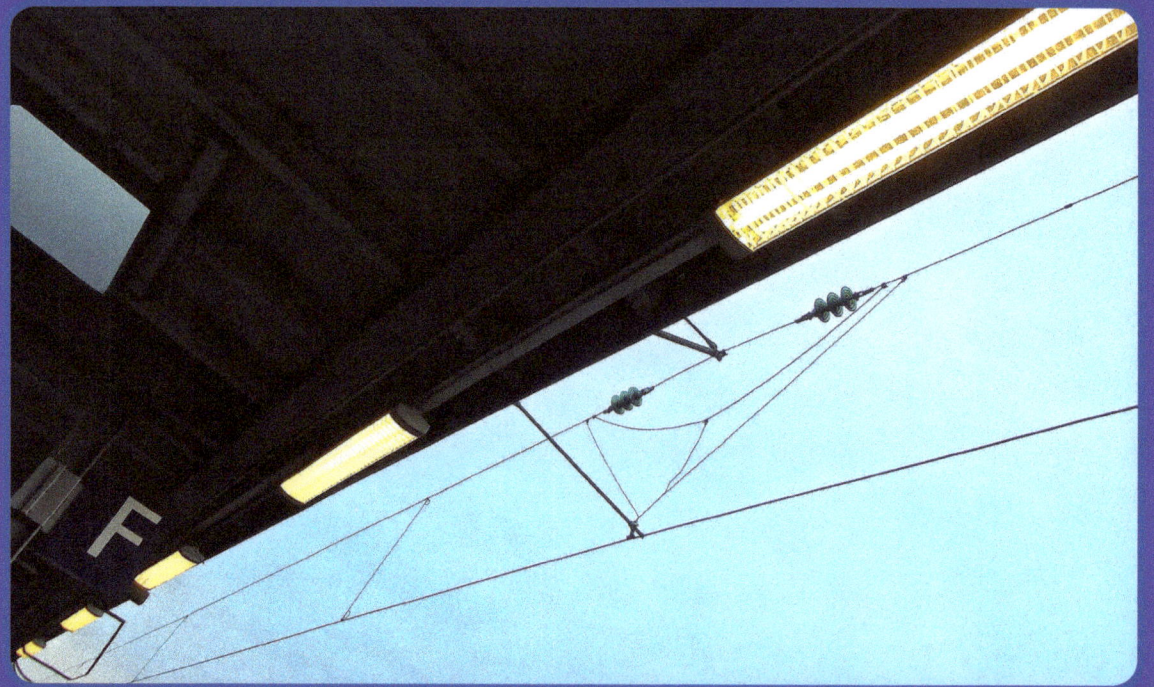

An outdoor platform roof above a train station in Bavaria.

Chapter 3:

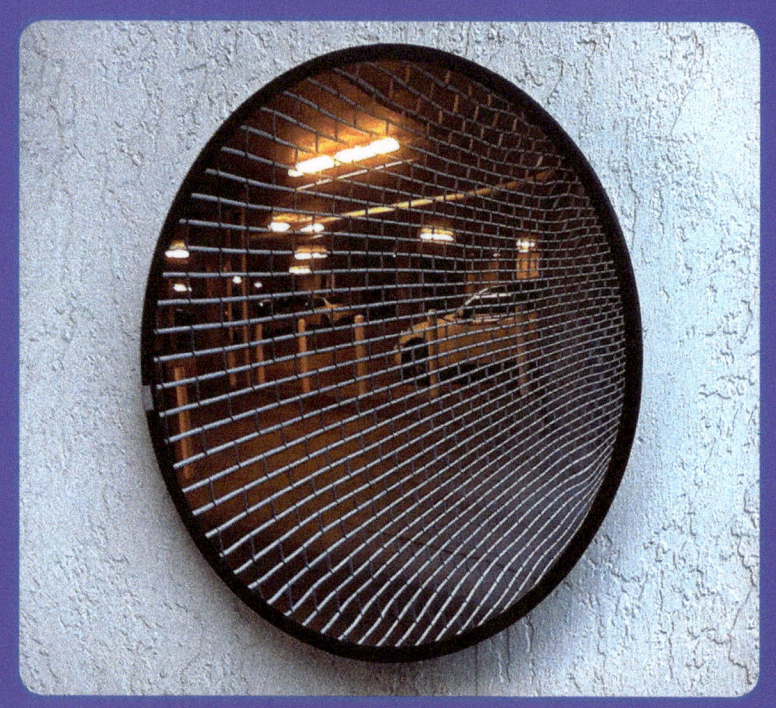

A mirror is mounted on an outside wall to cover a blind spot within an interior parking lot.

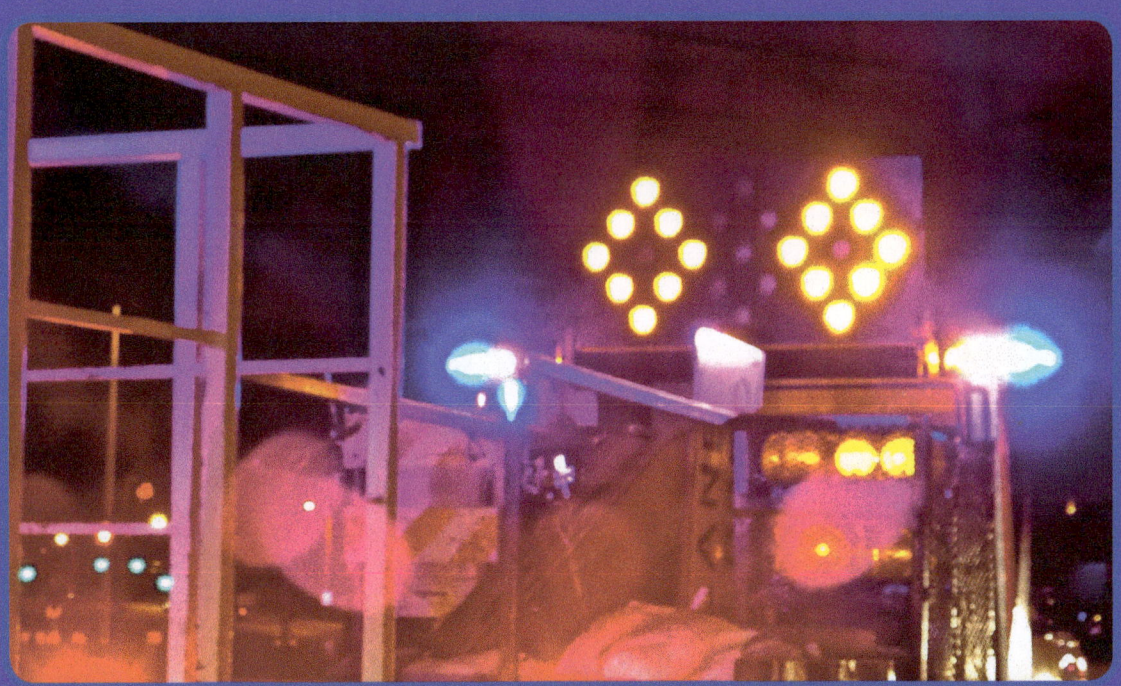

After midnight, a road repair truck (above) carries flashing emergency signs to post along a highway to warn drivers about repaving and lane closures. Below is a close up of the warning lights.

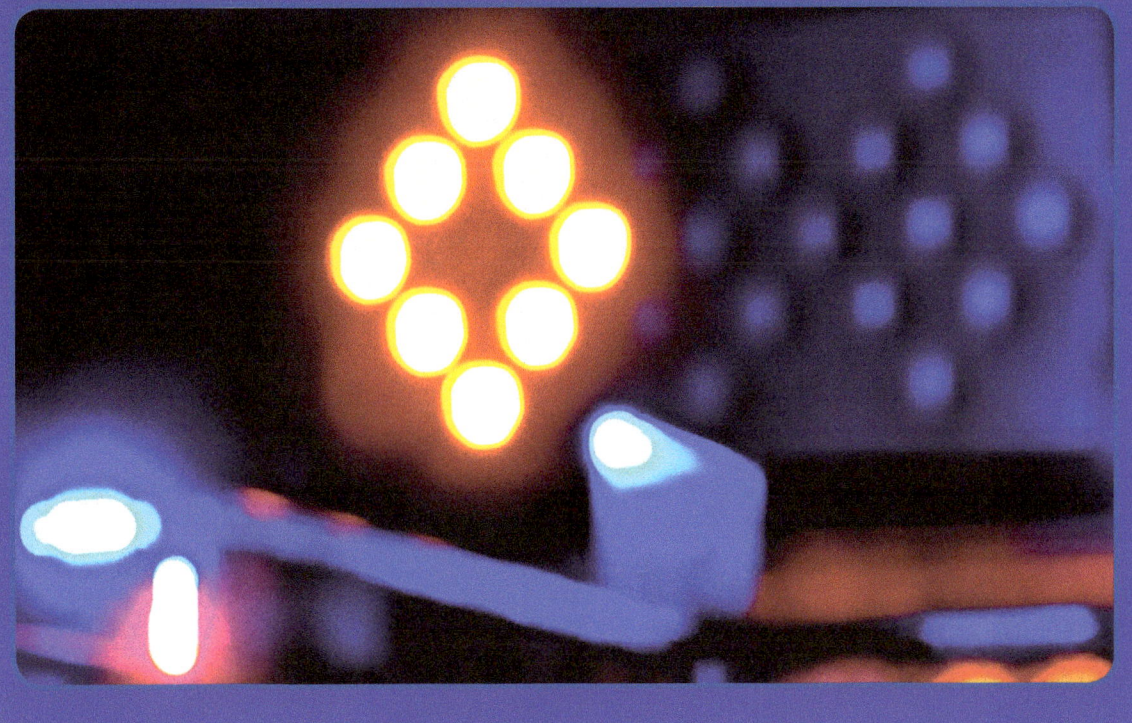

A light illuminates an underground parking lot.

Pathways in Time: Photo Journeys • 55

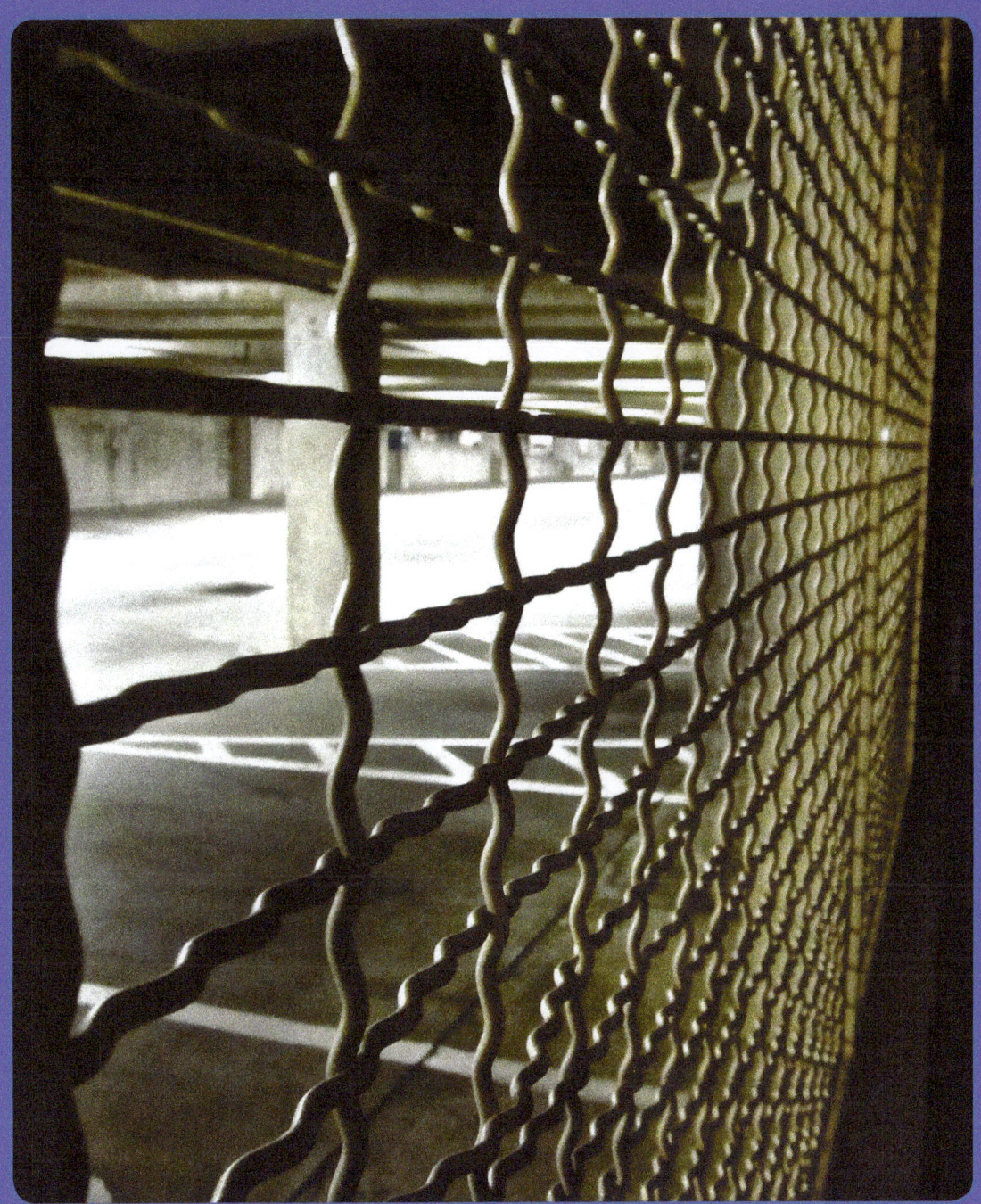

A metal grill prevents weekend access to an empty parking lot beneath a tall office building.

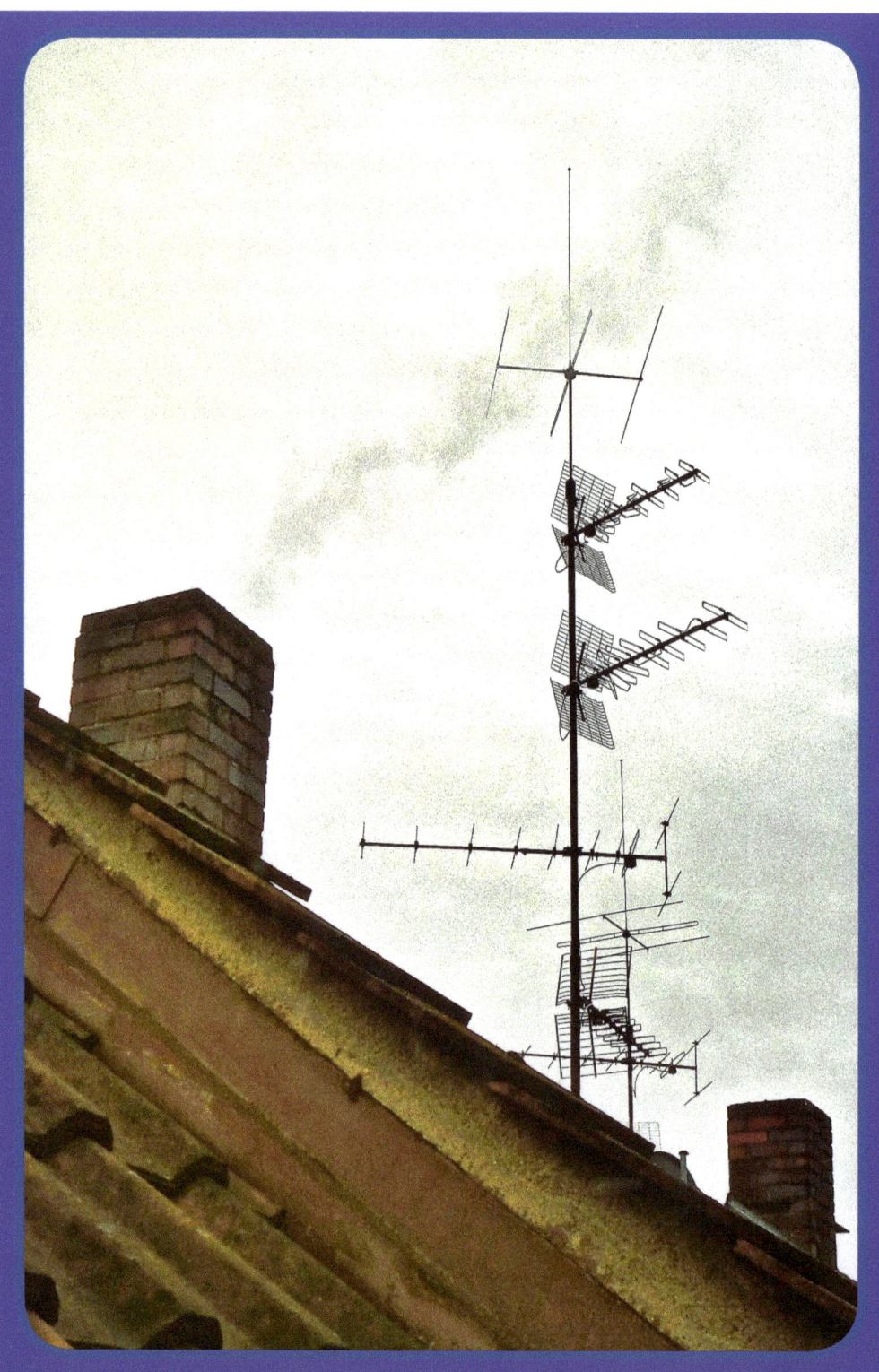

A rooftop in Germany.

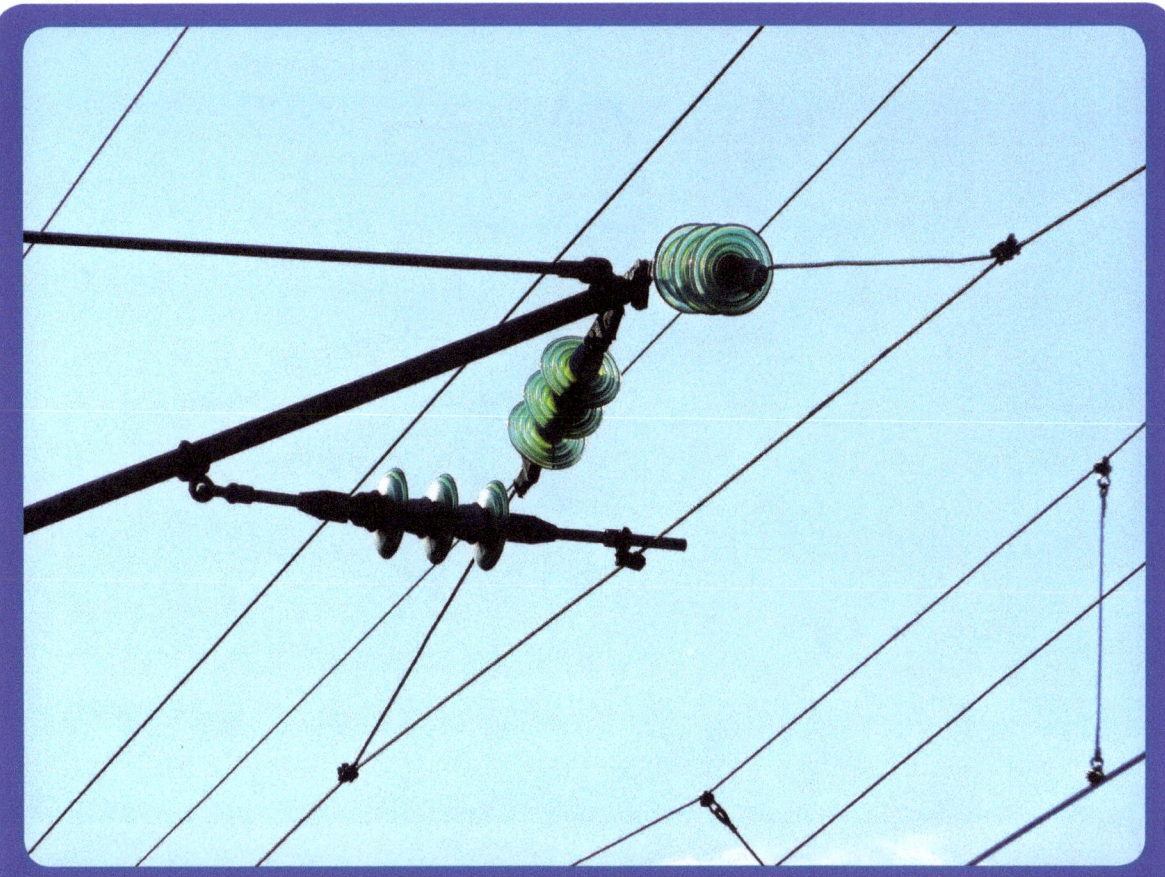
Rail lights are suspended above train tracks in Bavaria.

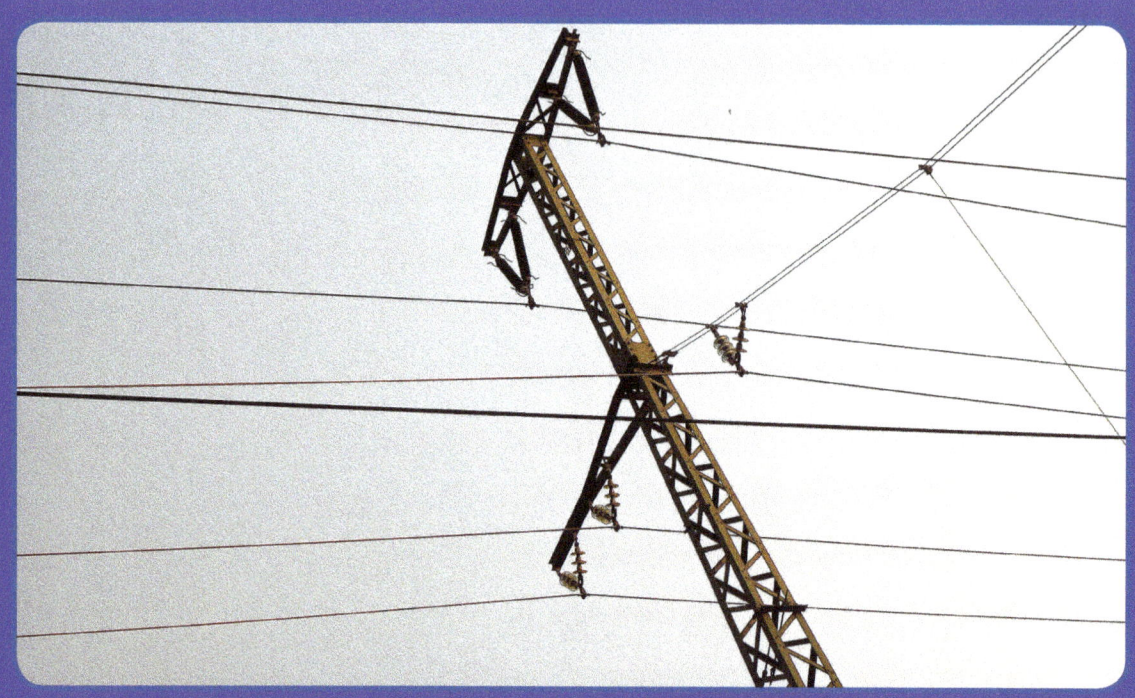
An electricity transmission line disrupts the view of the sky above.

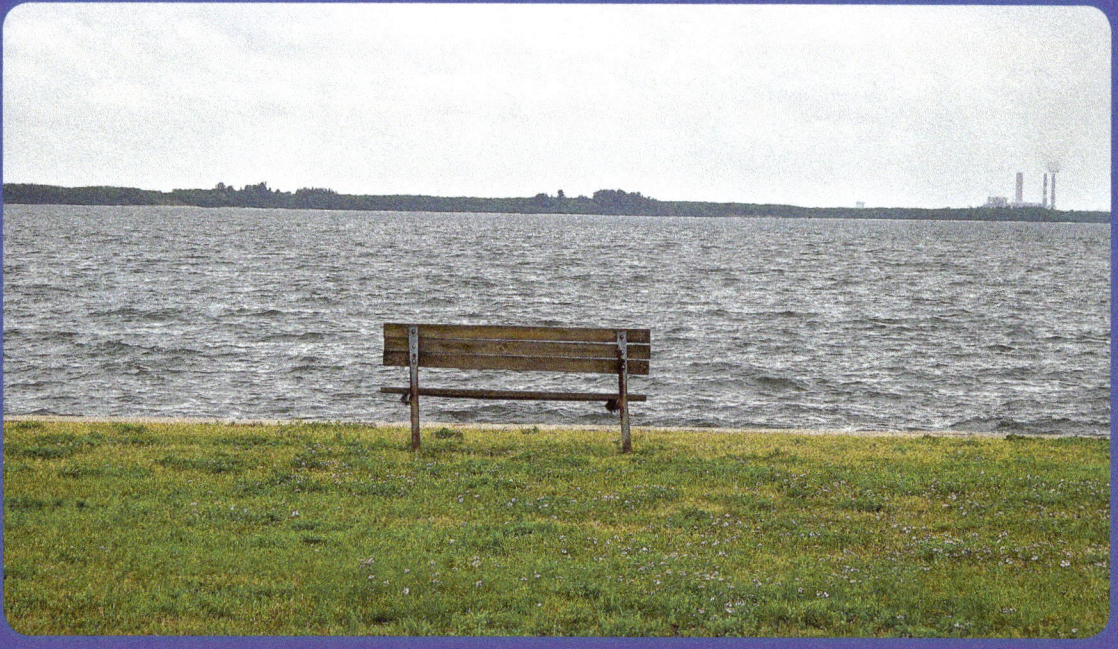
No one sits on an island park bench facing a view of ever-changing waters in a bay.

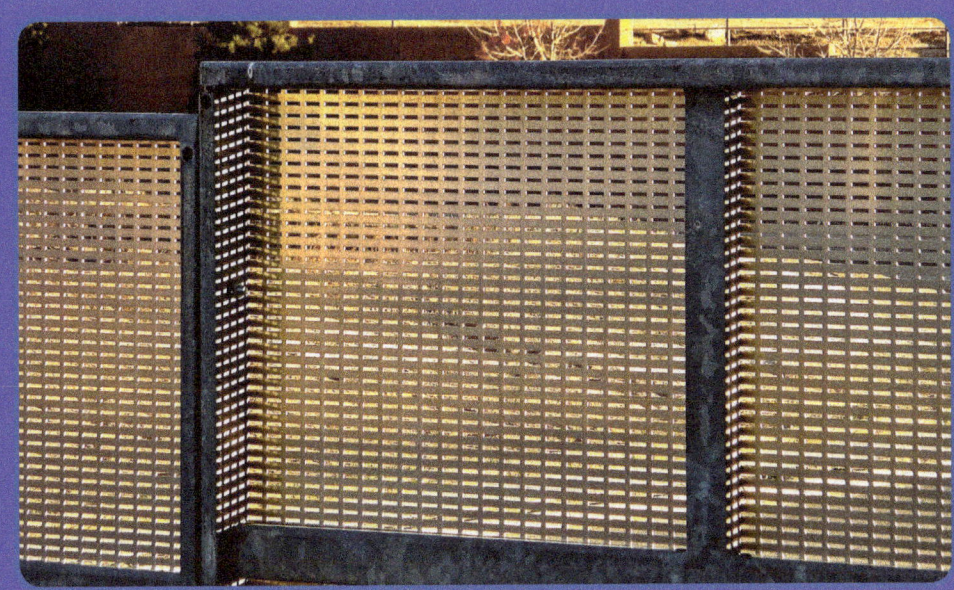
Setting sun's rays illuminate a metal fence along a walkway outside offices.

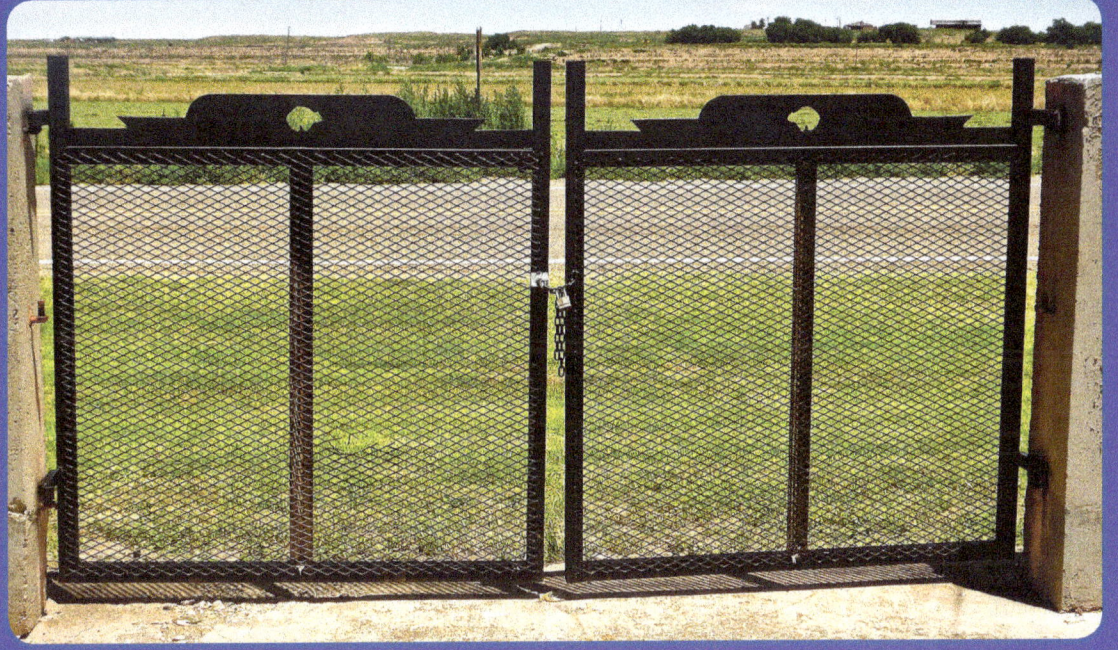
A handmade wrought iron gate with bears blocks street access to the graveyard where Billy the Kid (William Bonney) is buried near the place he died in an 1881 shootout. His grave is located a few feet away from one of his victims (Joe Grant) who was killed in 1880. Billy the Kid is buried in the same place and shares a headstone with 2 of his gang members (Tom O'Folliard and Charlie Bowdre), who died after gun battles in separate incidents in December 1880. All 3 died at the hands of Sheriff Pat Garrett.

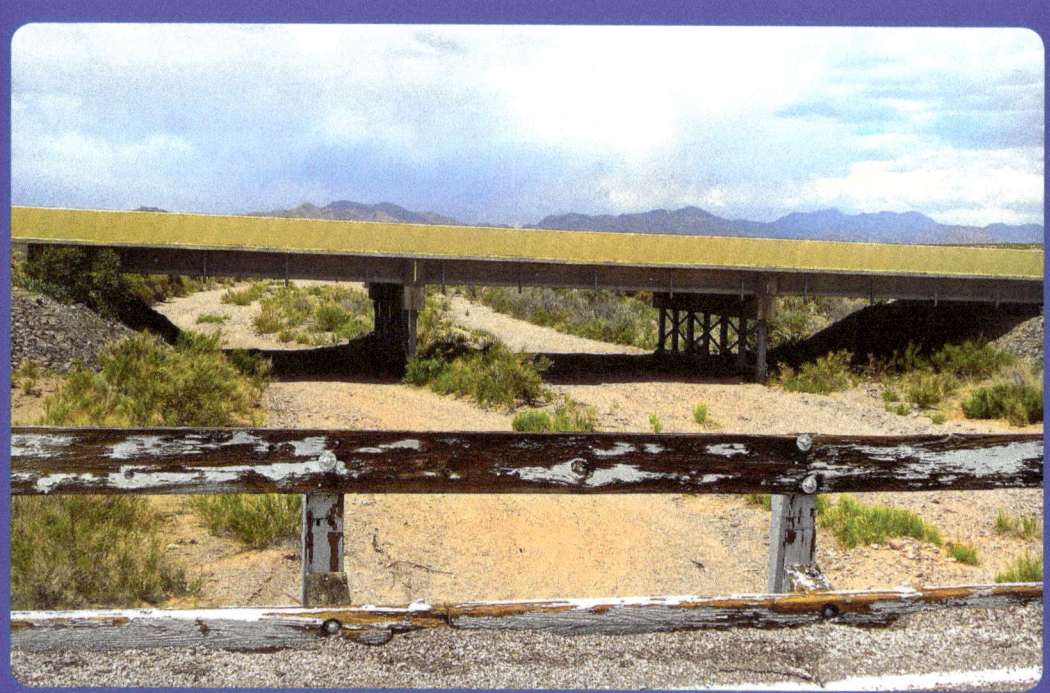

A double set of roadway bridges span an arroyo. The newer bridge for interstate traffic has replaced the older wooden structure in the forefront.

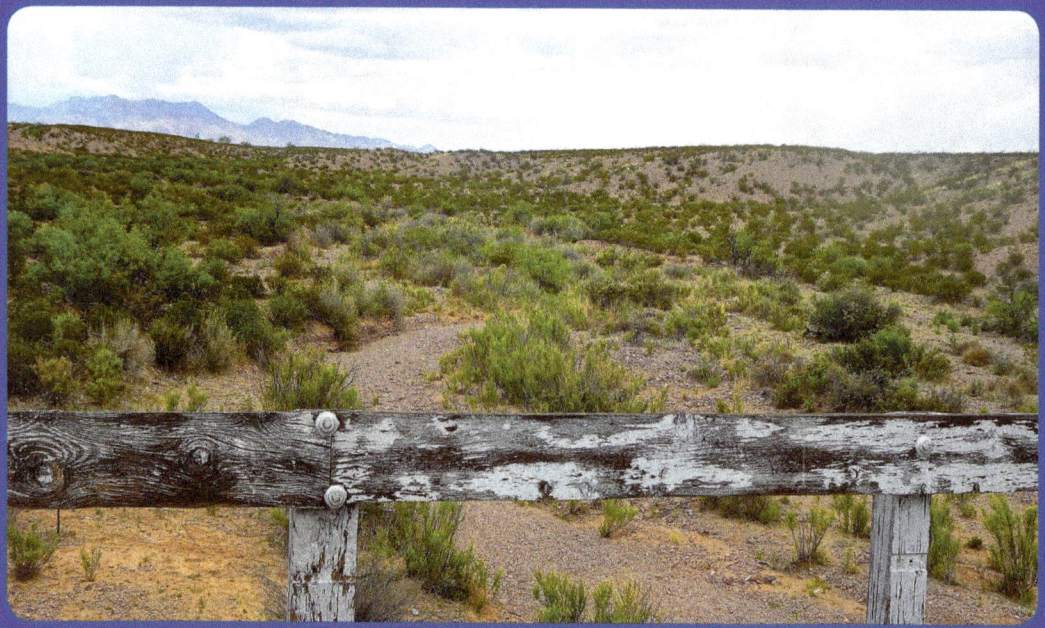

An old wooden highway bridge over a dry riverbed deteriorates in New Mexico.

Chapter 4: Trees

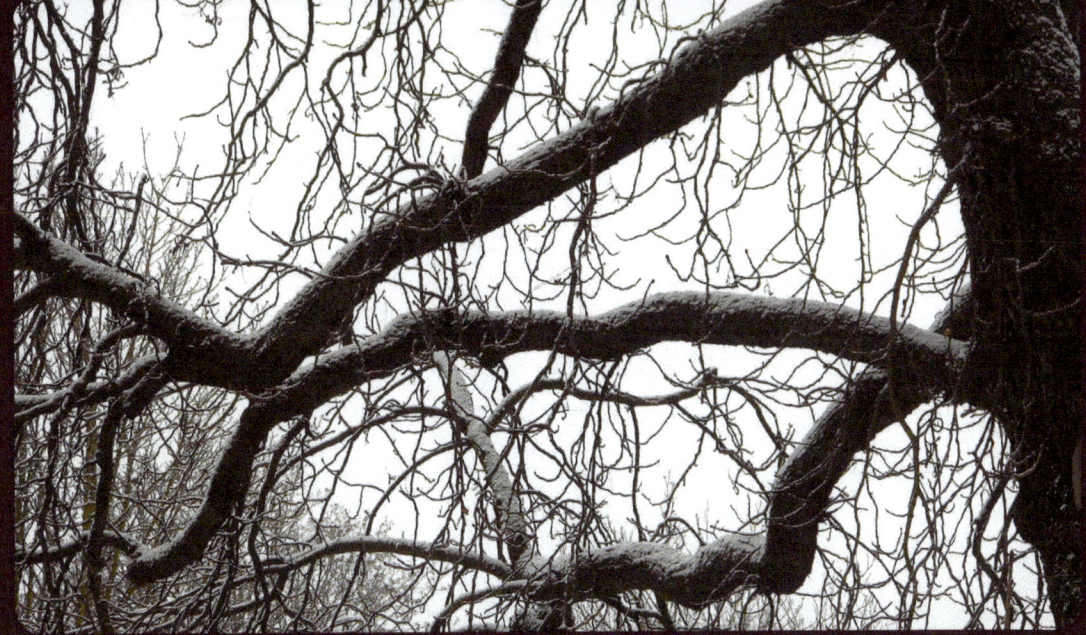
Snow attaches itself to tree branches during the winter.

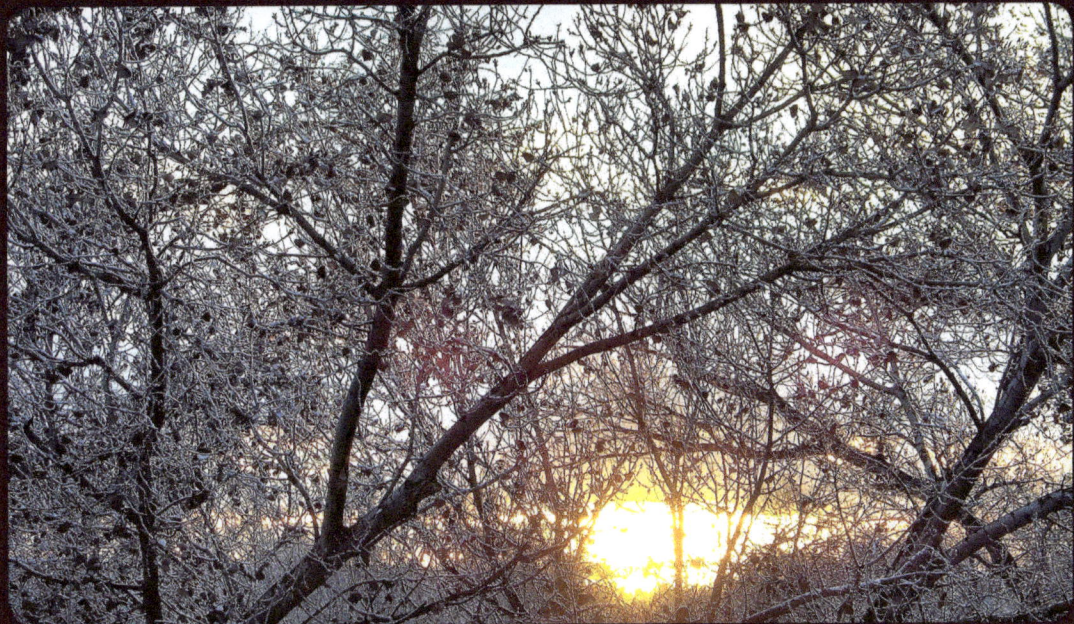
Frozen trees face a cold evening as the sun sets one winter day near a river.

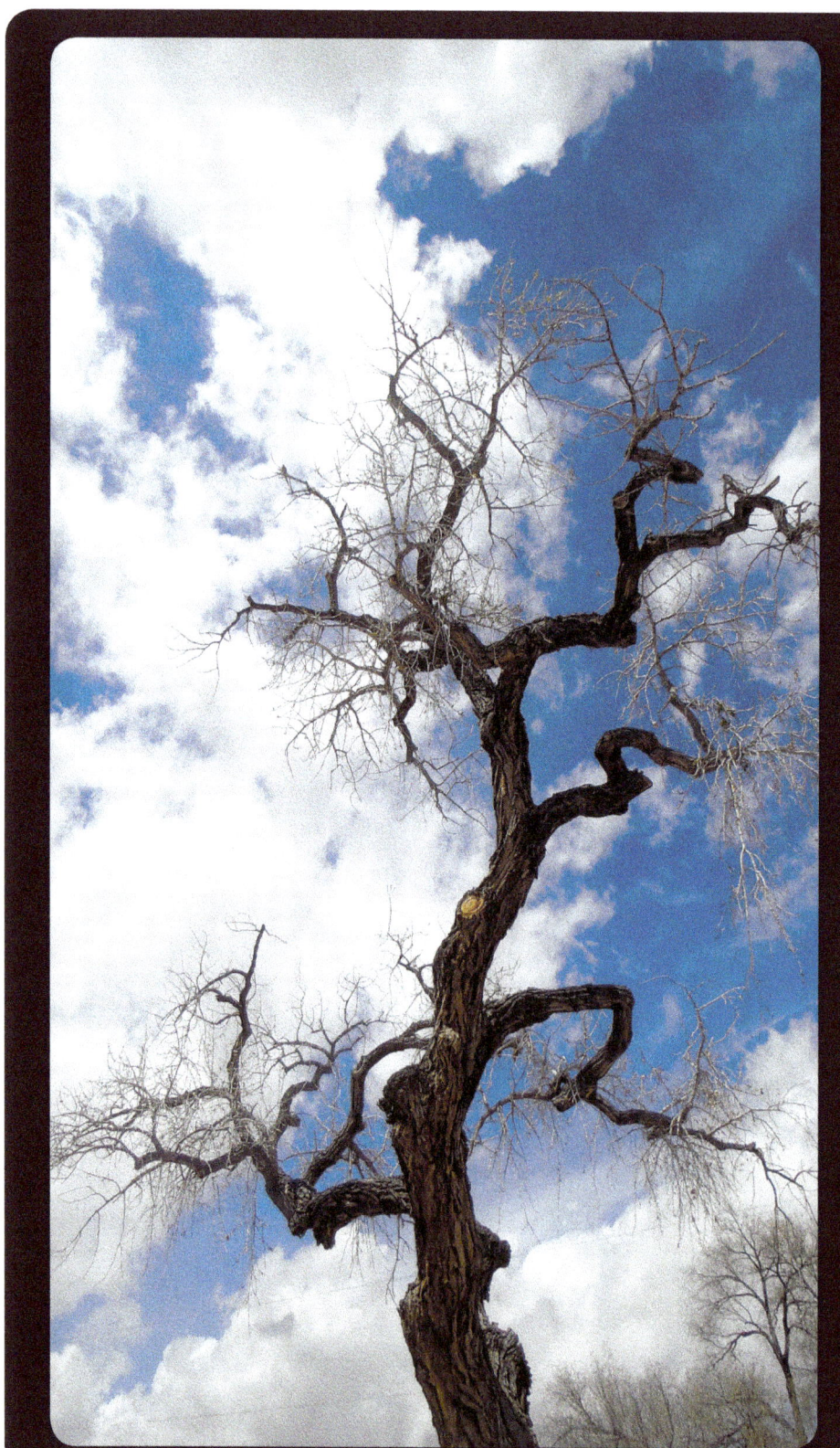

A cottonwood tree reaches upwards to the heavens.

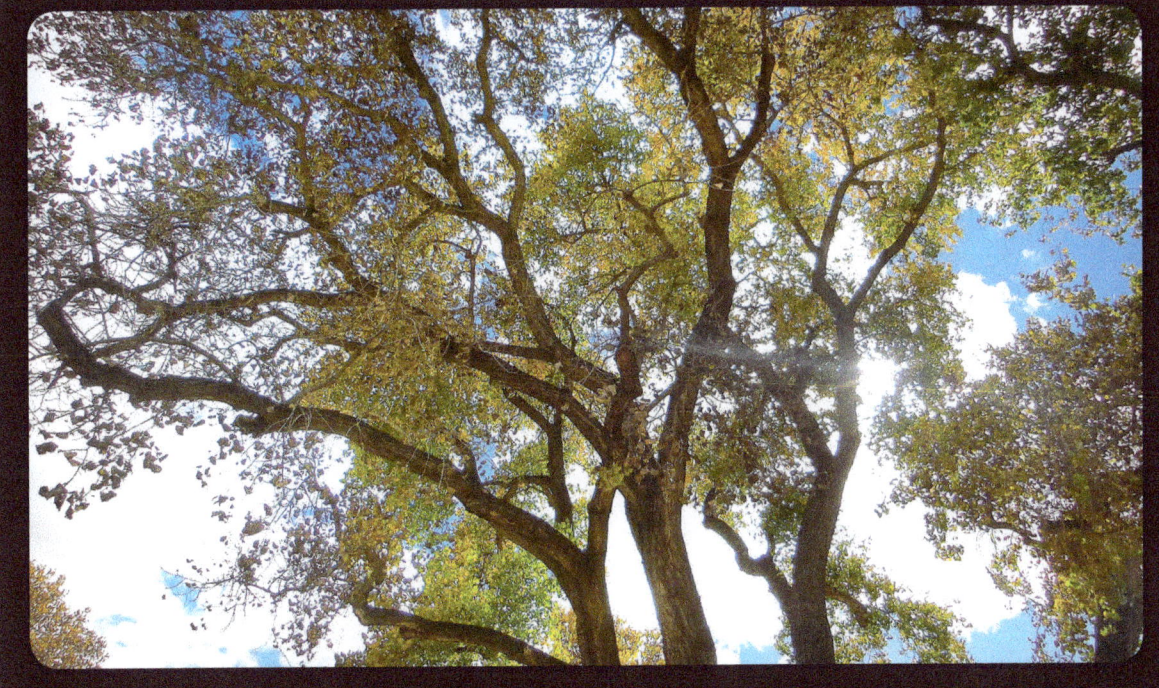
Rays of sunlight shimmer.

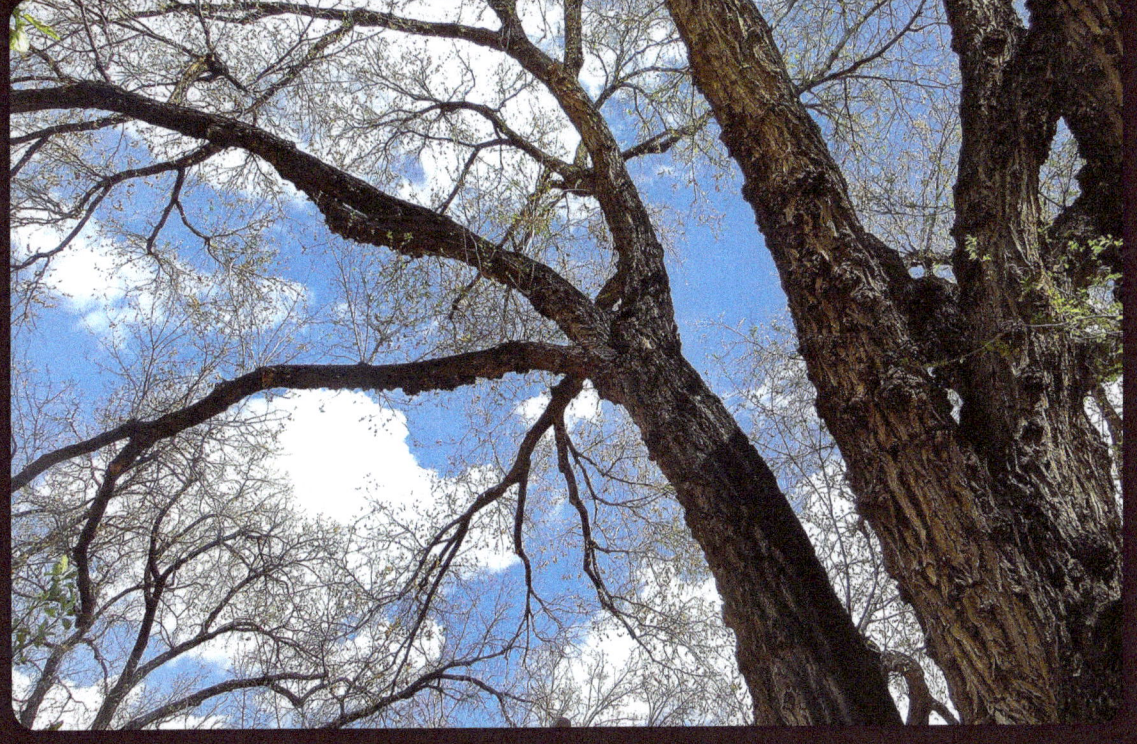
Buds appear on a tree at the start of spring.

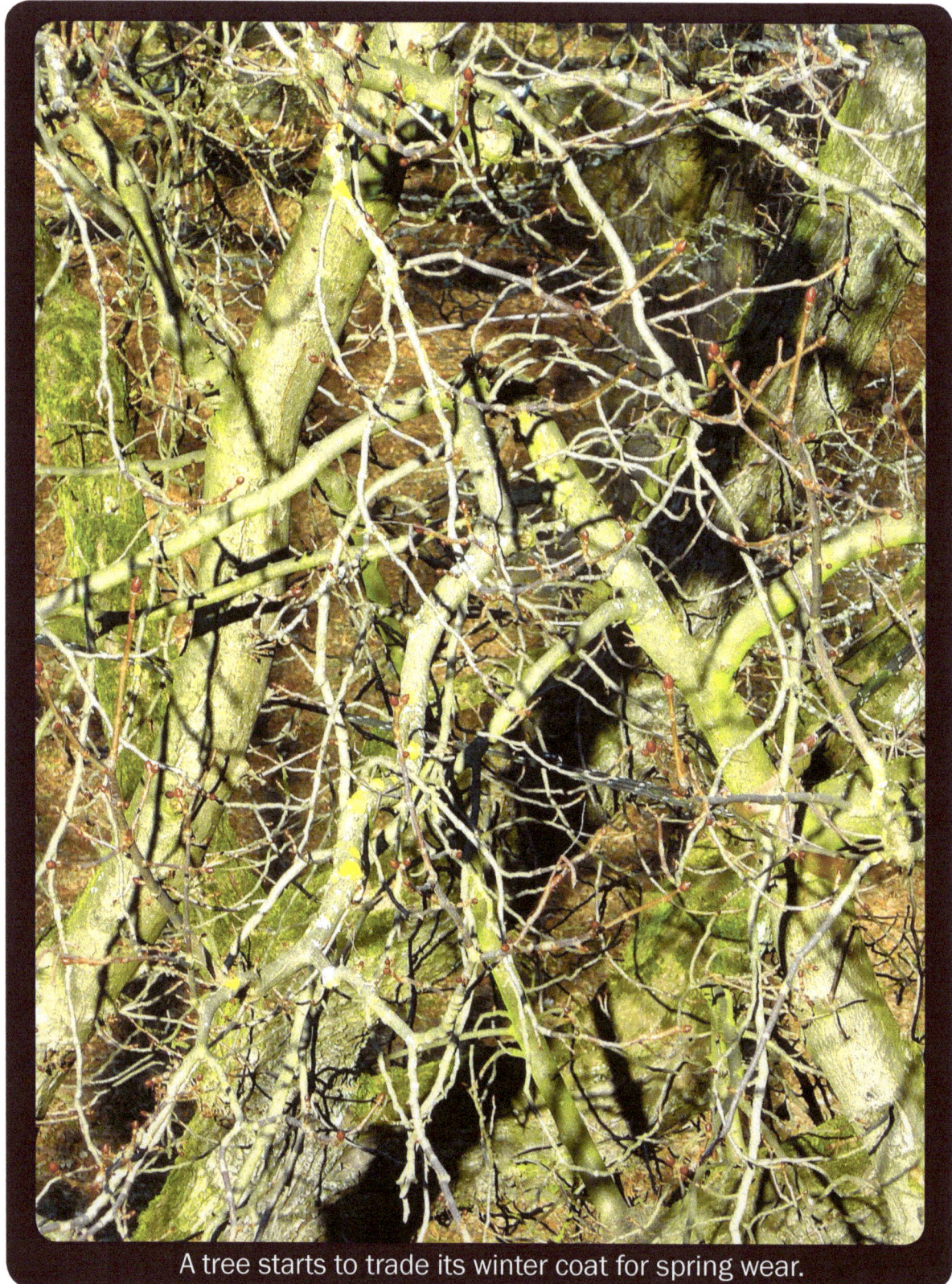
A tree starts to trade its winter coat for spring wear.

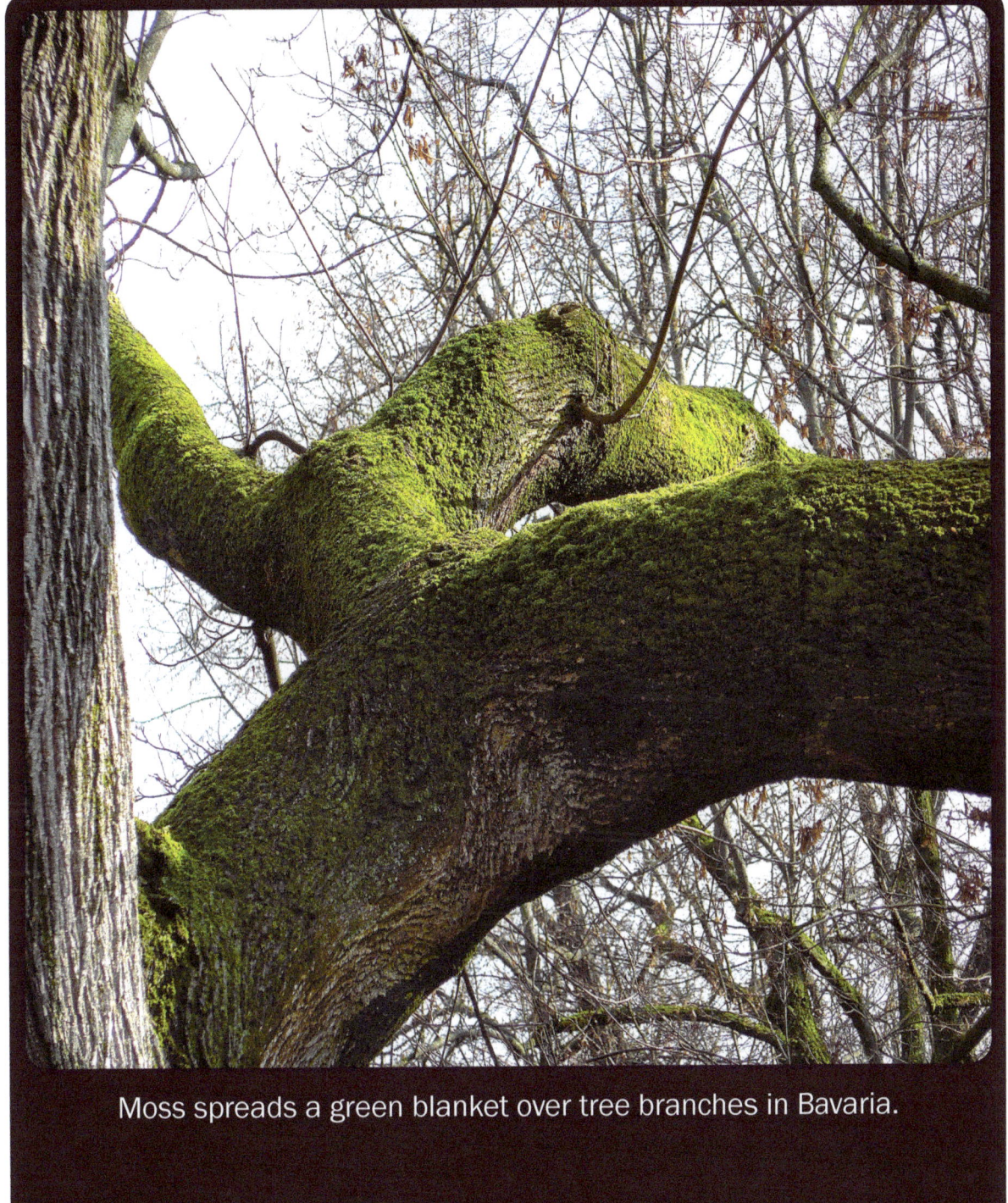
Moss spreads a green blanket over tree branches in Bavaria.

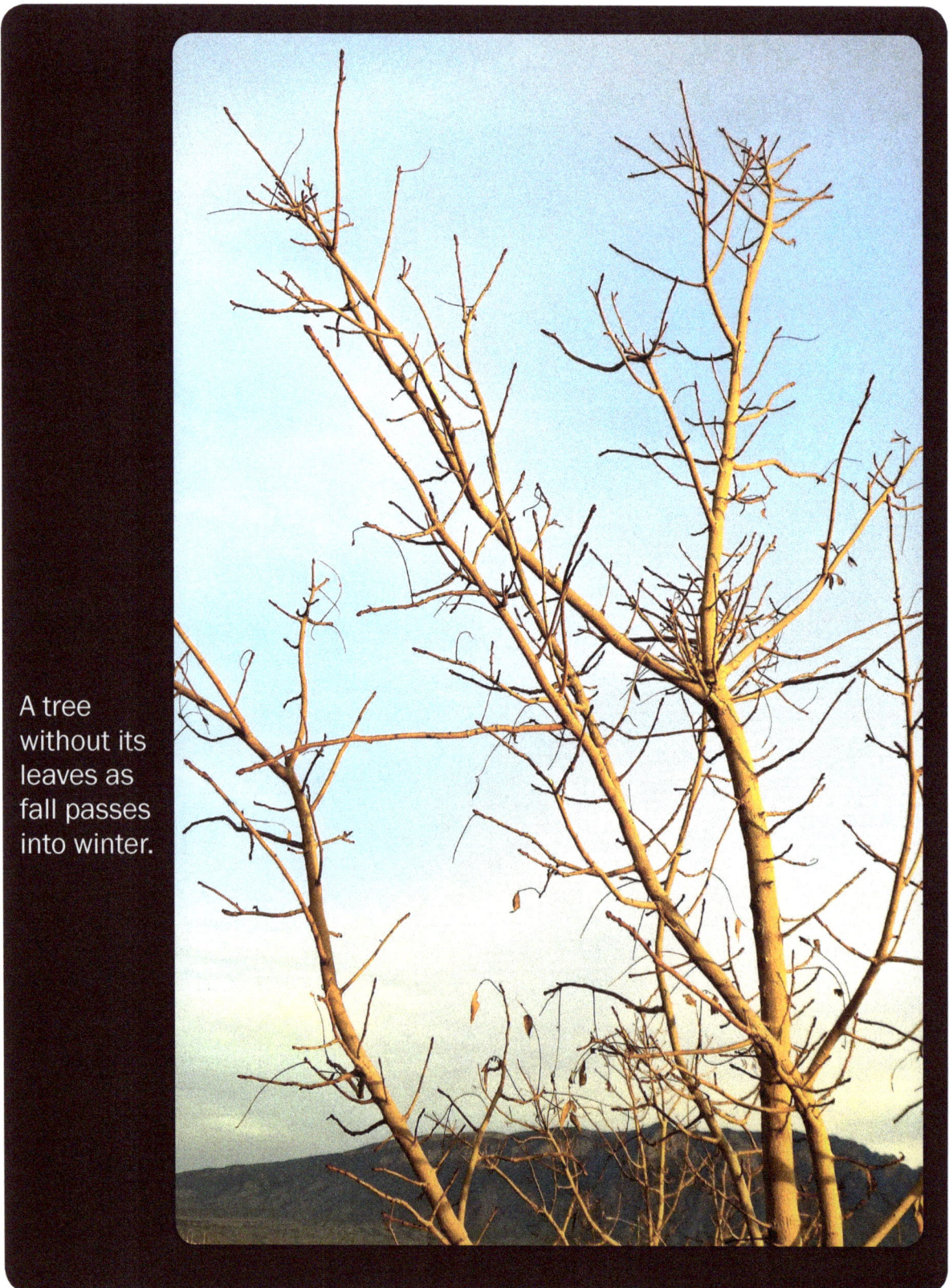
A tree without its leaves as fall passes into winter.

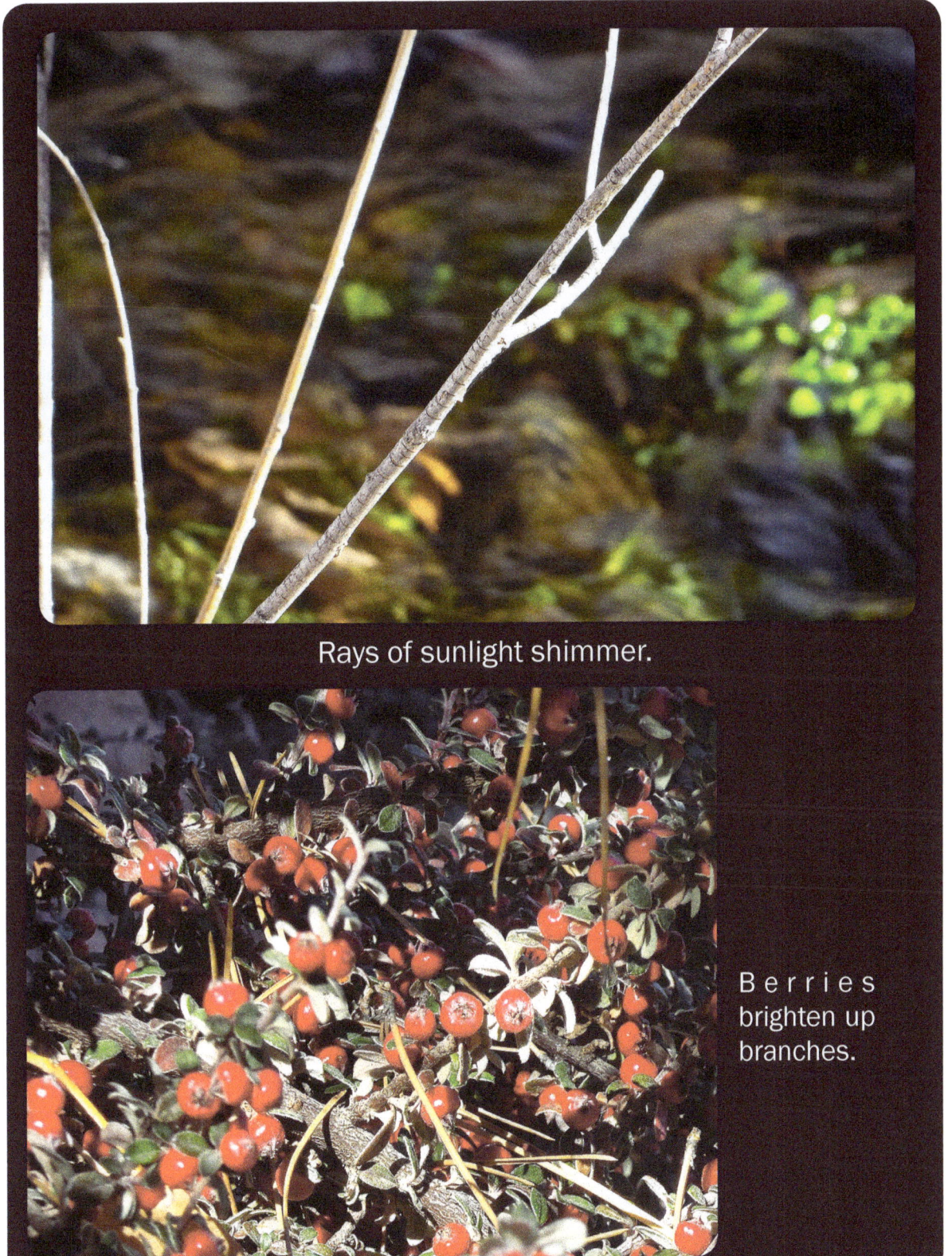

Rays of sunlight shimmer.

Berries brighten up branches.

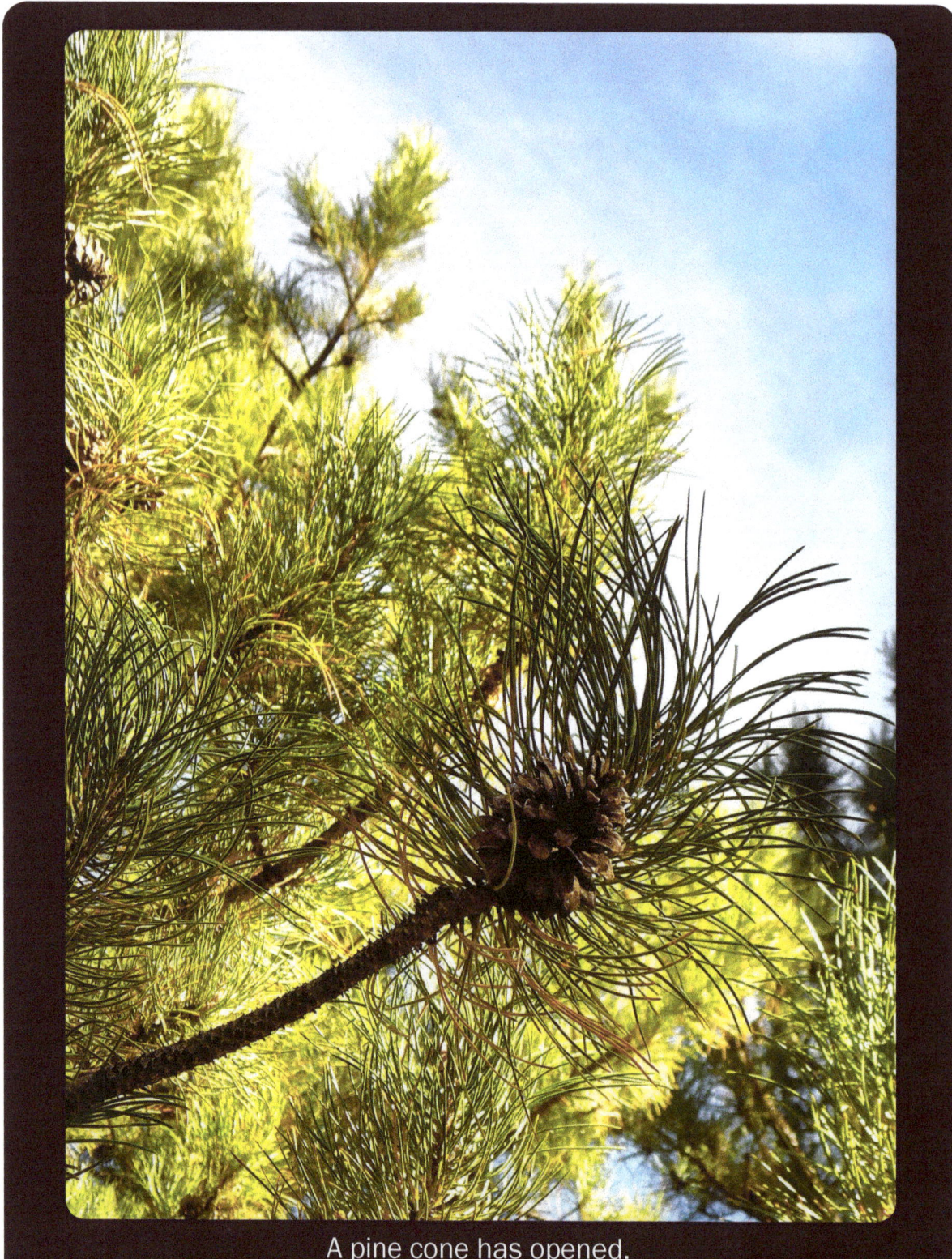

A pine cone has opened.

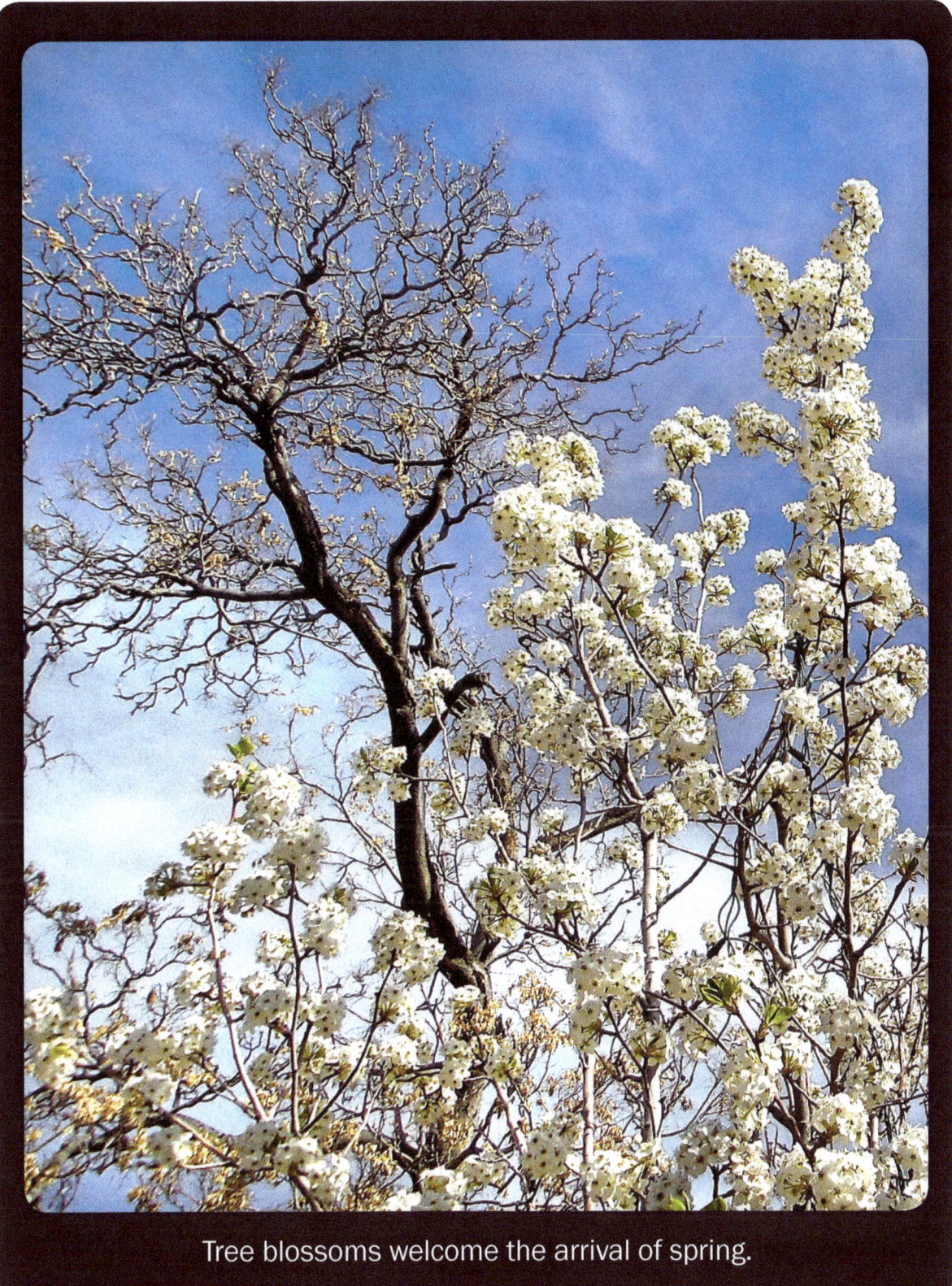
Tree blossoms welcome the arrival of spring.

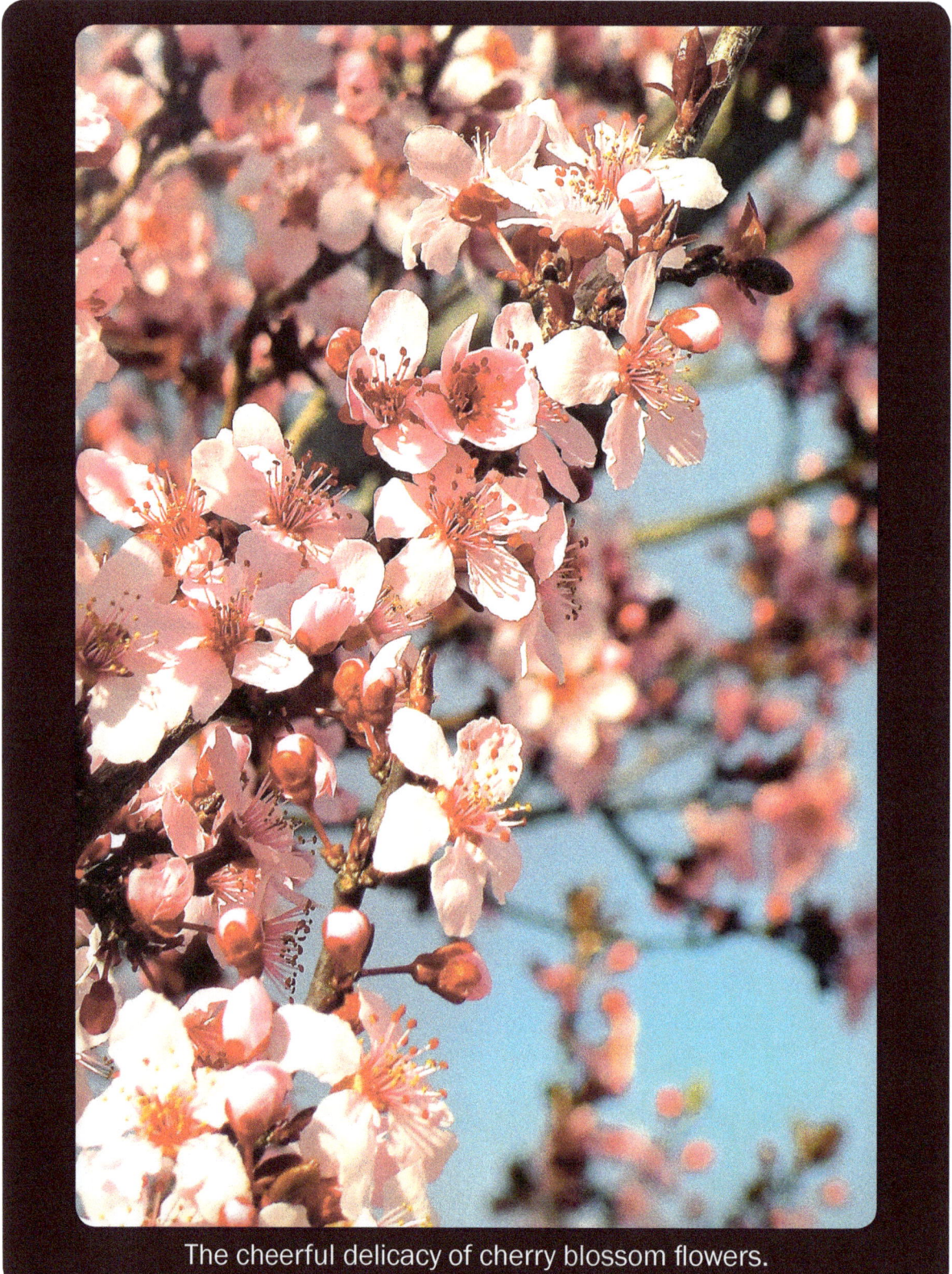
The cheerful delicacy of cherry blossom flowers.

Pathways in Time: Photo Journeys

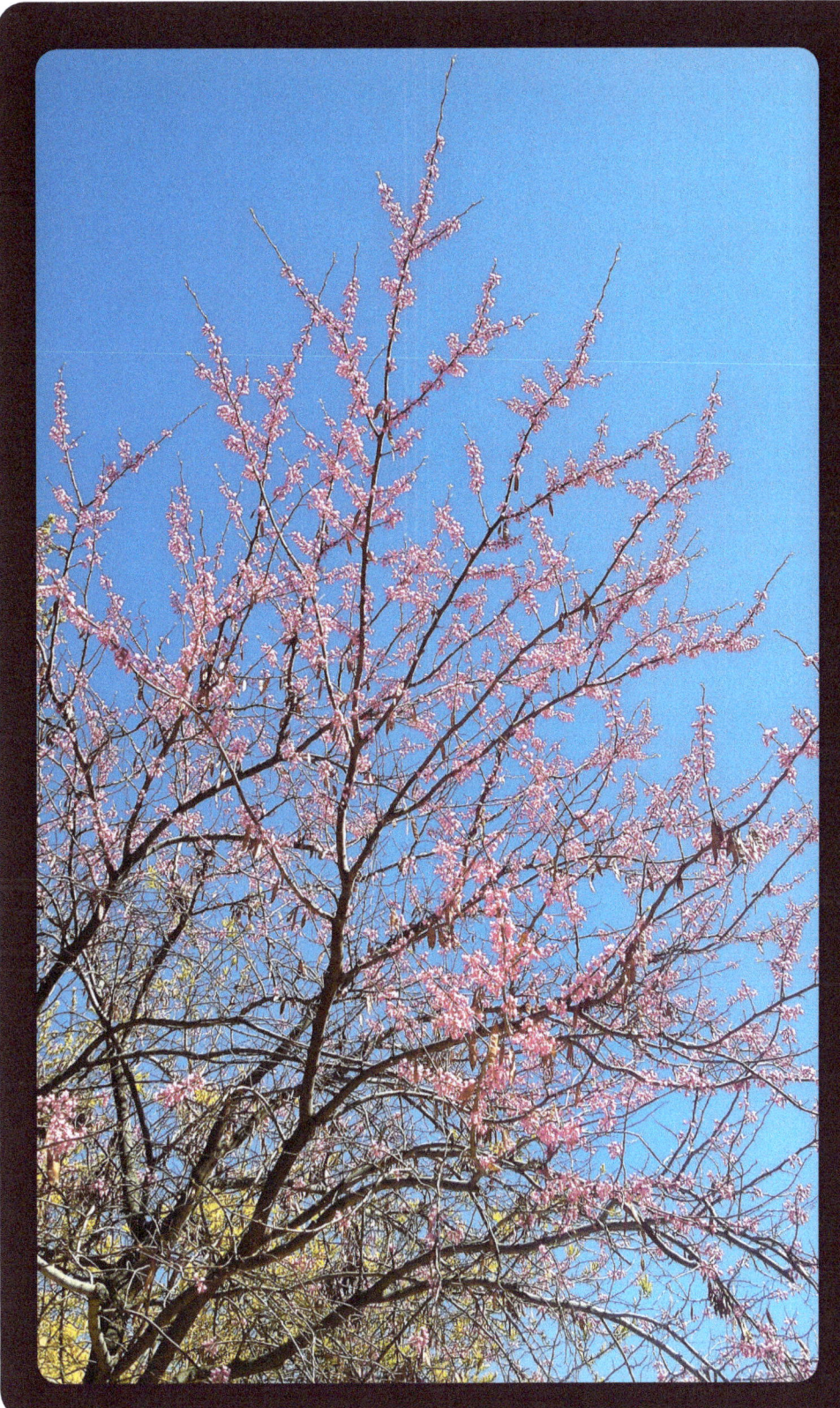

Colors contrast cherry blossoms against a clear blue sky.

Chapter 5: Leaves

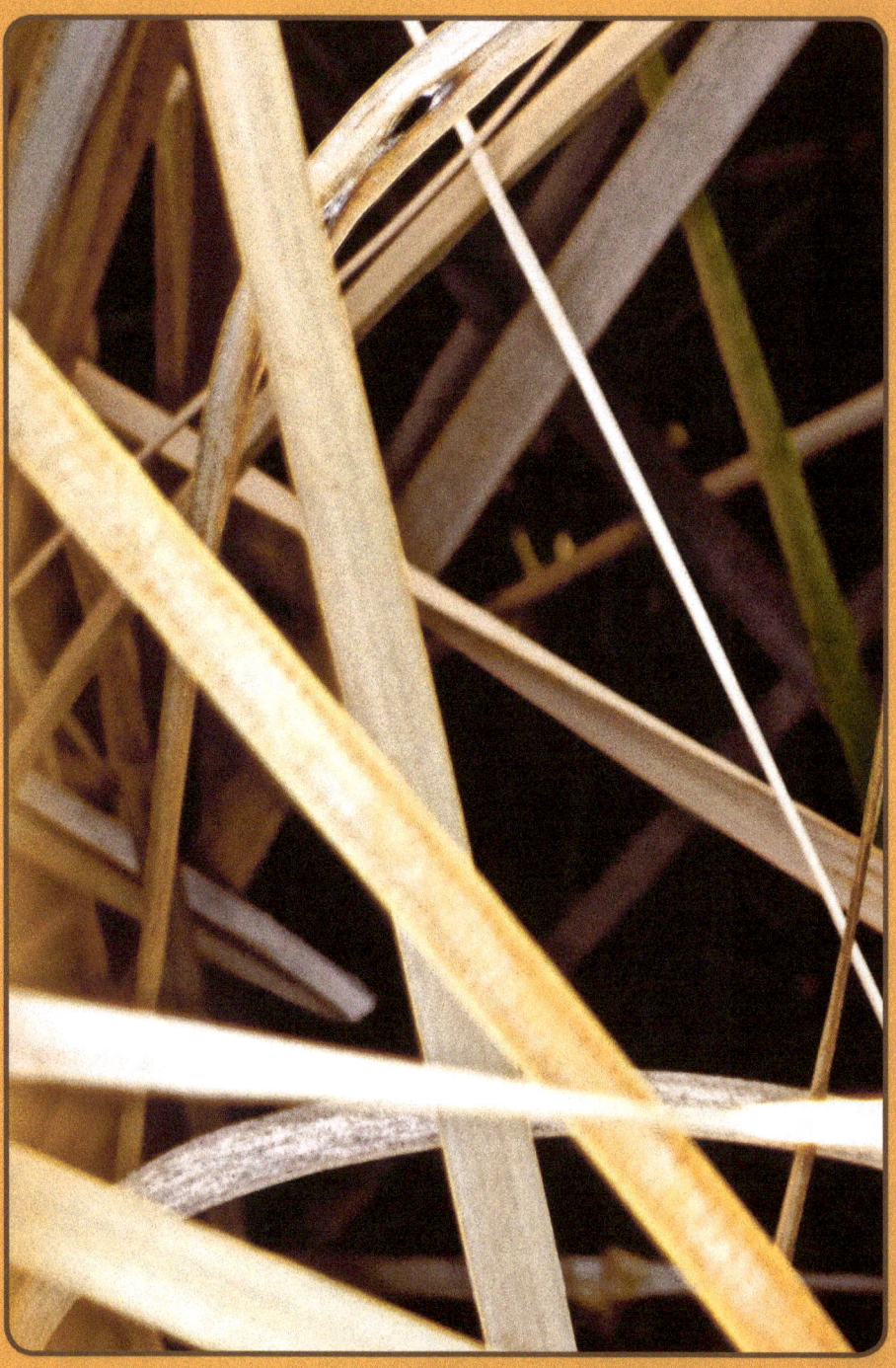

Leaves intertwine just above the ground surface in a barren pond in a wildlife preserve.

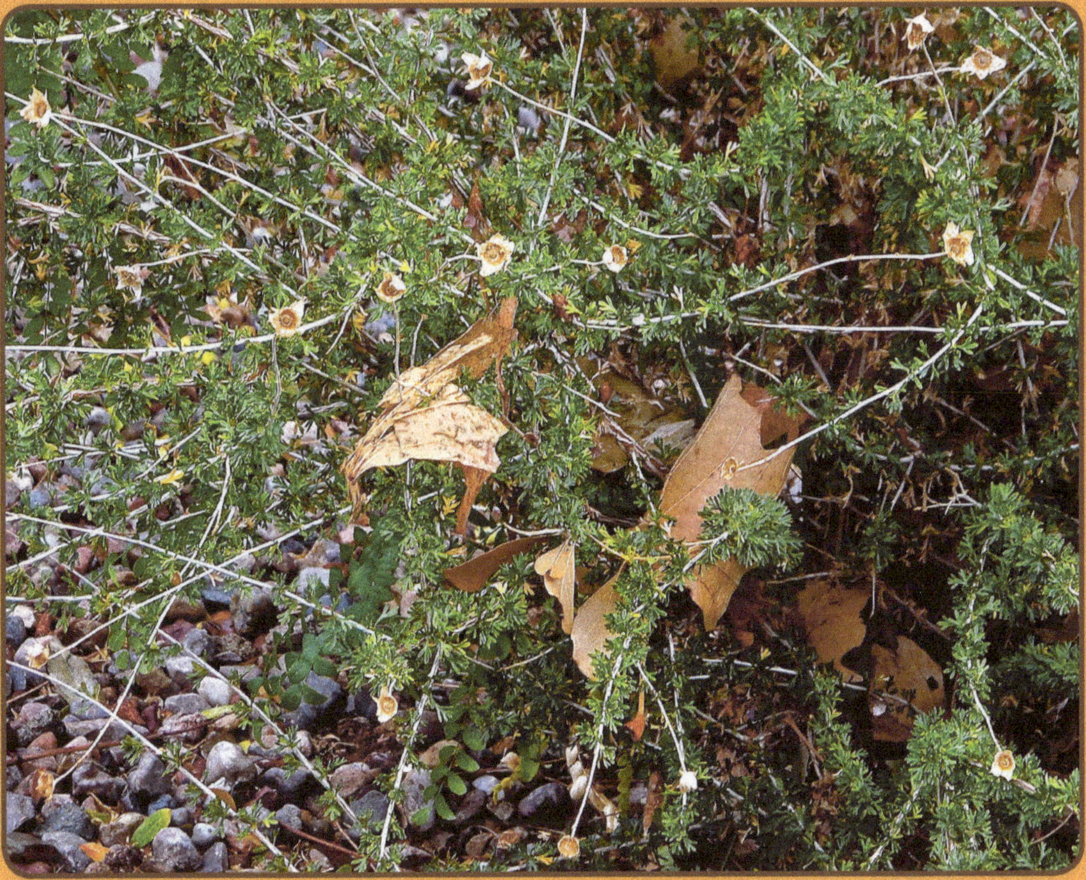

🌿 • Pathways in Time: Photo Journeys • 🌿   73

Autumn leaves nestle in a bush after falling from a tree near medical offices.

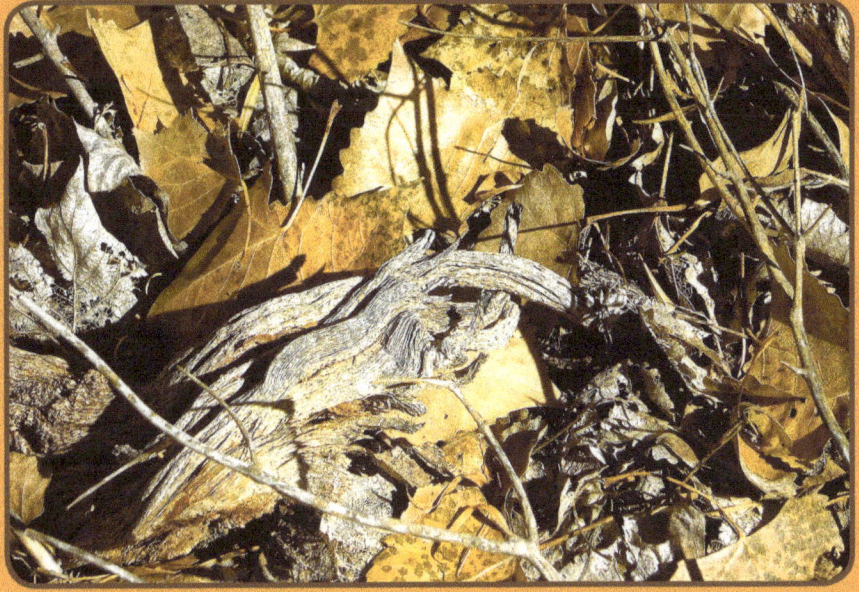

Leaves and driftwood cover the ground in a forest.

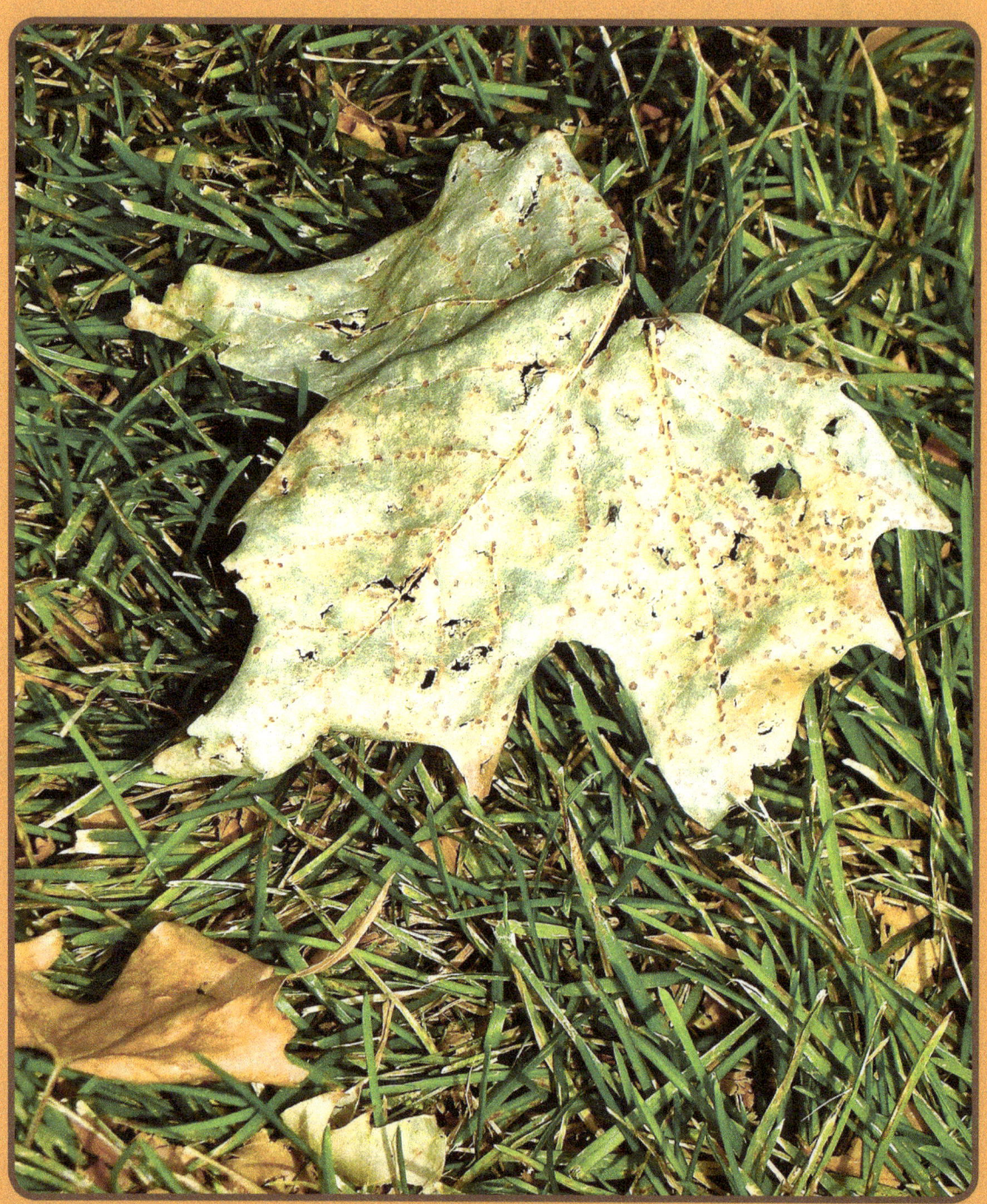

Traces of green fade to brown on a fallen leaf outside a restaurant.

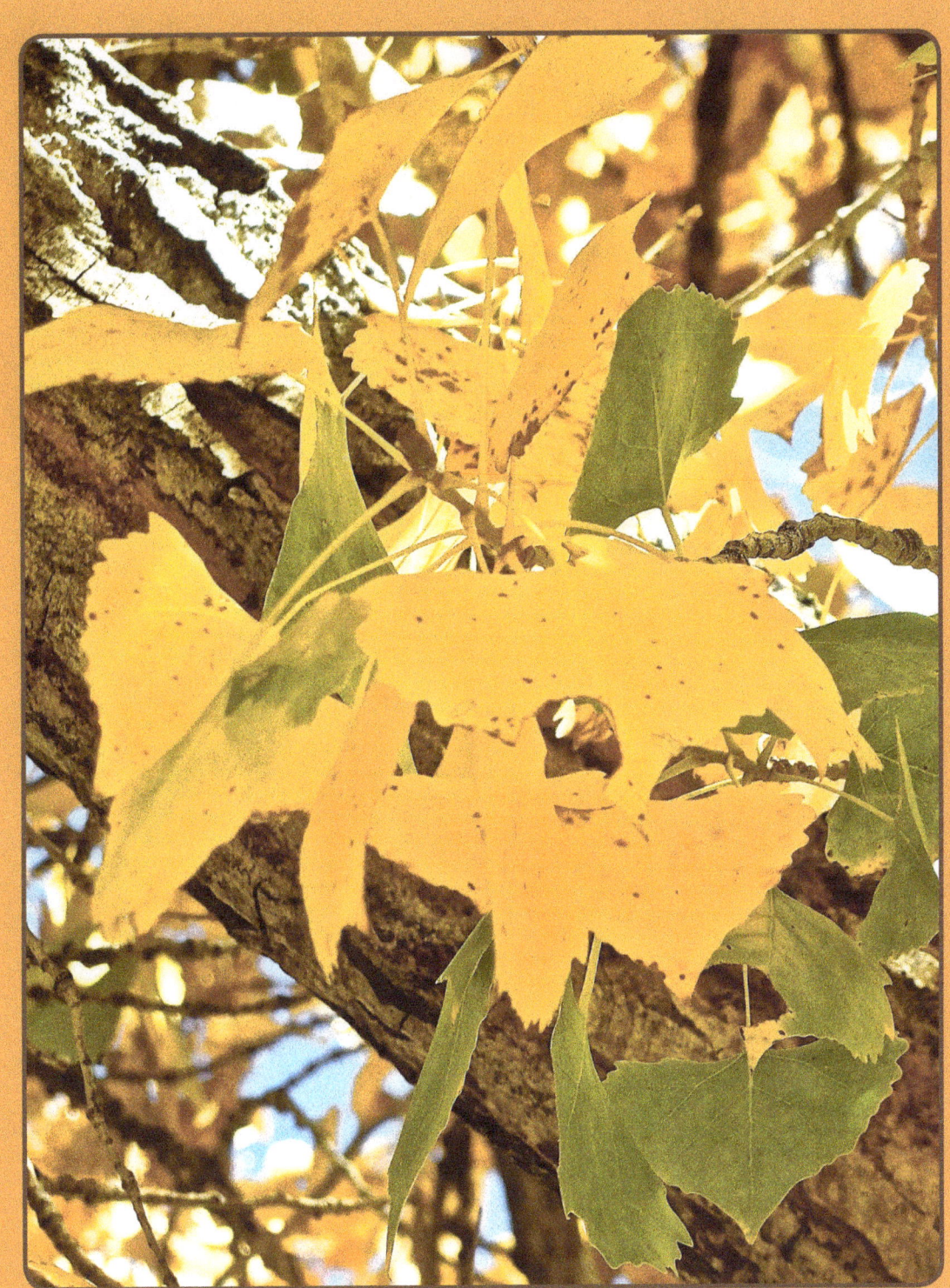
Fall colors replace warm summer greens on a cottonwood tree along a bike path.

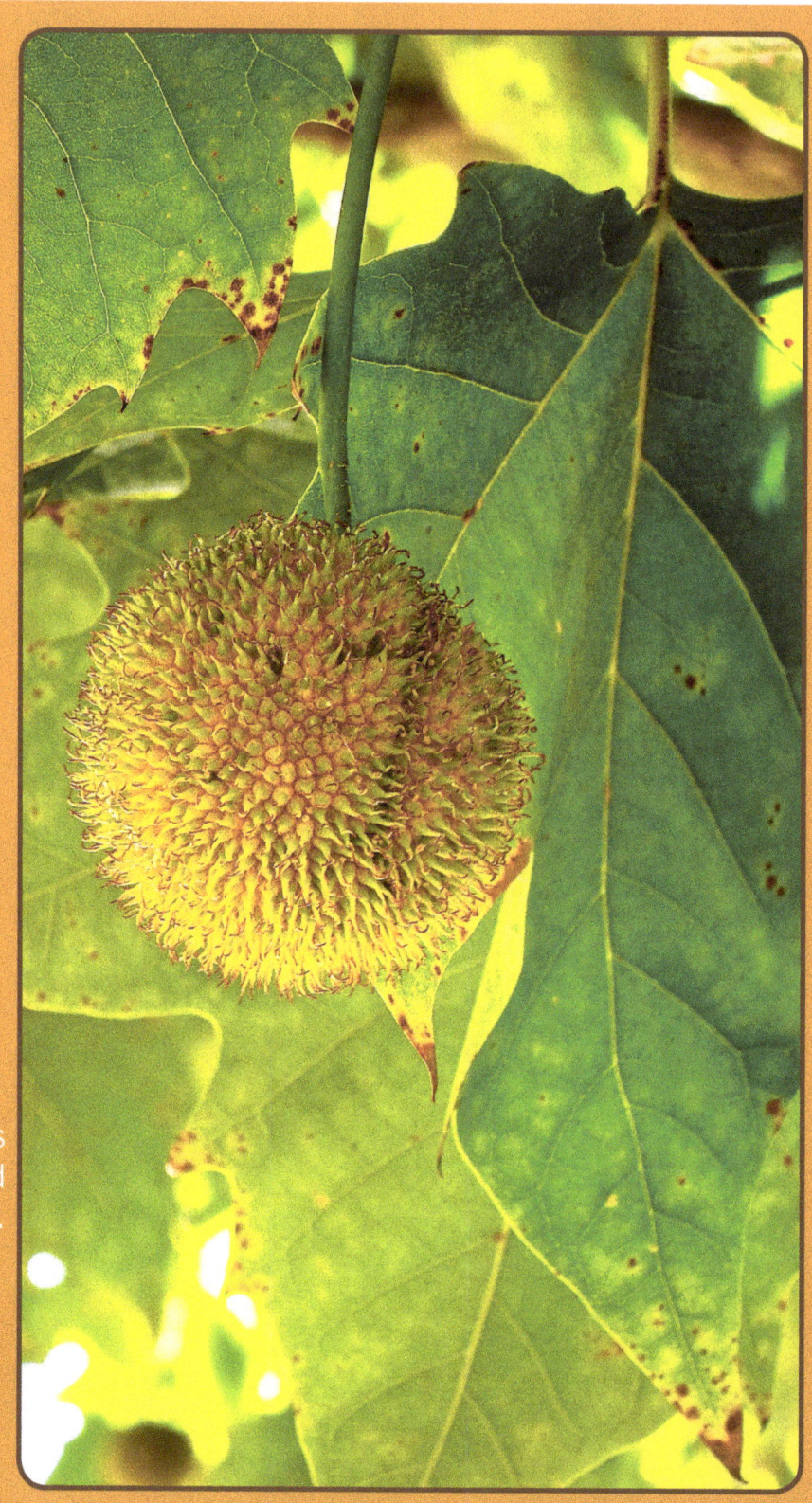

Foliage brightens up the background at a cultural event.

Pathways in Time: Photo Journeys

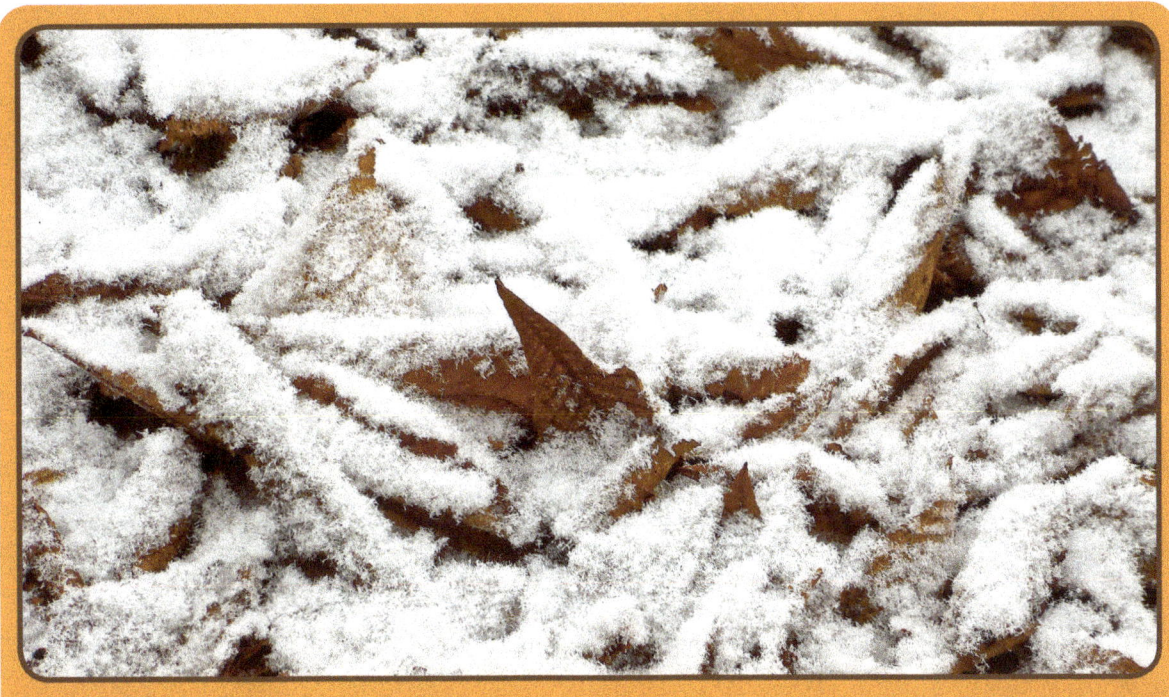

Leaves peer out from a blanket of snow near an old church in Germany.

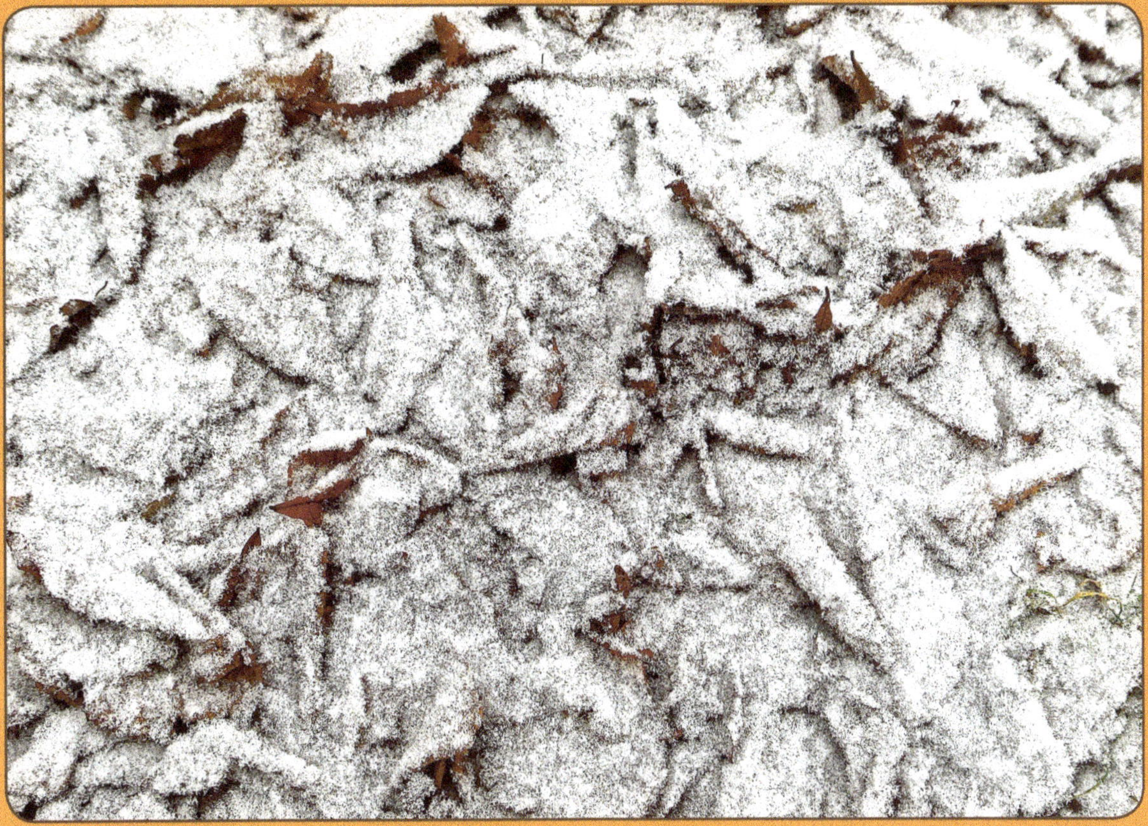

Chapter 6: Earth

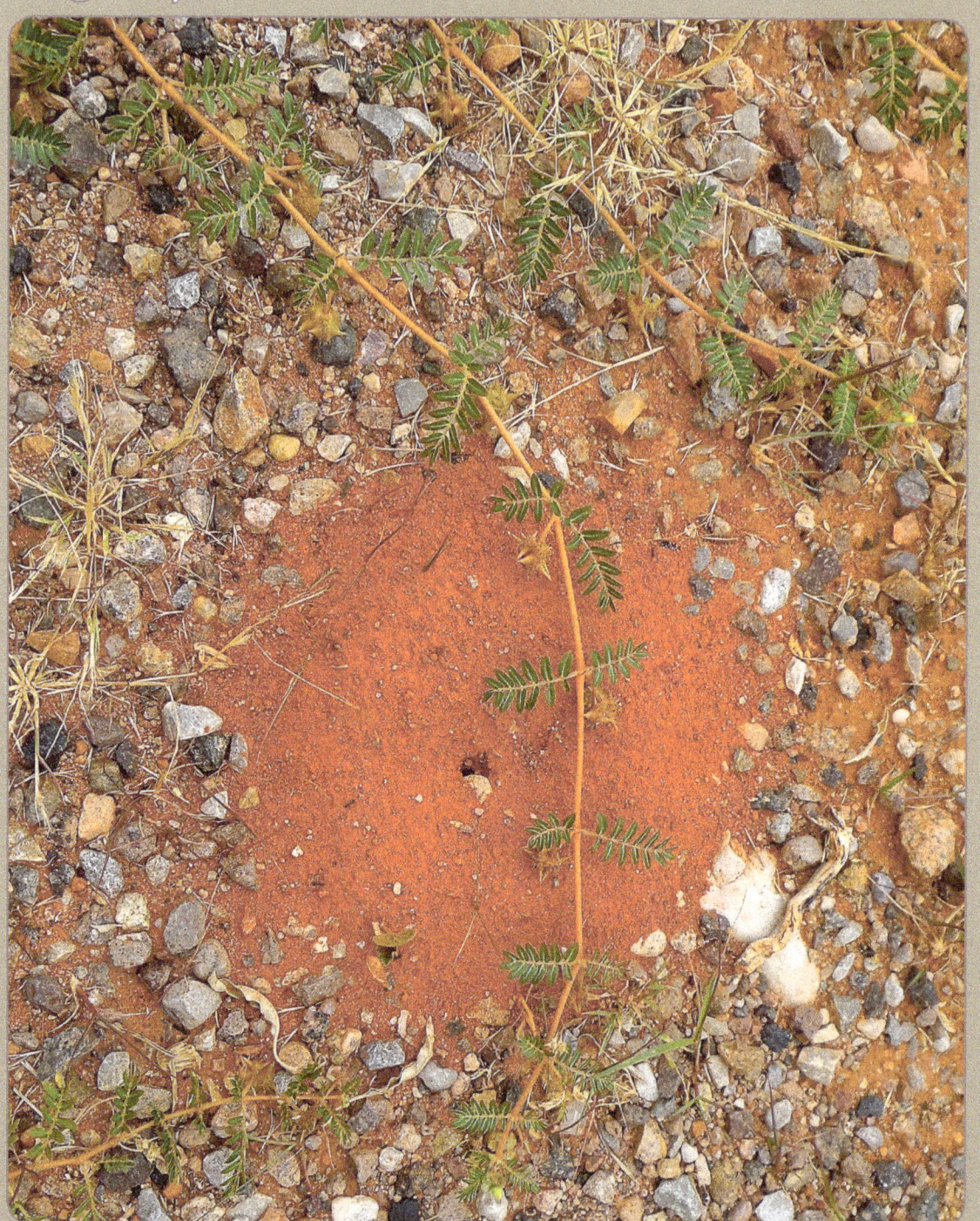

A goat head weed traverses an anthill outside a picnic area in New Mexico.

• Pathways in Time: Photo Journeys •

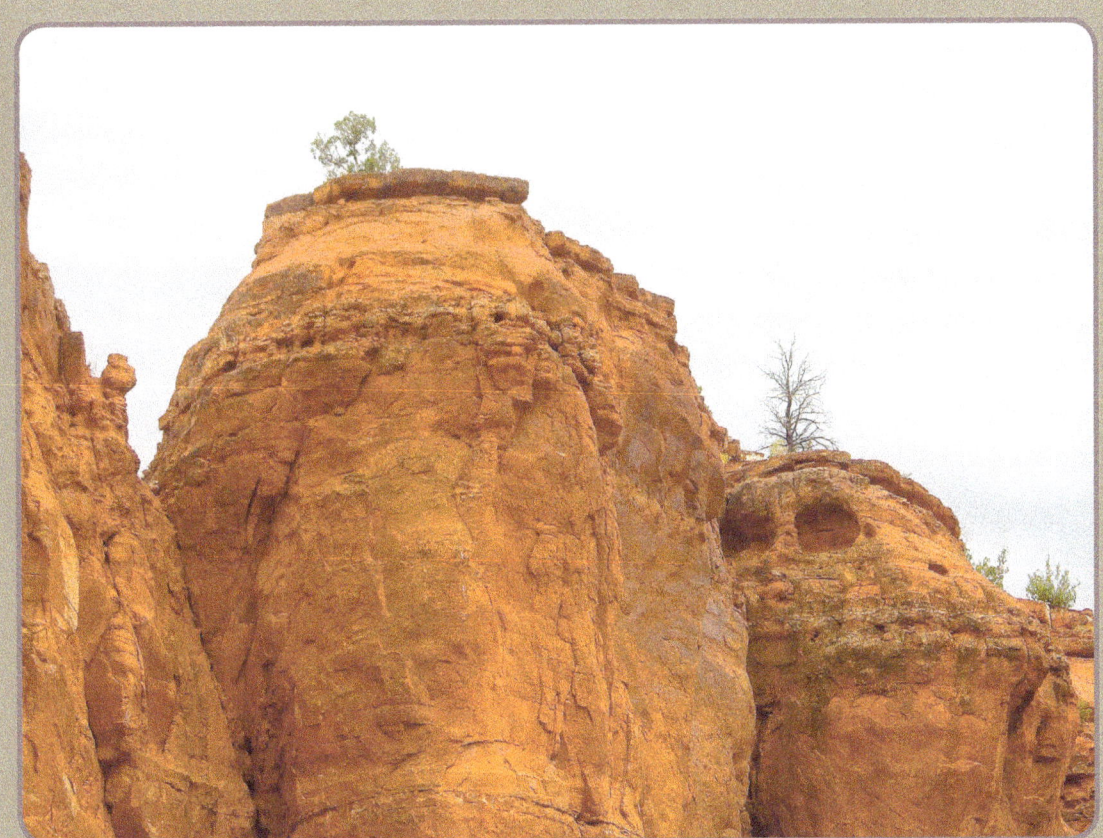

Facial features appear in an ancient sandstone rock formation in New Mexico.

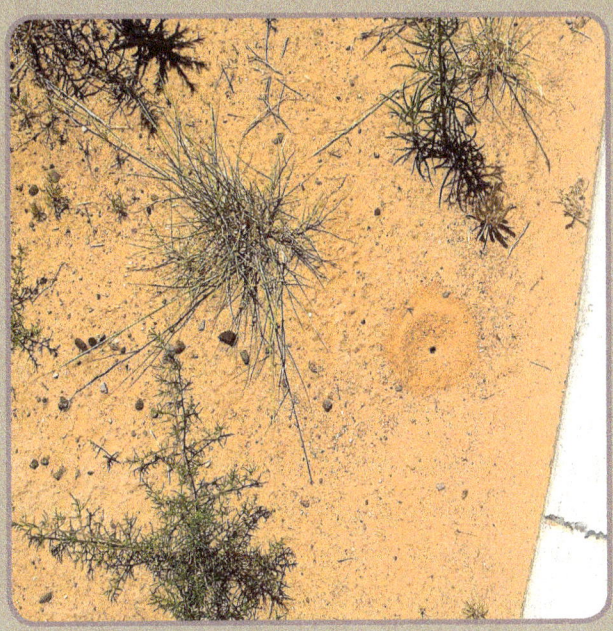

Ants create a perfect oval shape in rich soil bordered by a cement curb in a parking lot outside a fire station.

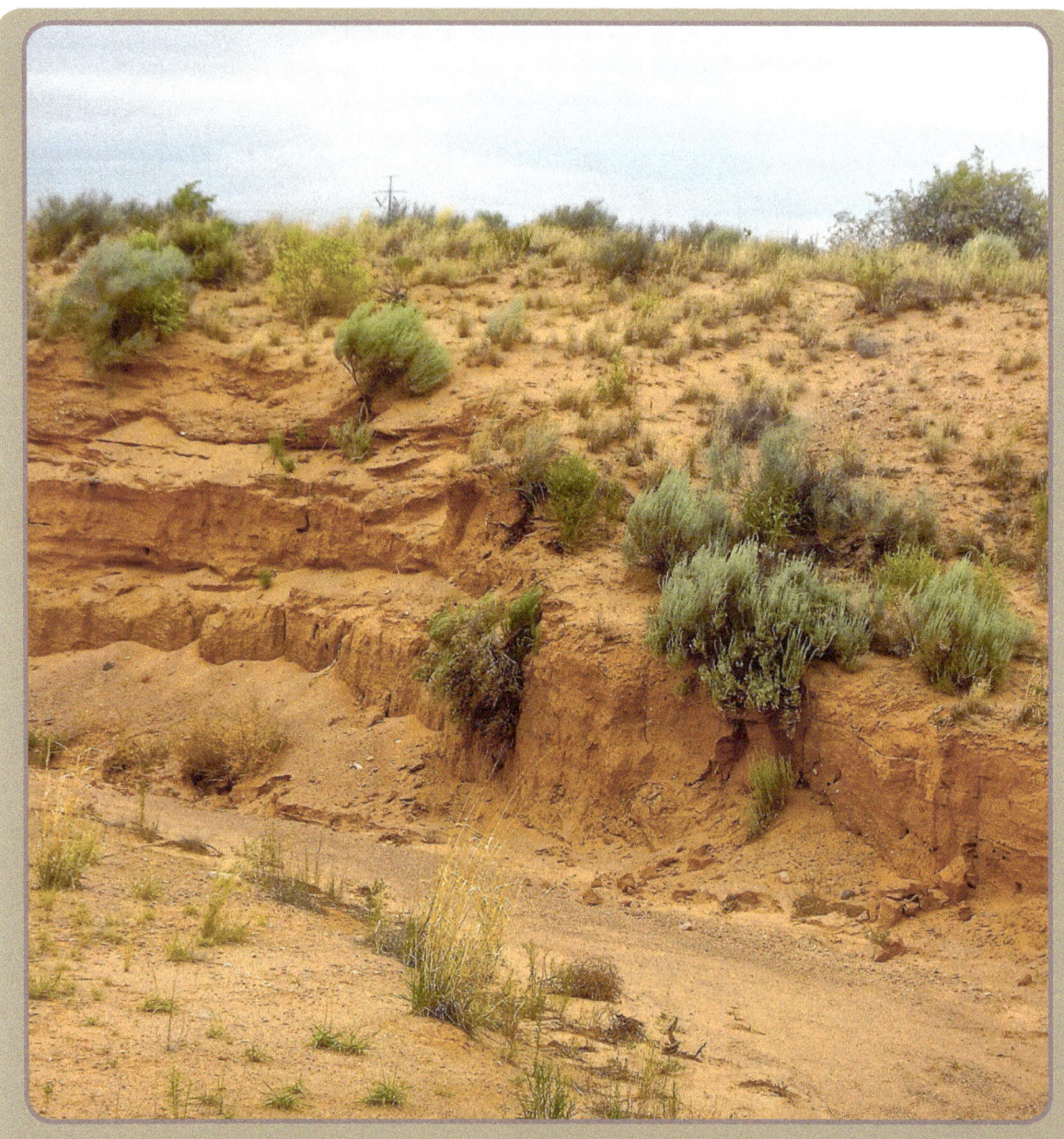

Clumps of dusty green sagebrush arise from an arroyo carved into the earth by raging flashfloods in summer rainstorms.

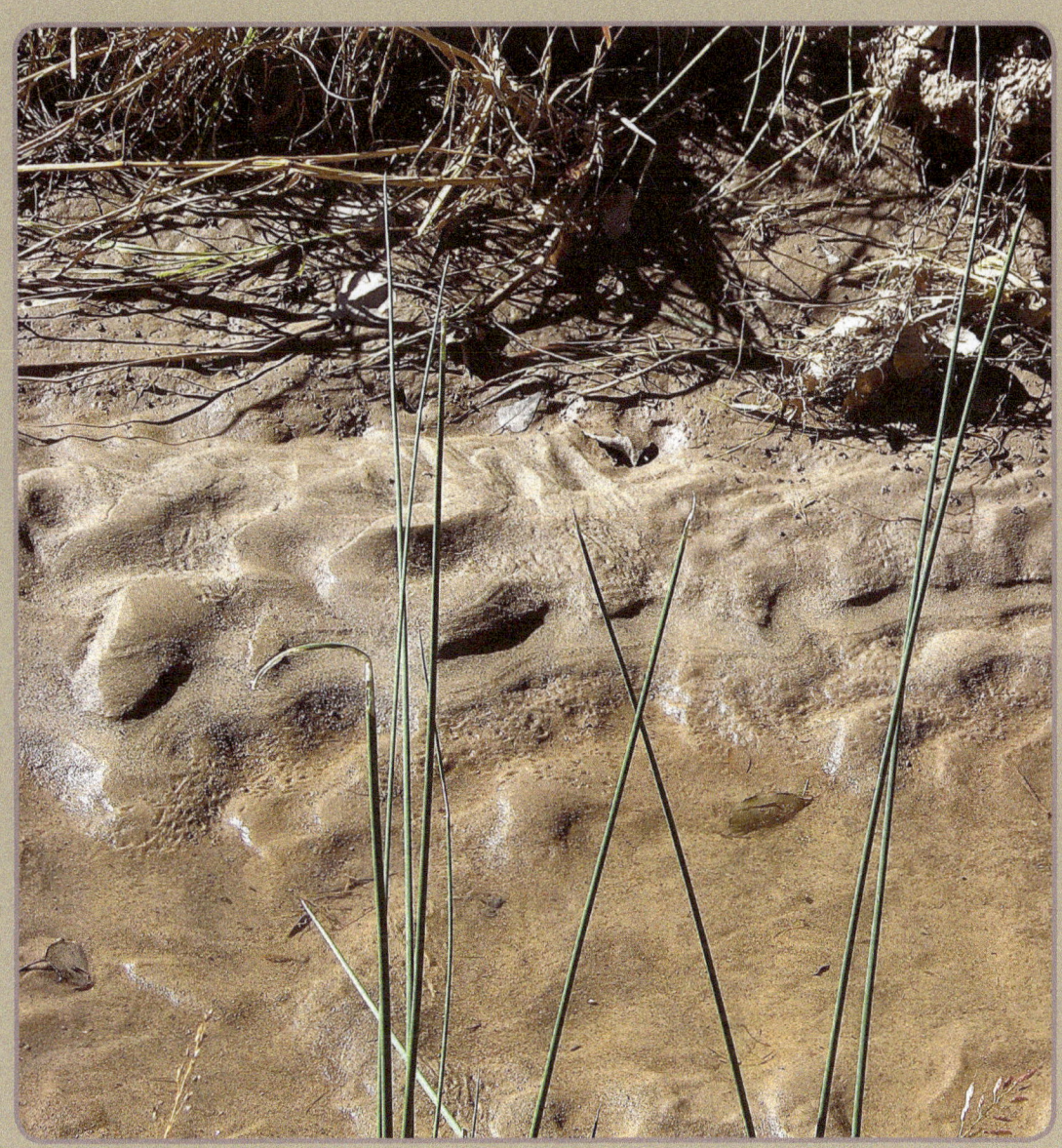

Receding water leaves soft mud formations in the bottom of an irrigation ditch next to a walking path.

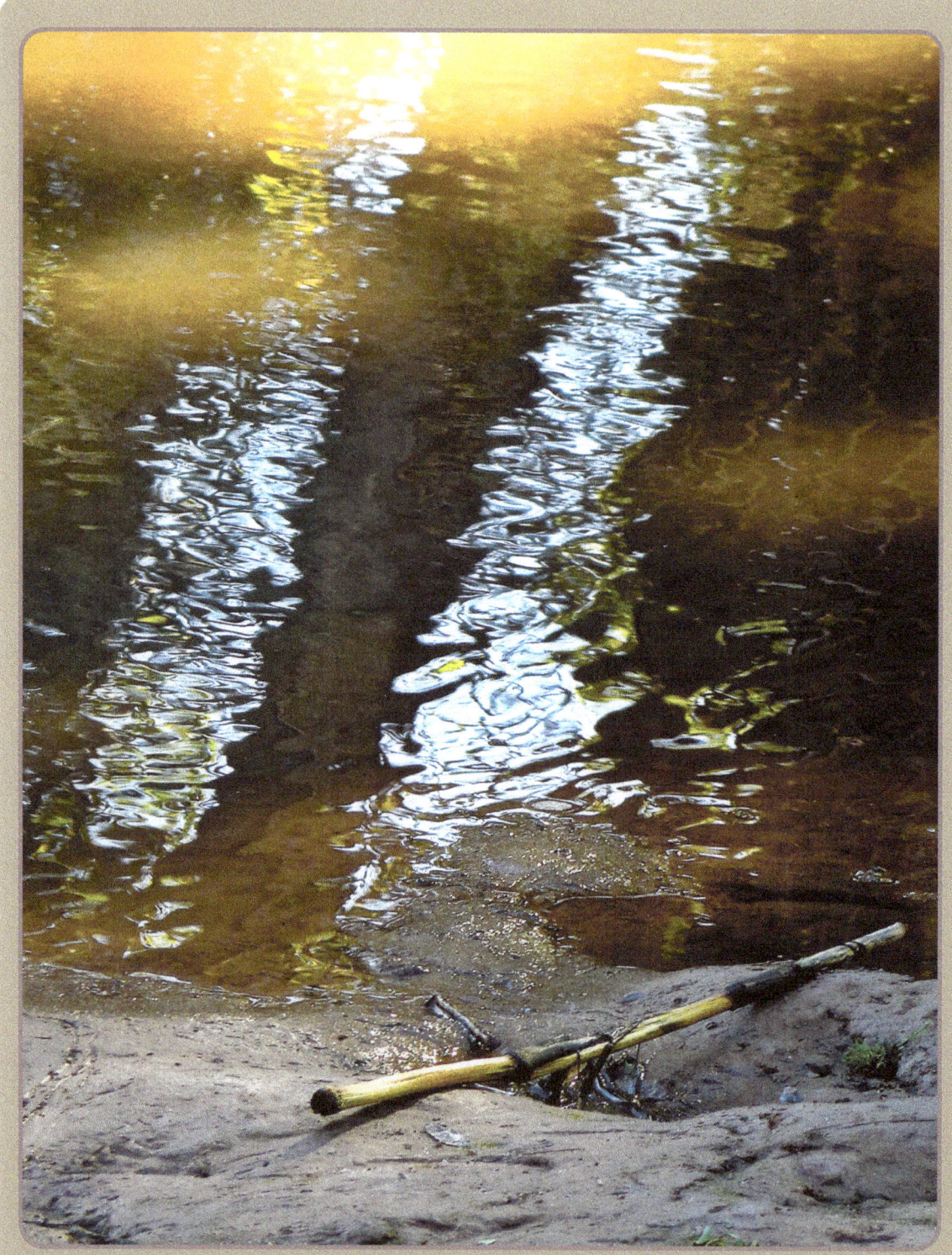
A reed has been carried to its resting place on a muddy riverbank next to the Rio Grande.

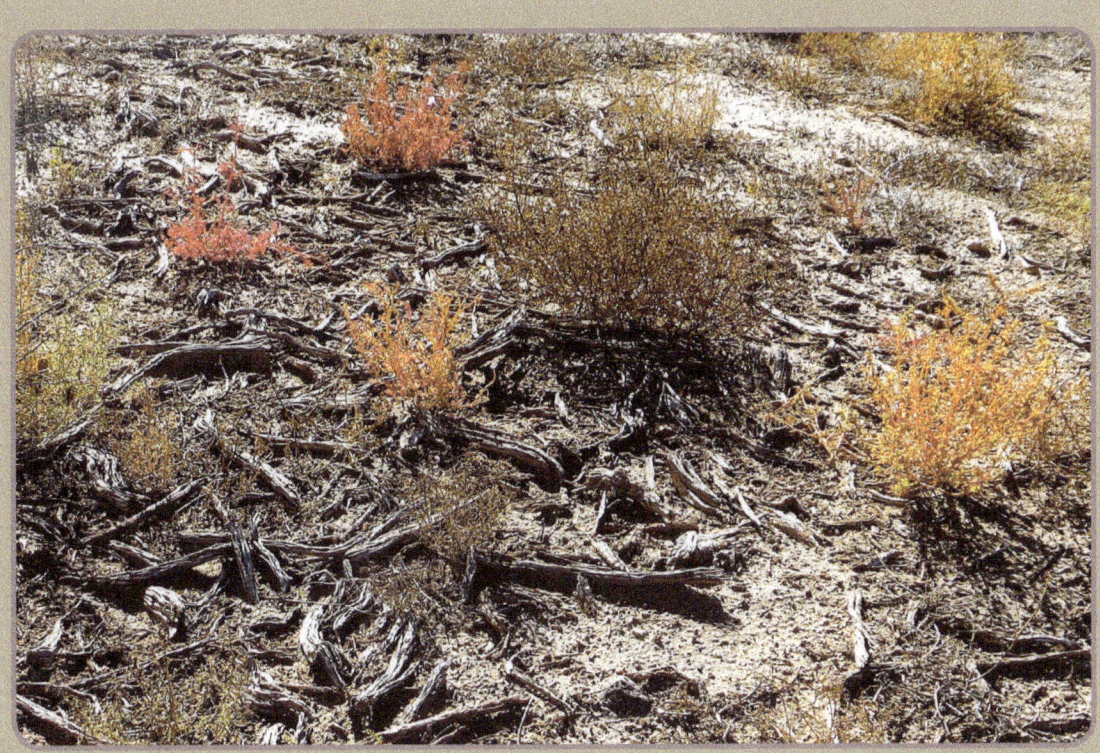
Weeds provide vibrant ground color to decaying vegetation outside an abandoned cemetery where my Perea relatives are buried.

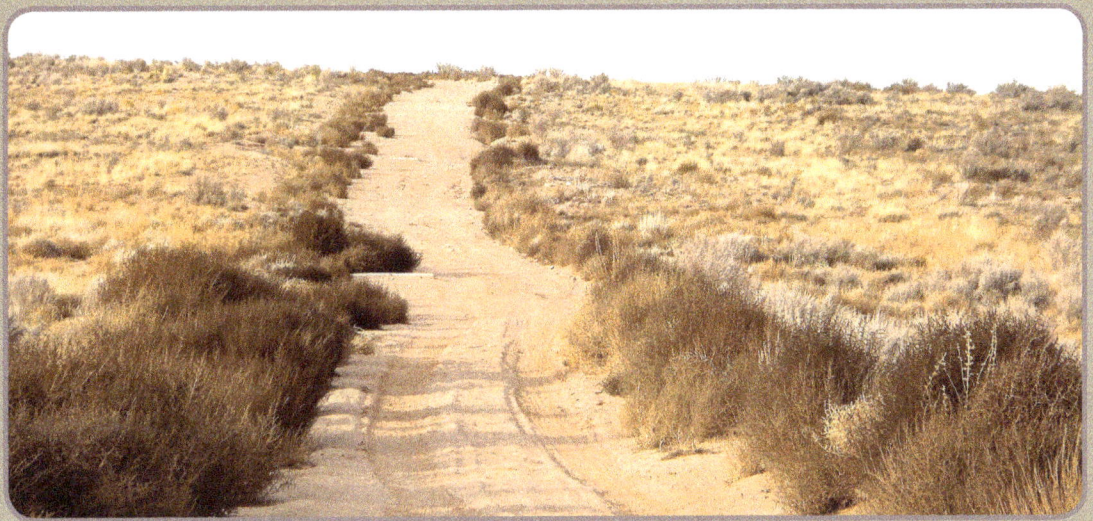
A sandy road for utility vehicles near a medical facility is boarded by fuzzy brown tumbleweeds.

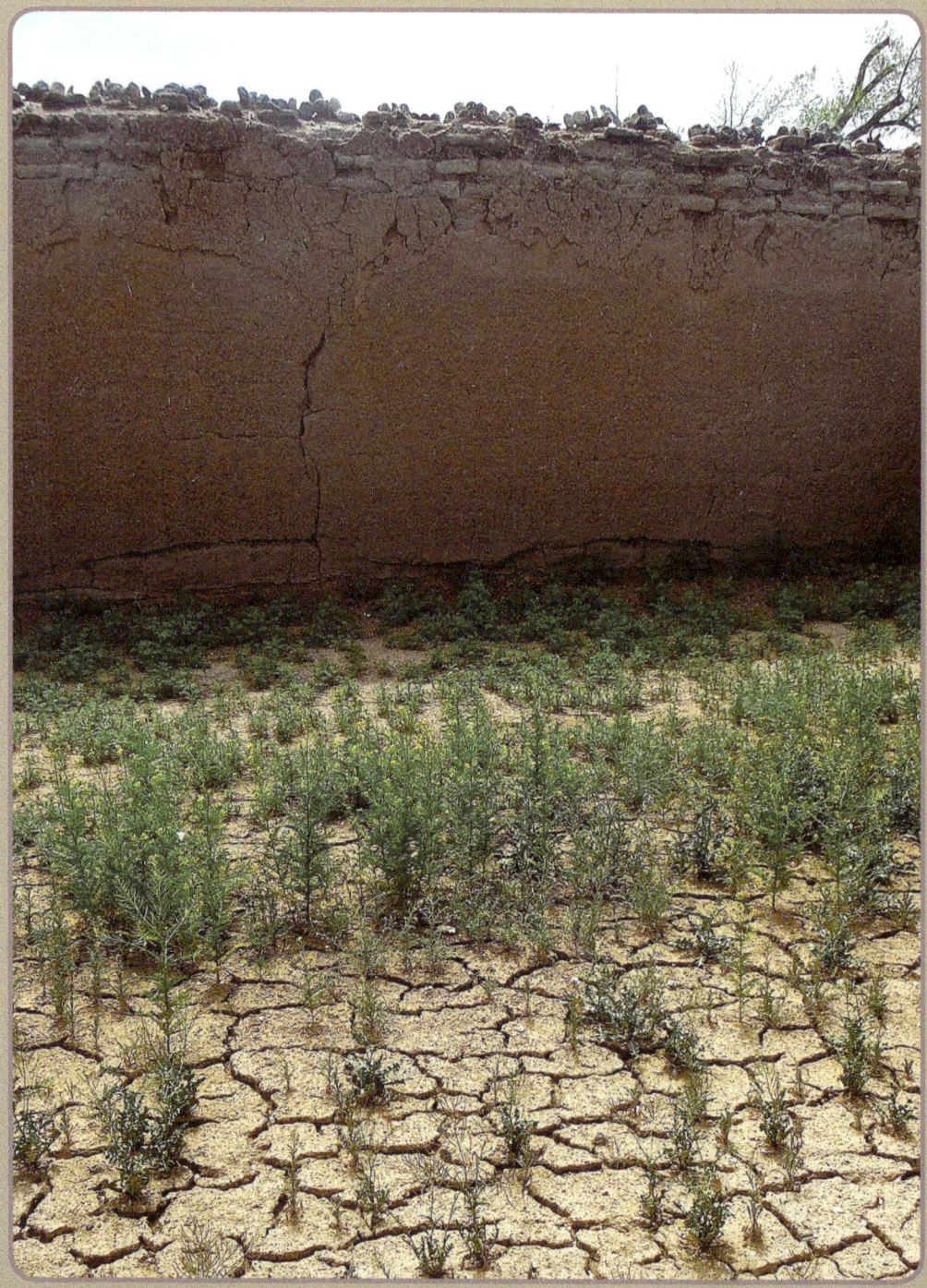

Cracked earth on the ground mirrors cracks in the adjacent crumbling adobe building, topped with cactus on the roof in a traditional New Mexico way to deter intruders.

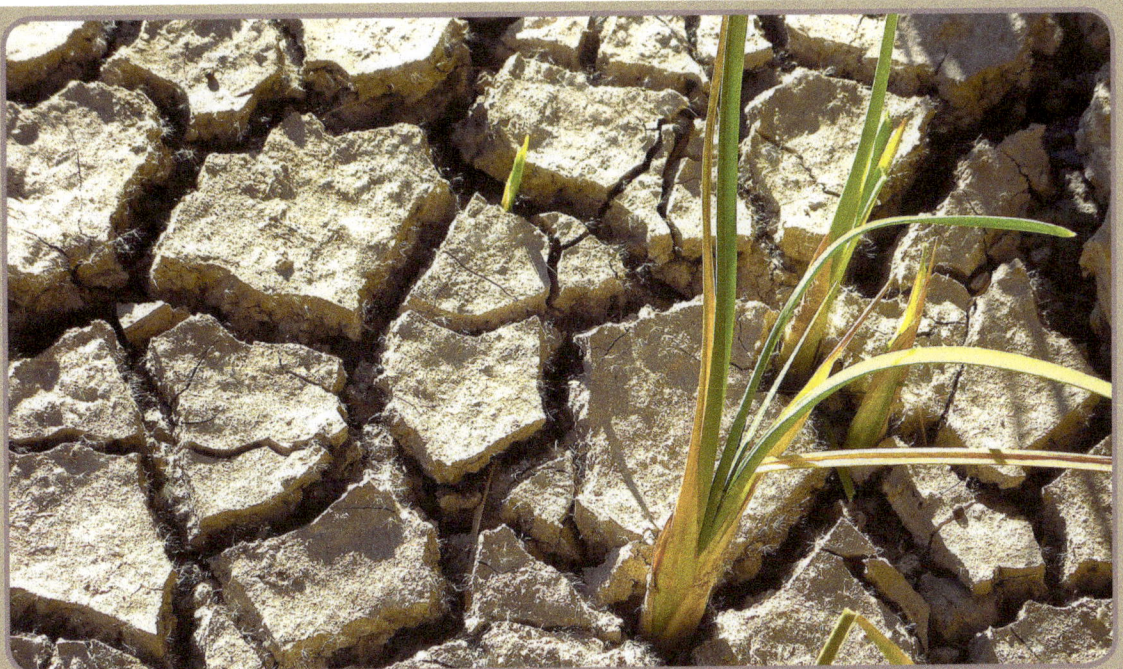

Vegetation struggles to grow from the ground in a dry pond near the famed desert area called the *Jornada del Muerto* (Dead Man's Journey) in southern New Mexico.

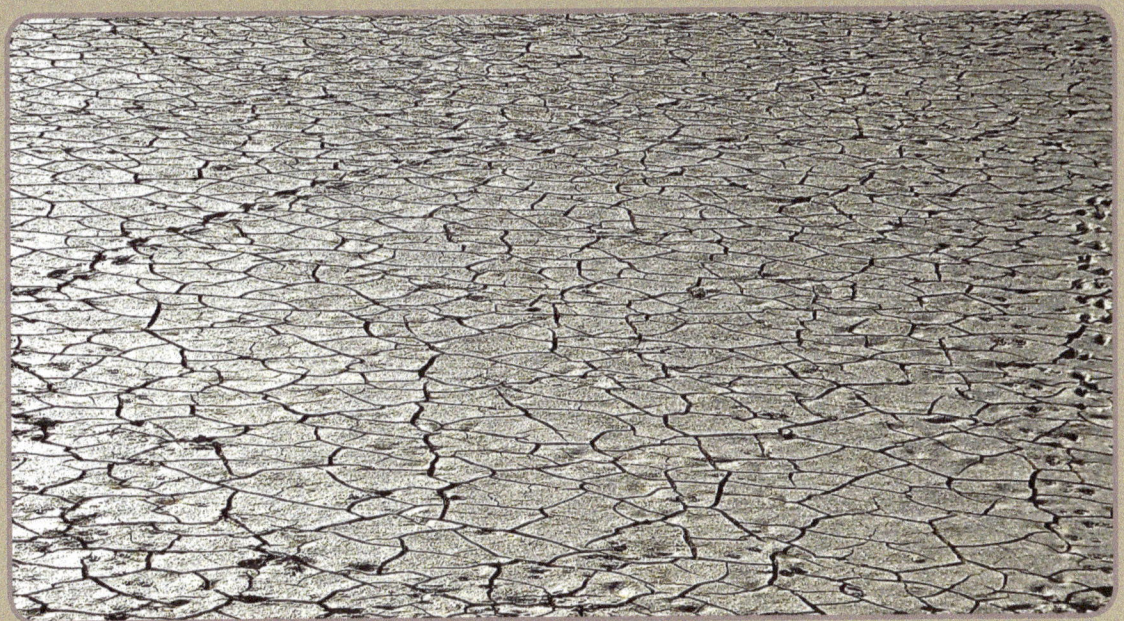

A close up of parched earth in dried pond inside a nature preserve where Apaches used to winter.

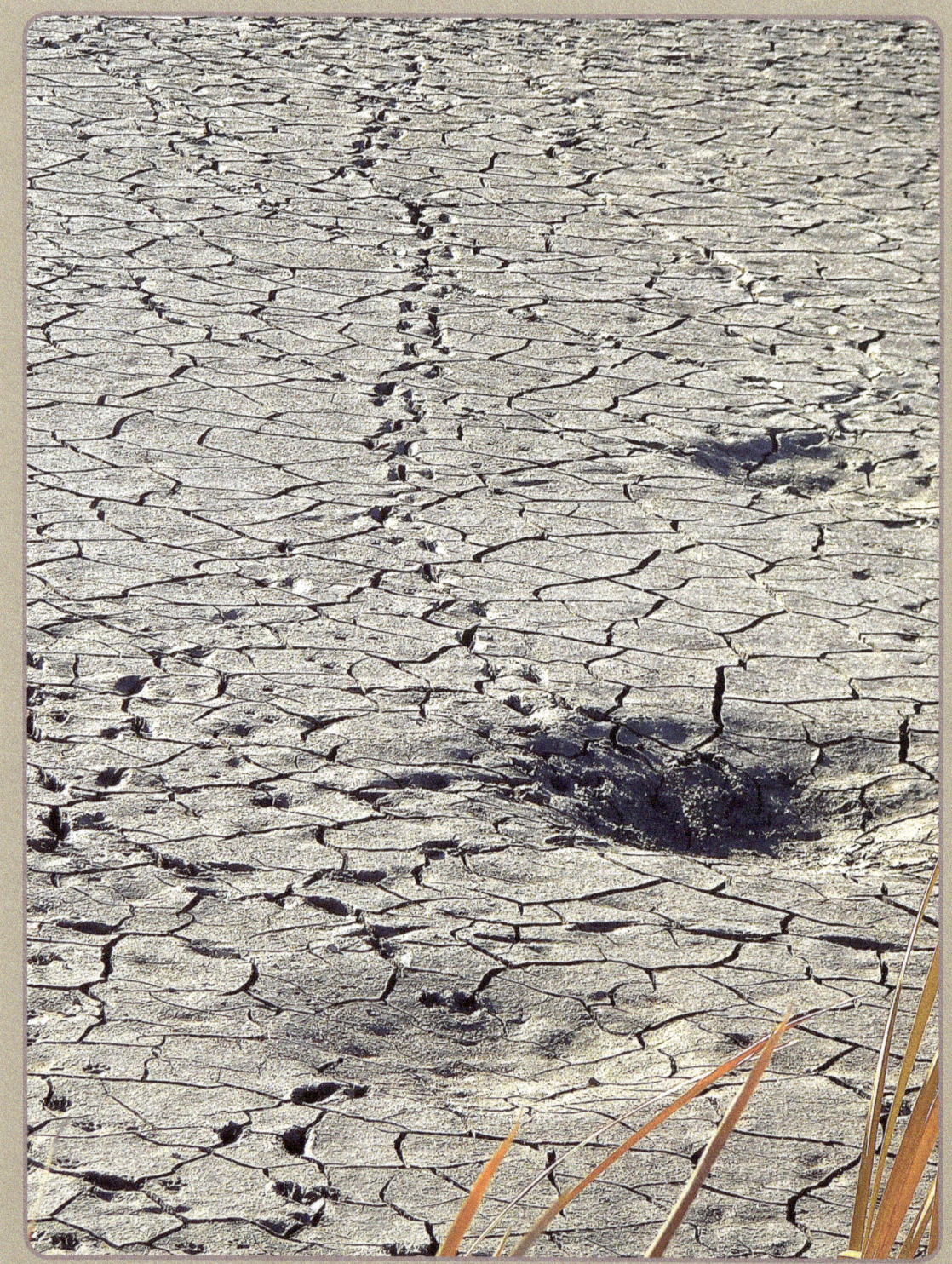

An animal left its tracks behind as it crossed a drying pond in a nature preserve in New Mexico.

Chapter 7: Rainbows

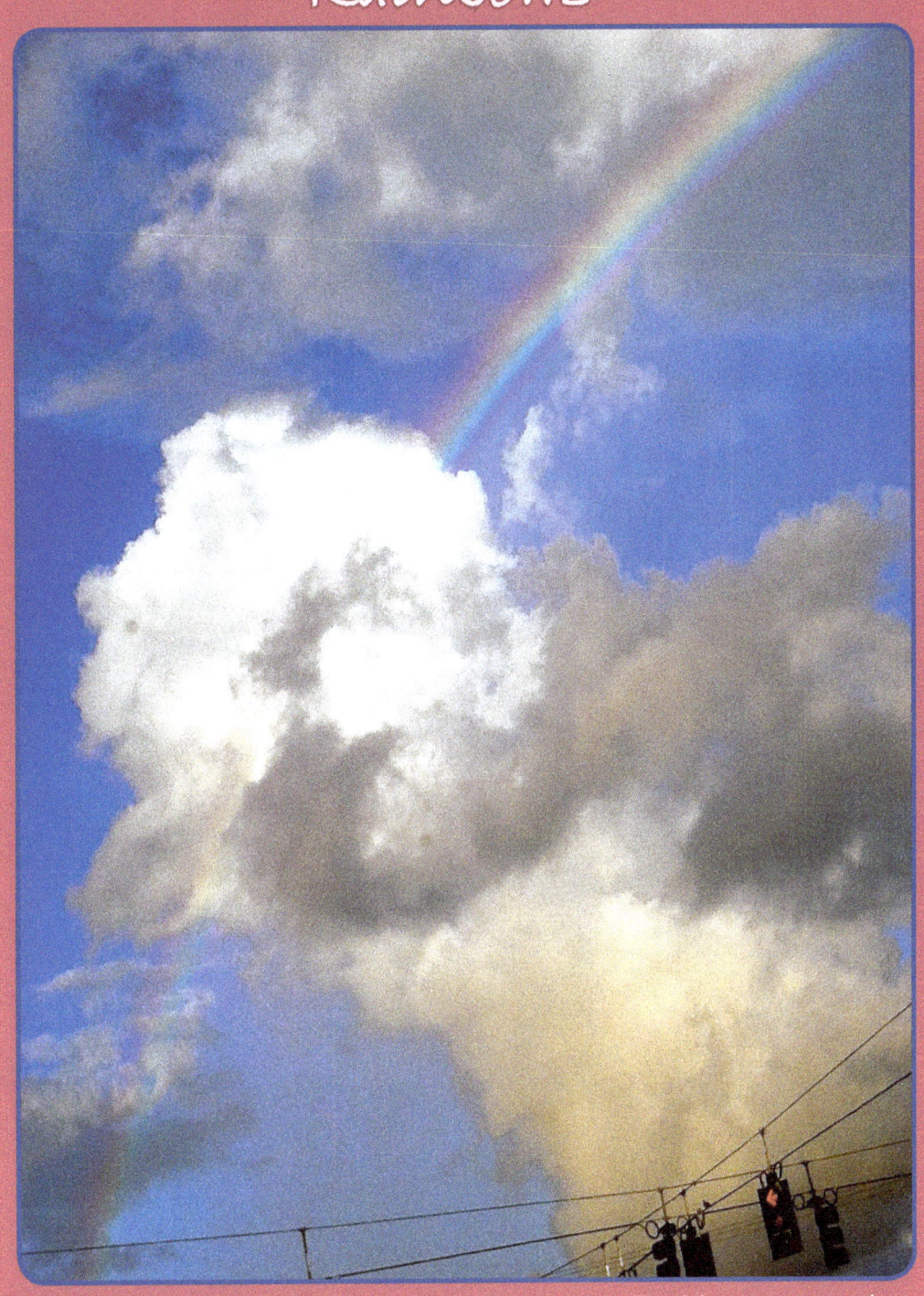

A rainbow darts through a cloud in a south Florida summer sky.

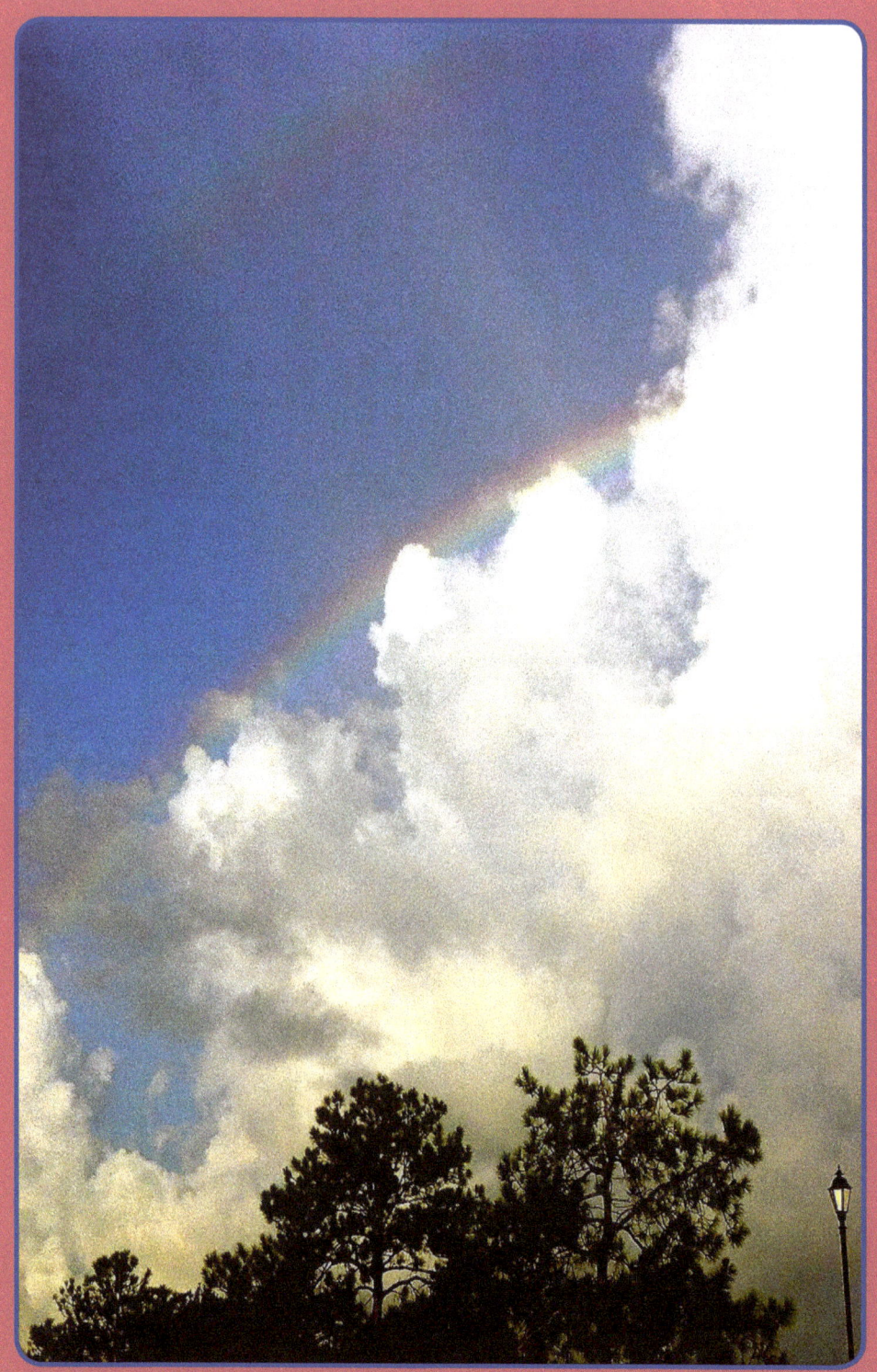

A double rainbow graces the skies above a parking lot near offices.

• Pathways in Time: Photo Journeys • 89

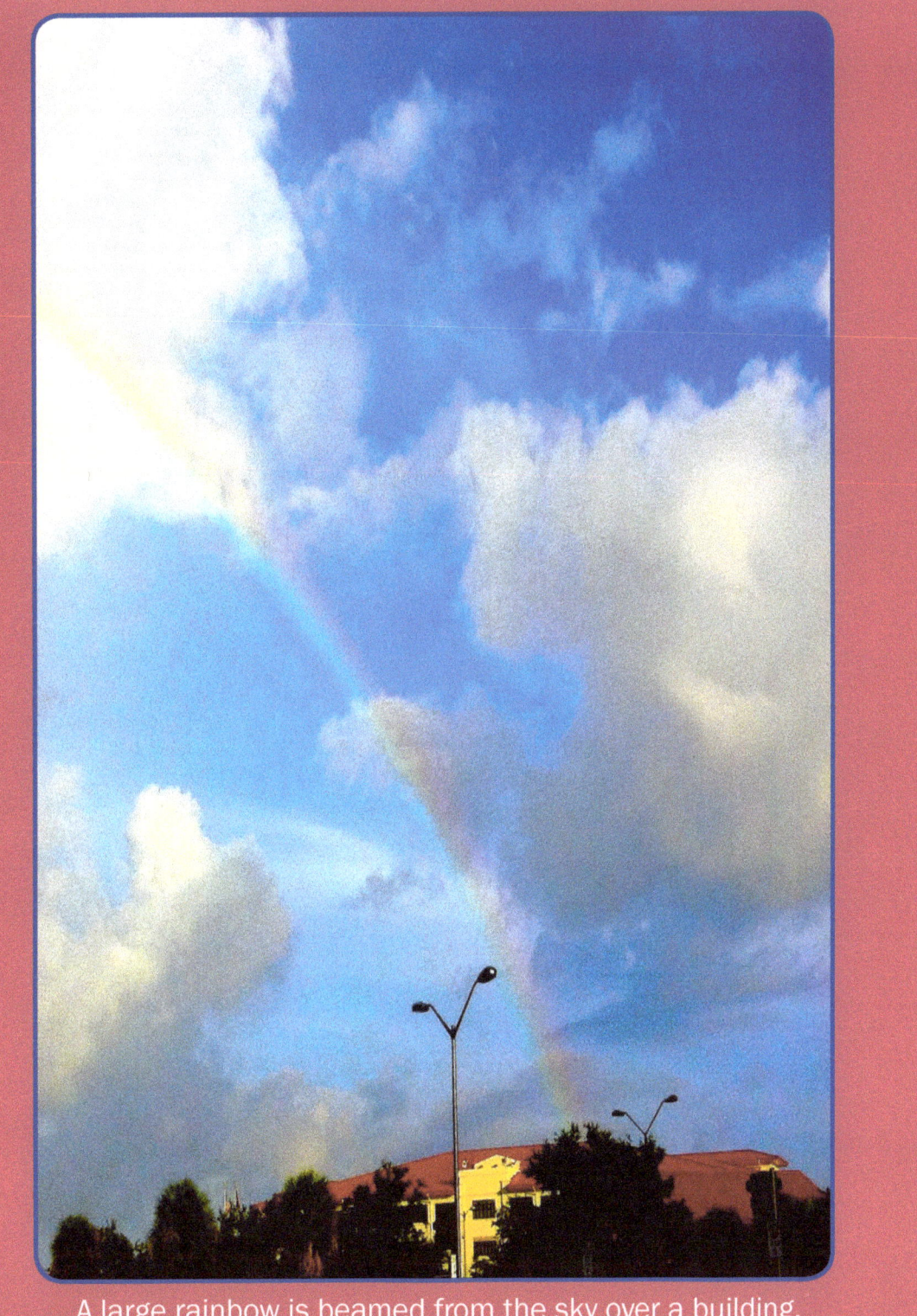
A large rainbow is beamed from the sky over a building.

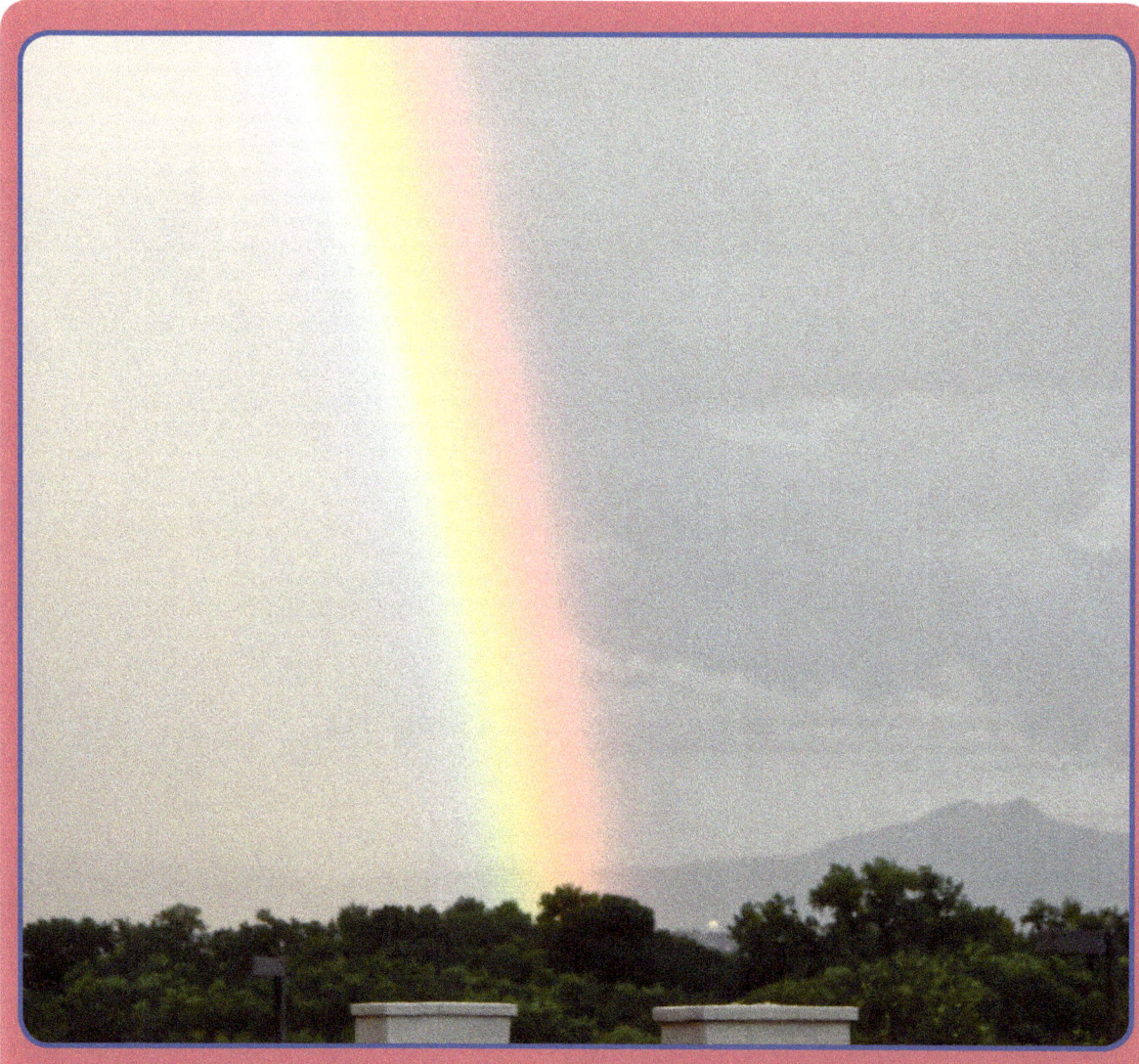

A wide rainbow shines between a residential area and a mountain range in mid-summer.

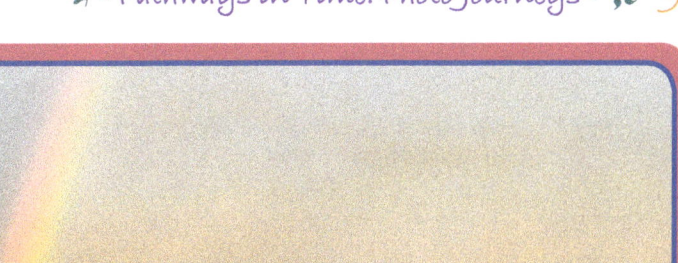

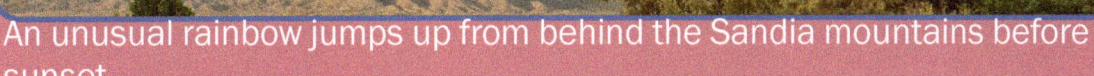
An unusual rainbow jumps up from behind the Sandia mountains before sunset.

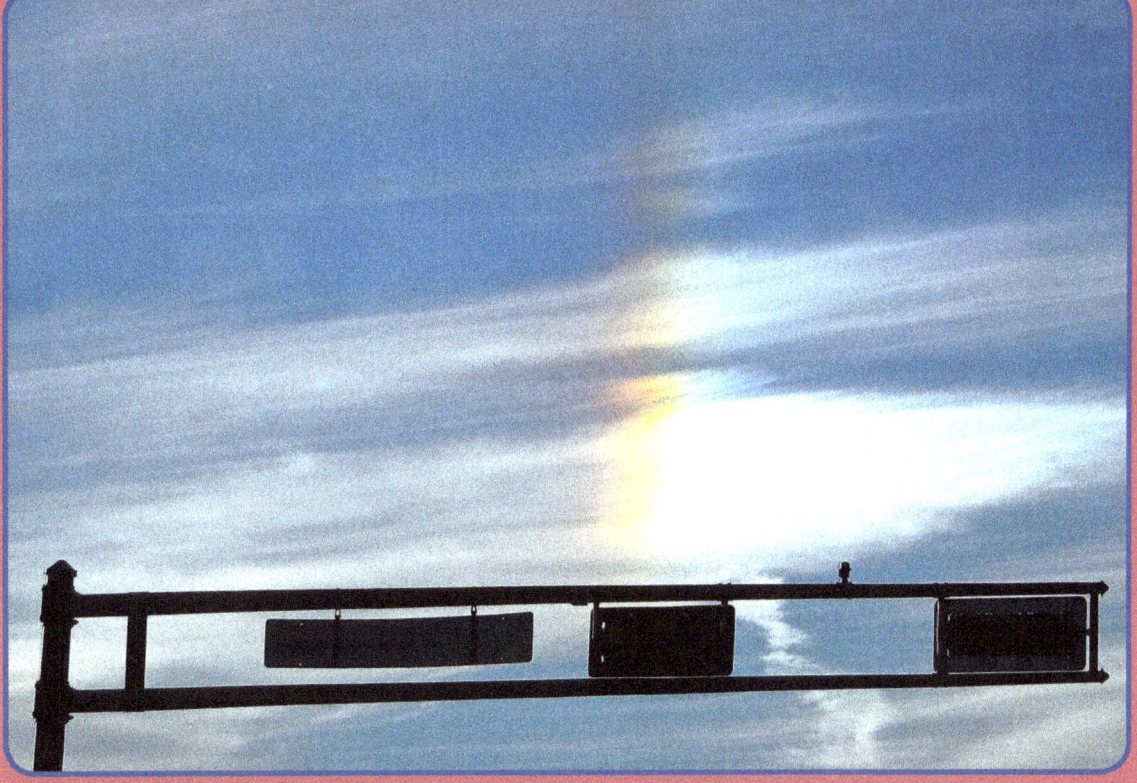
A strange rainbow appears in the sky on a hot, dry summer's day.

Chapter 8: Sunsets

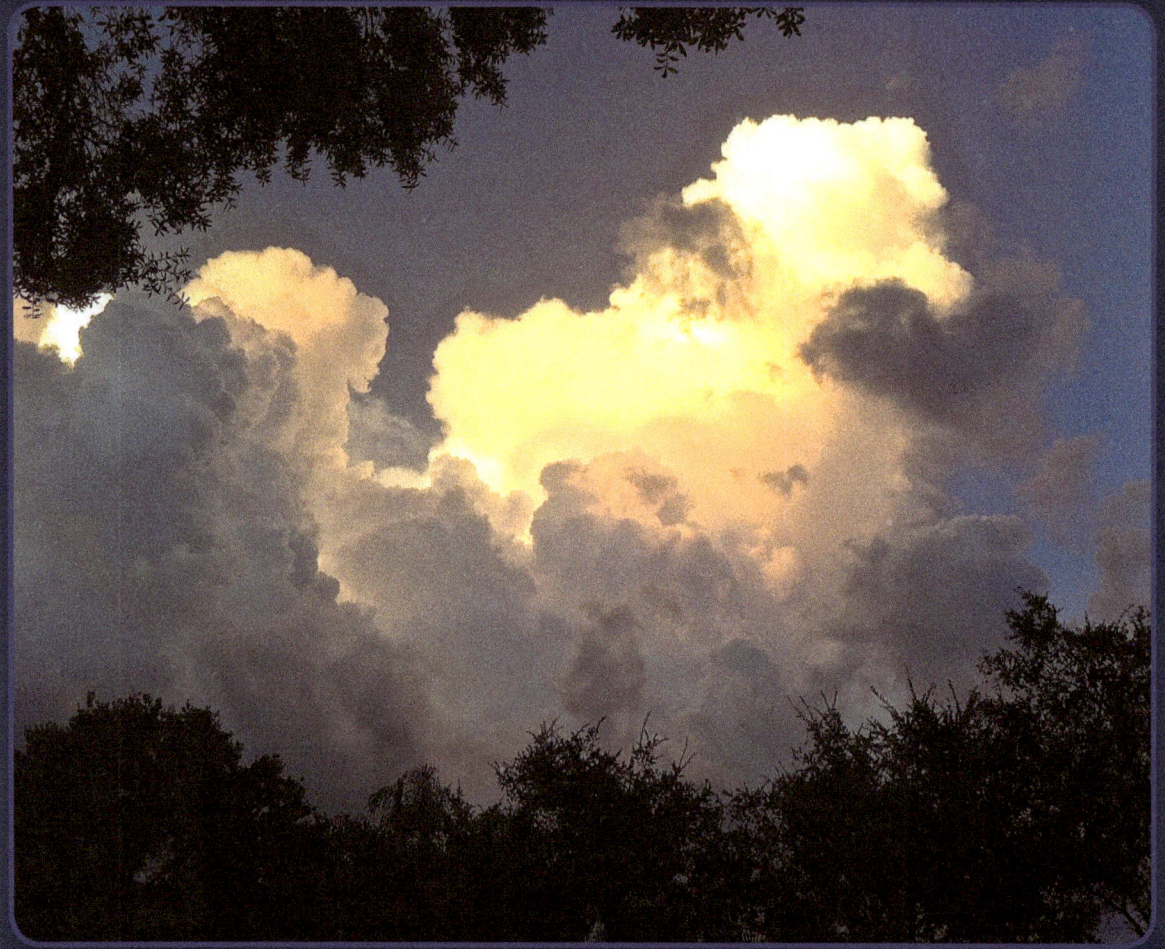

Sun rays illuminate a cloud before dusk turns to night.

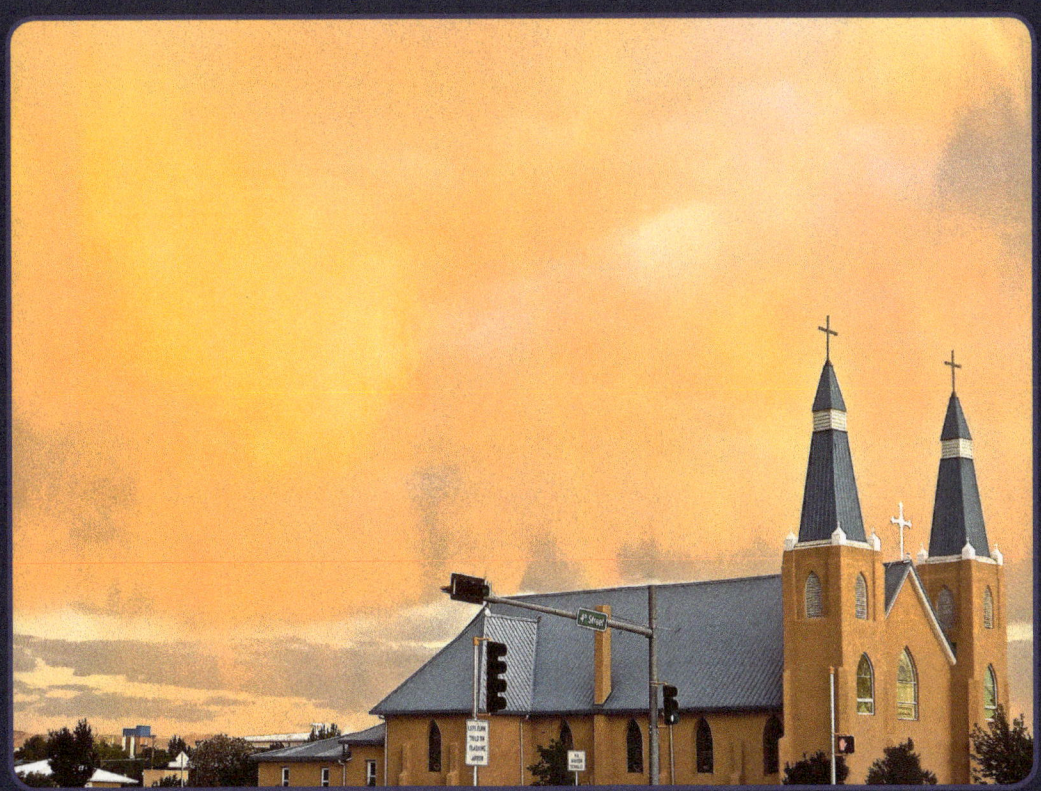
Majestic clouds in mixed hues fill the sky over a Catholic church.

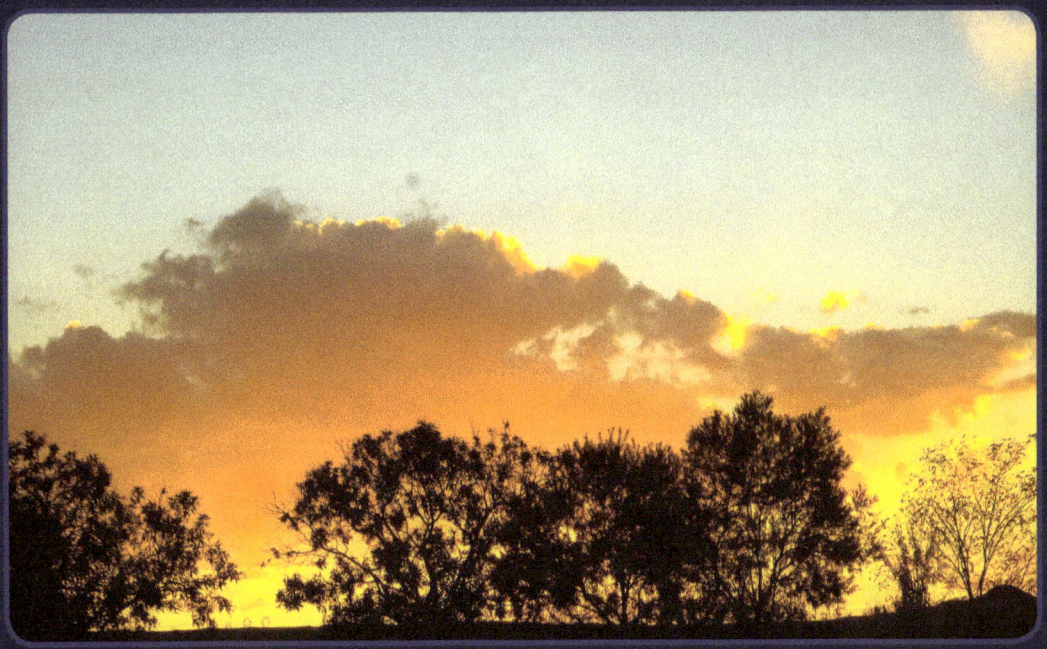
A calm green sky rises above glowing golden clouds.

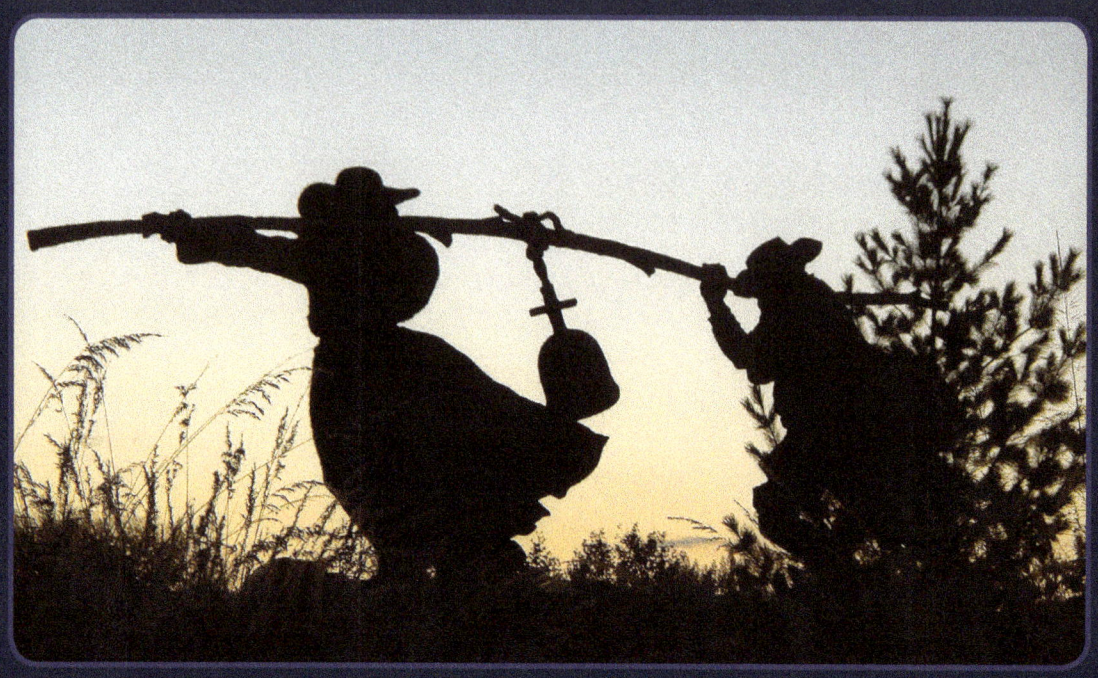
The last glow of daylight creates a dramatic illumination behind a bronze sculpture depicting Spanish colonists in New Mexico.

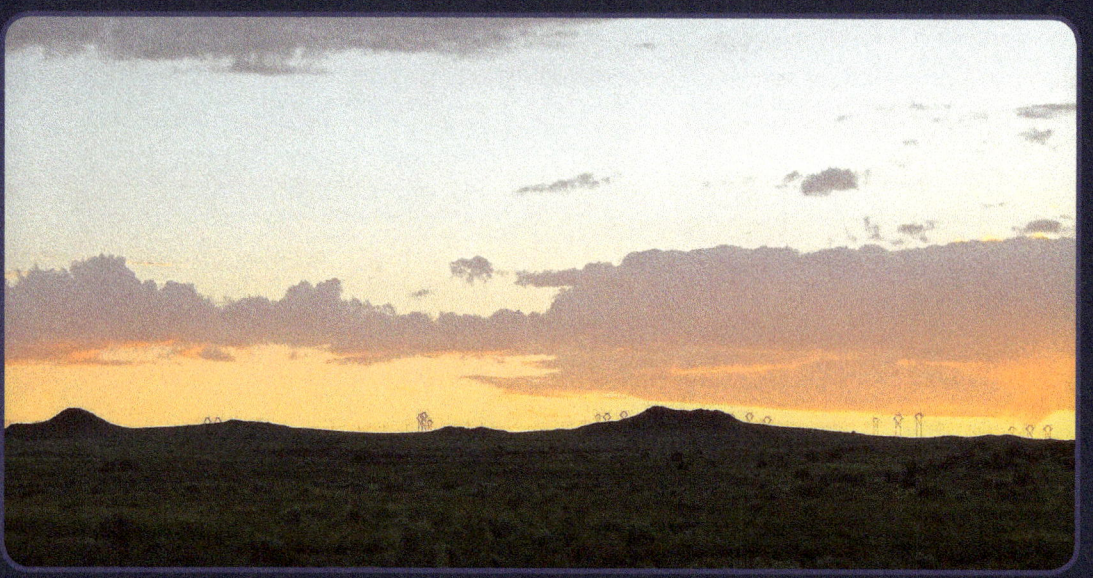
Volcanos along a ridge witness an apricot sunset.

• Pathways in Time: Photo Journeys • 95

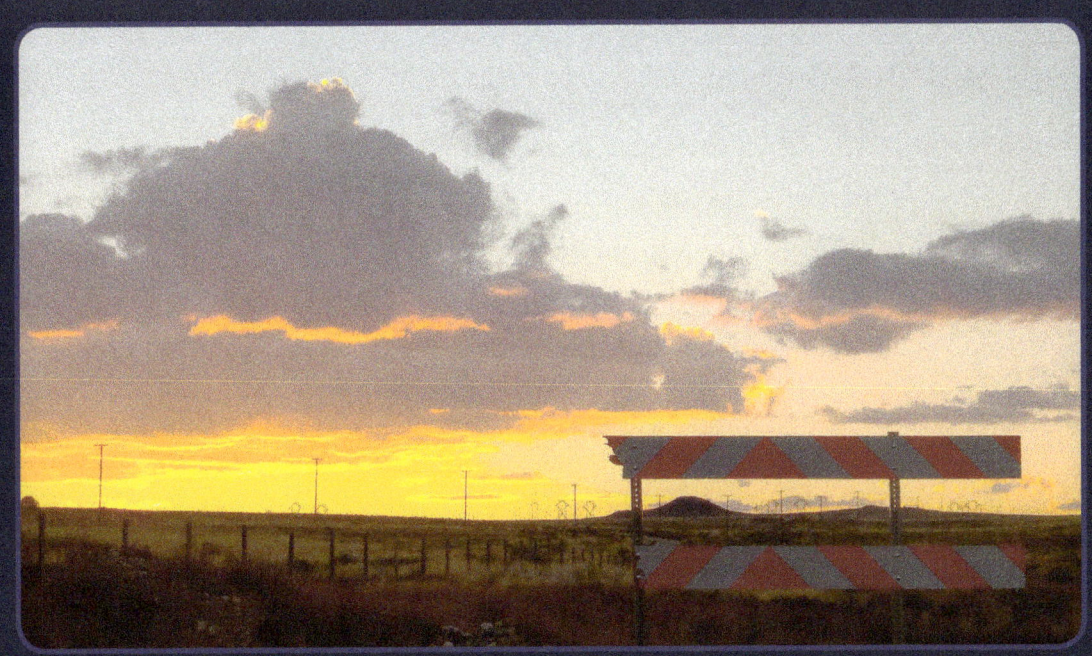

A thunderhead cloud rises above a volcano and expanse of wilderness that stretches beyond a sign marking the end of the road.

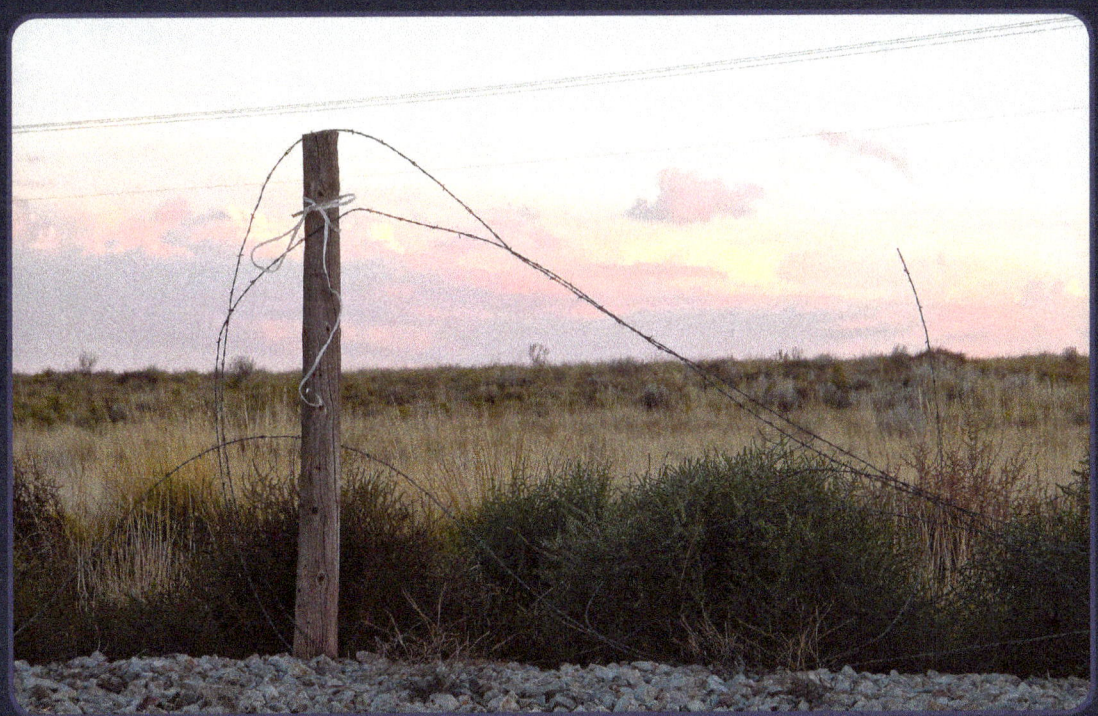

Pink and purple hues fill the sky over the desert beyond a fence post.

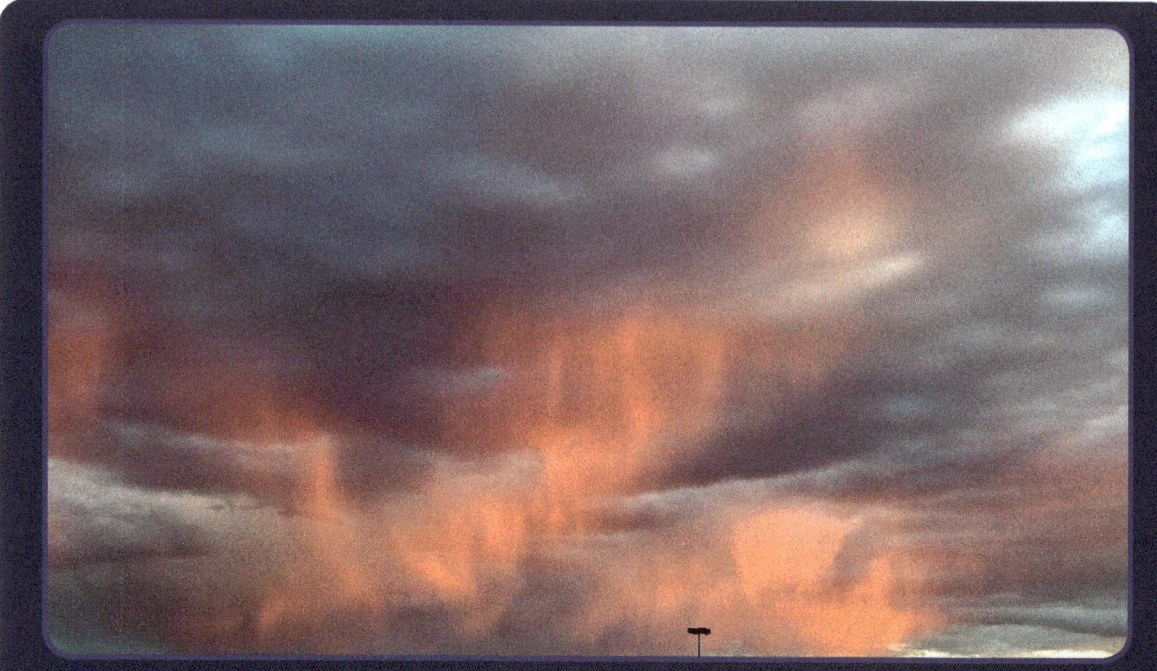
Red fringed clouds cascade down the sky over a shopping center light pole.

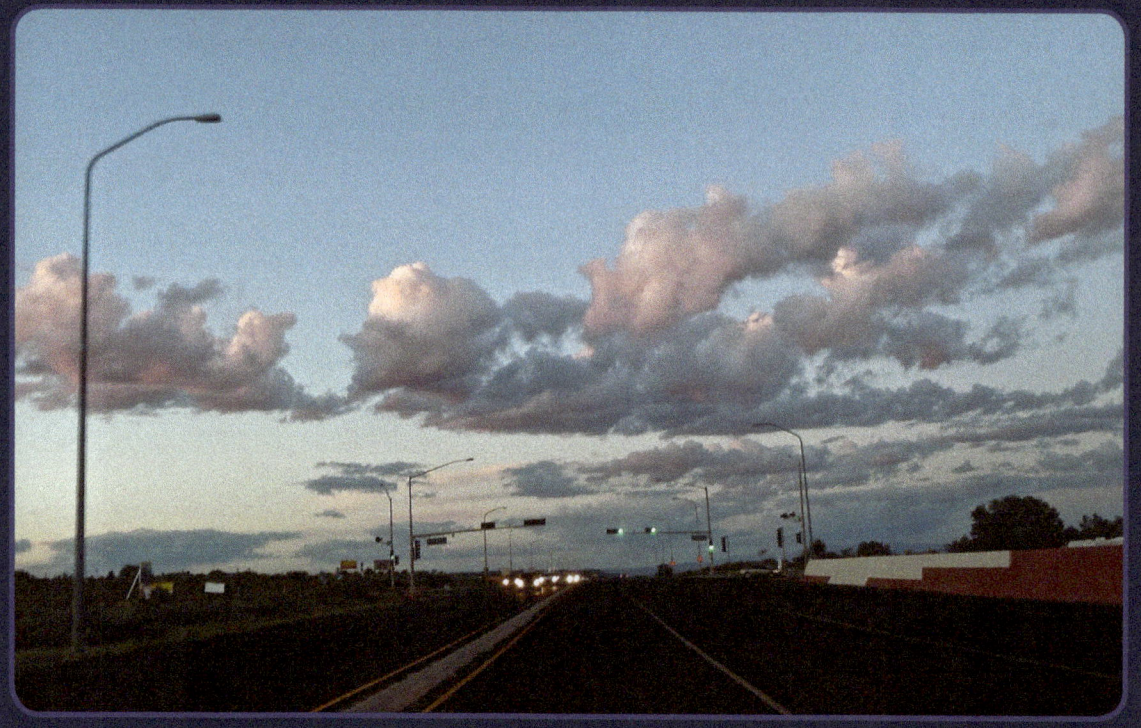
Cars fill the streets at rush hour under an army of billowing clouds.

• Pathways in Time: Photo Journeys • 97

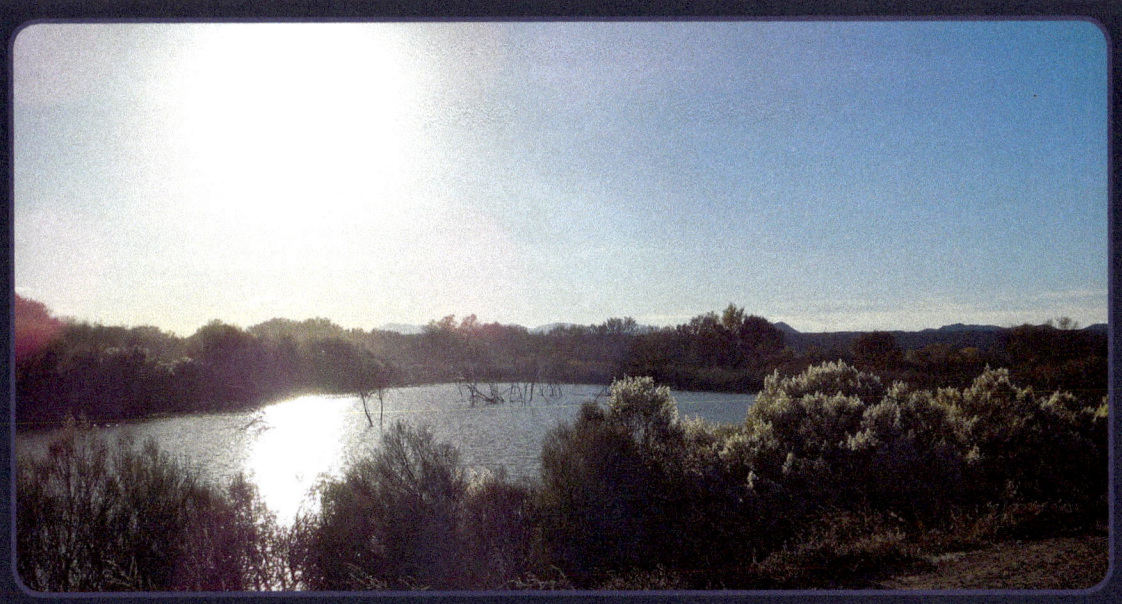

Sun fades into the sky at the onset of a wintery day in November.

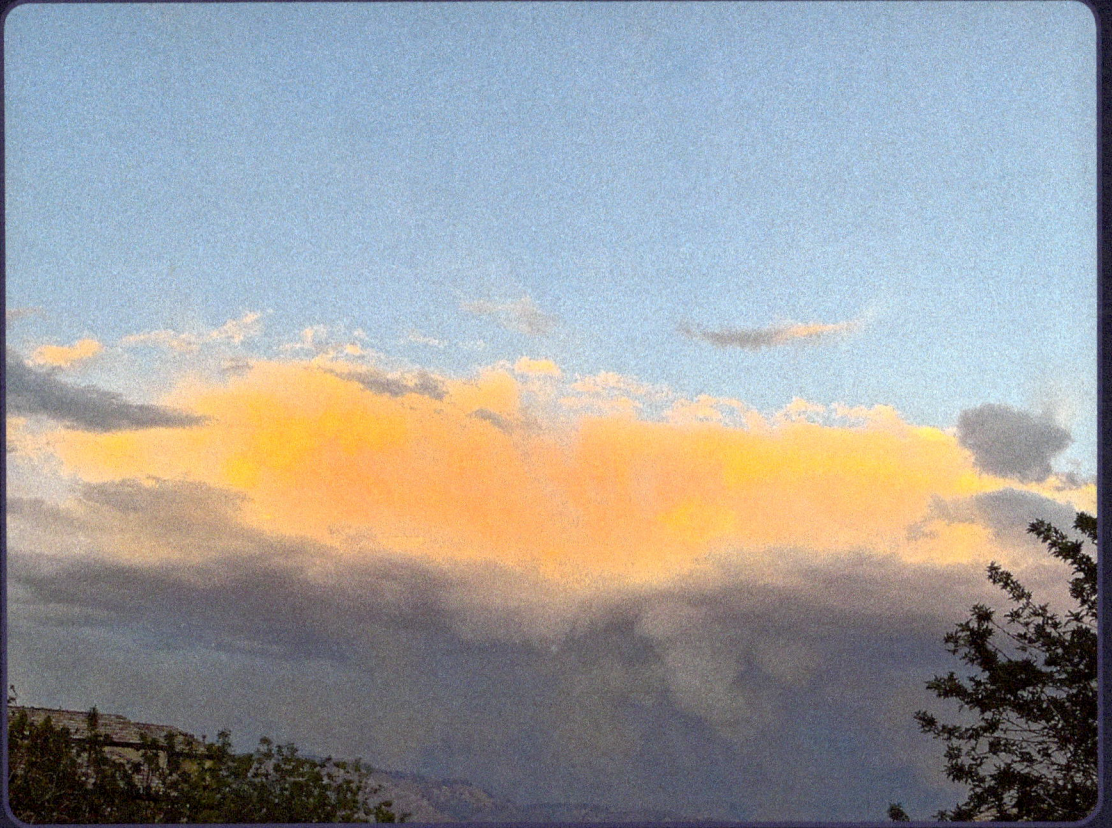

An ominous cloud formation blocks a view of the mountains behind it.

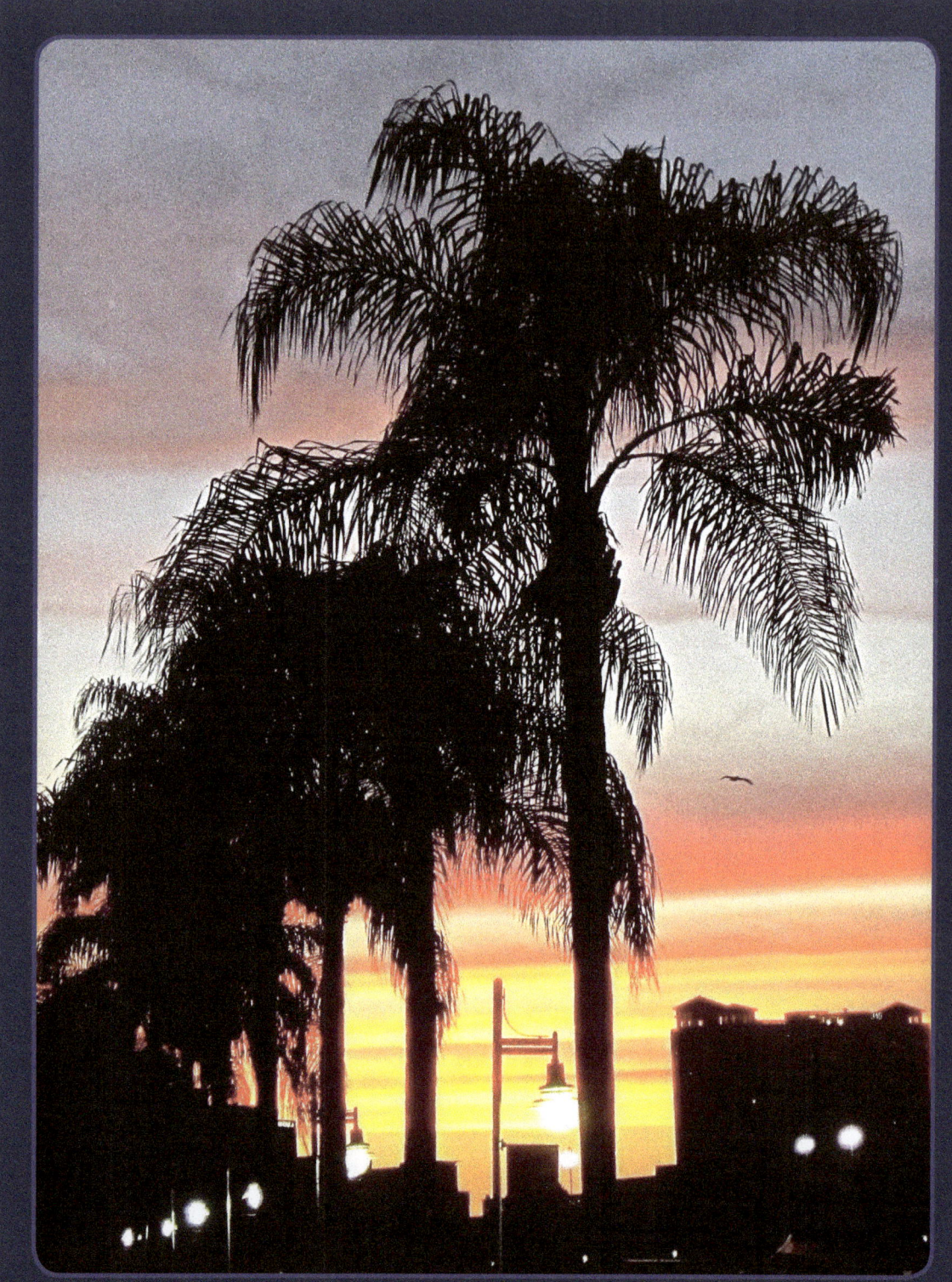
A bird flies alongside a row of palm trees as darkness approaches.

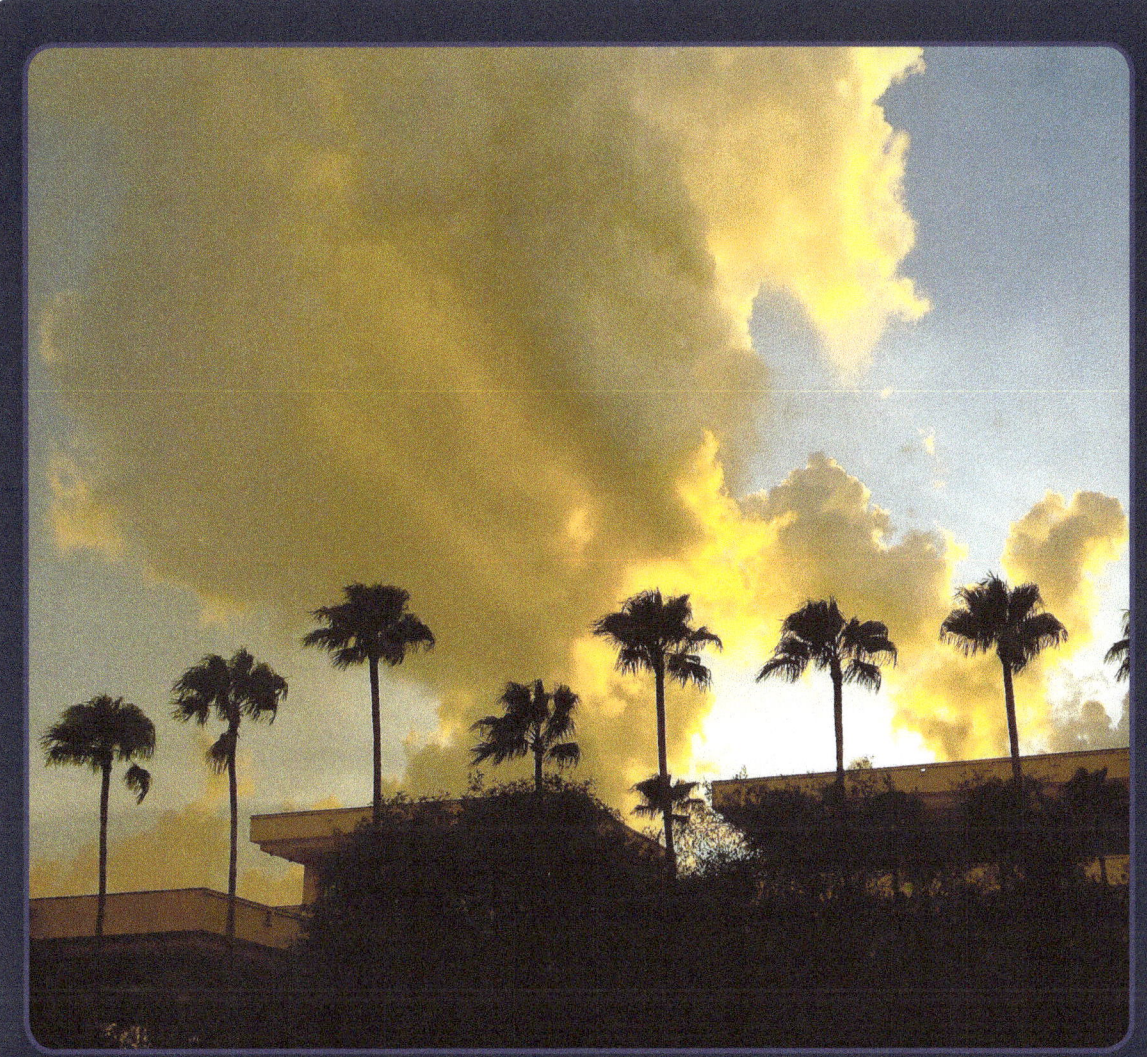

The setting sun illuminates clouds behind a shopping center at the end of the day.

A glowing moon begins its ascent into the clouds.

Purple waters in a Florida bay mirror the colors of the sky above.

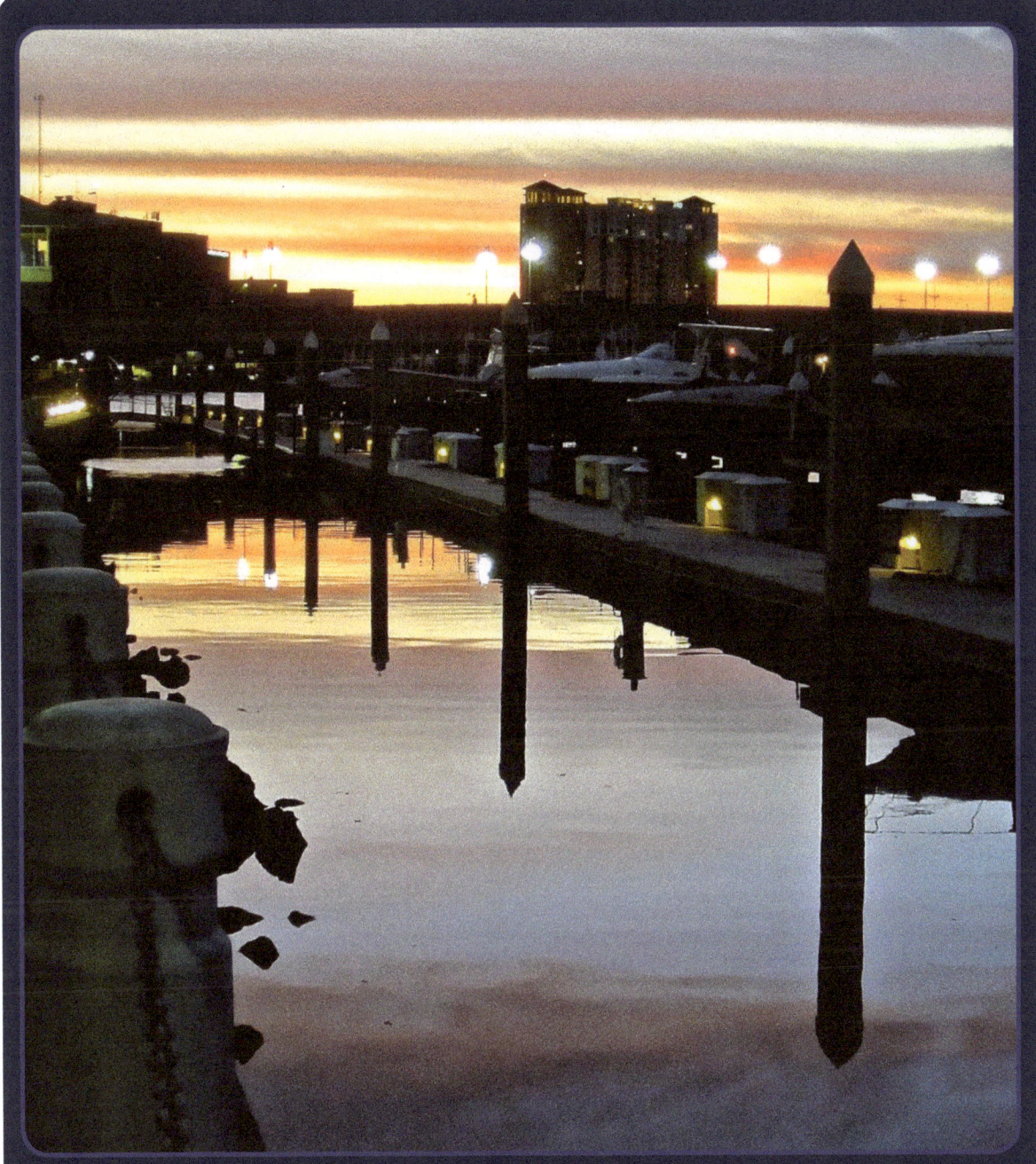

Harbor waters reflect the setting sun's rays overhead.

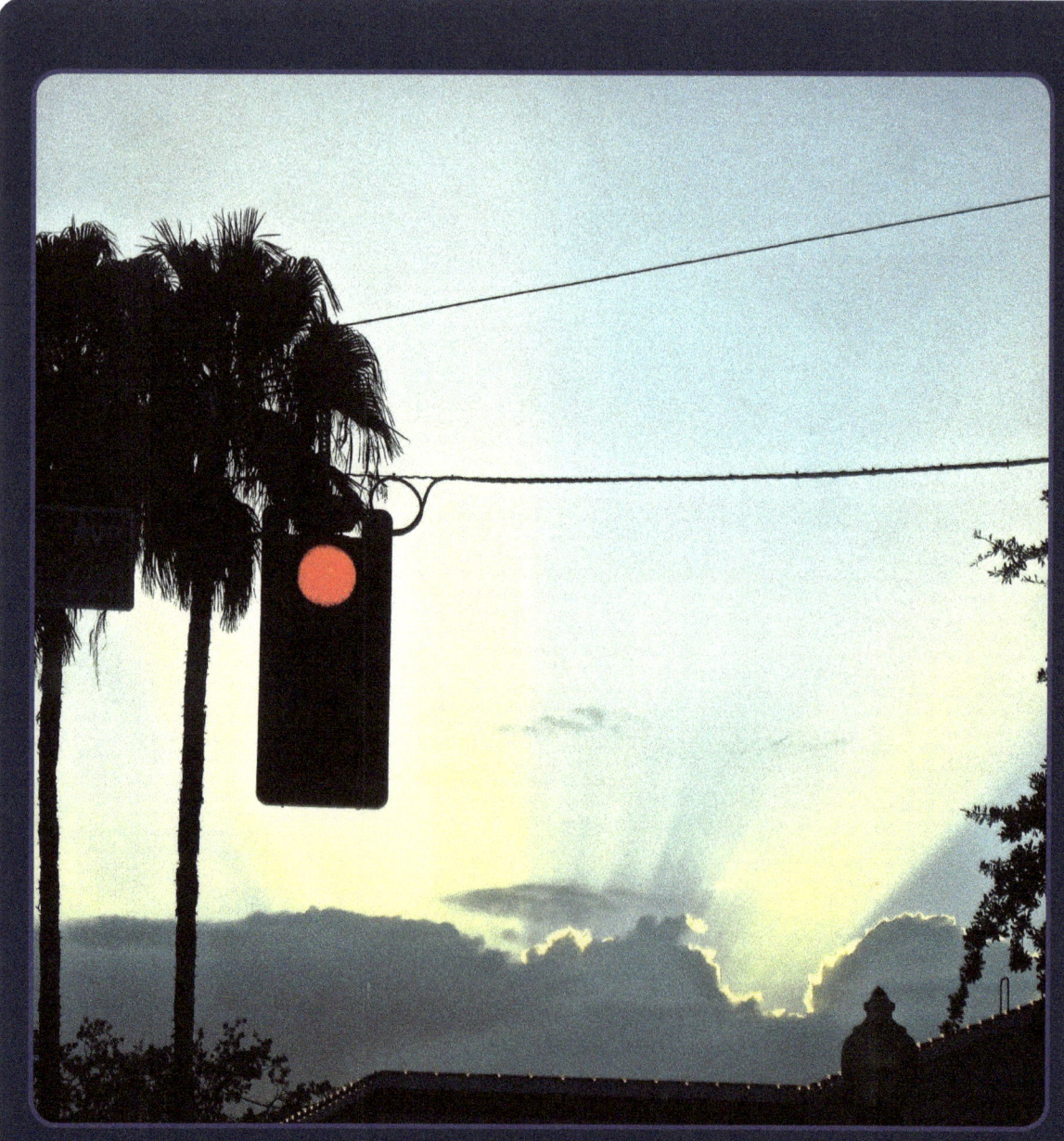

The bright setting sun outlines dark rays and clouds behind a restaurant at the end of a summer's day.

Night

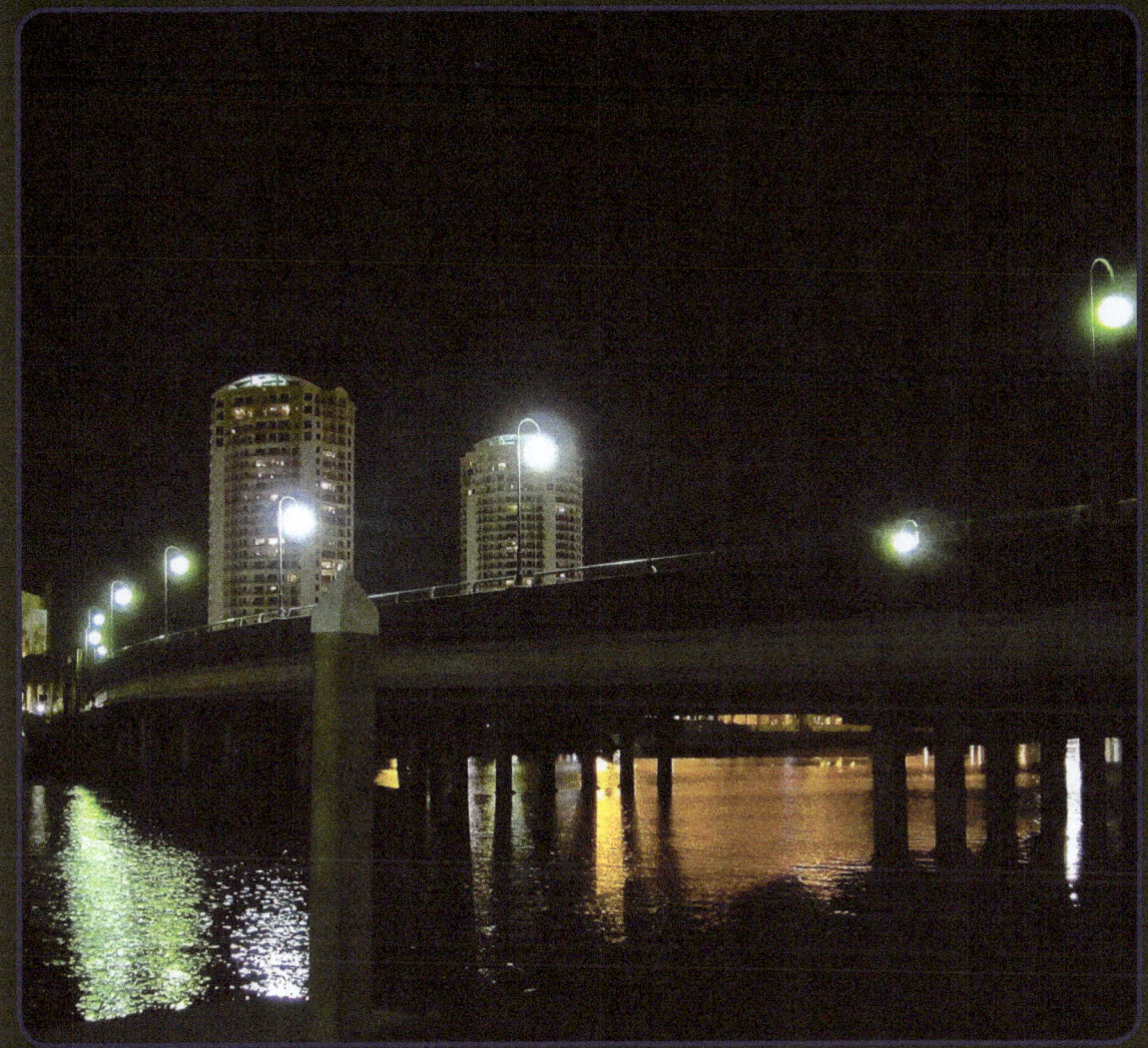

Waters sparkle in emerald green and amber colors under a bridge in Florida.

chapter 9:

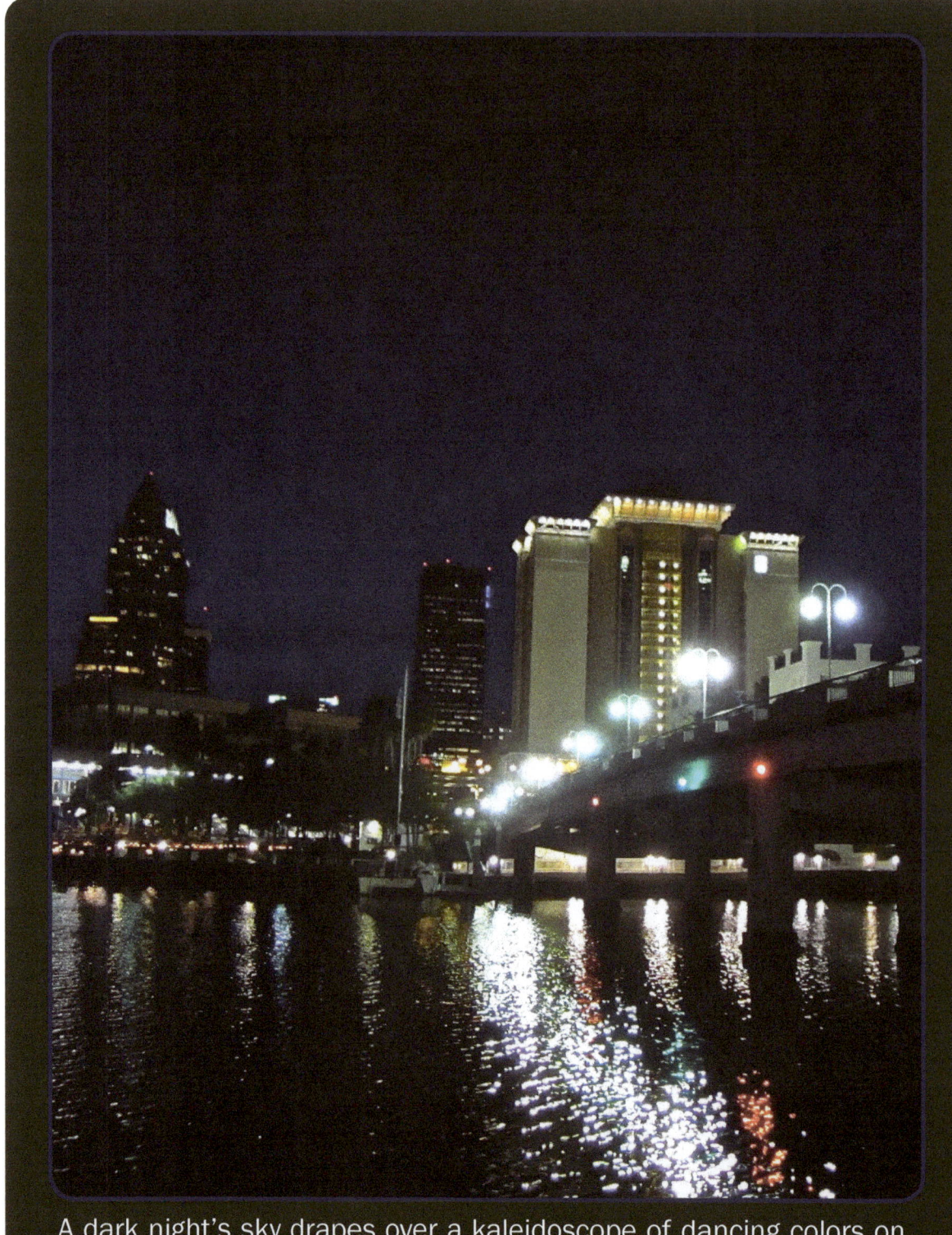

A dark night's sky drapes over a kaleidoscope of dancing colors on the water.

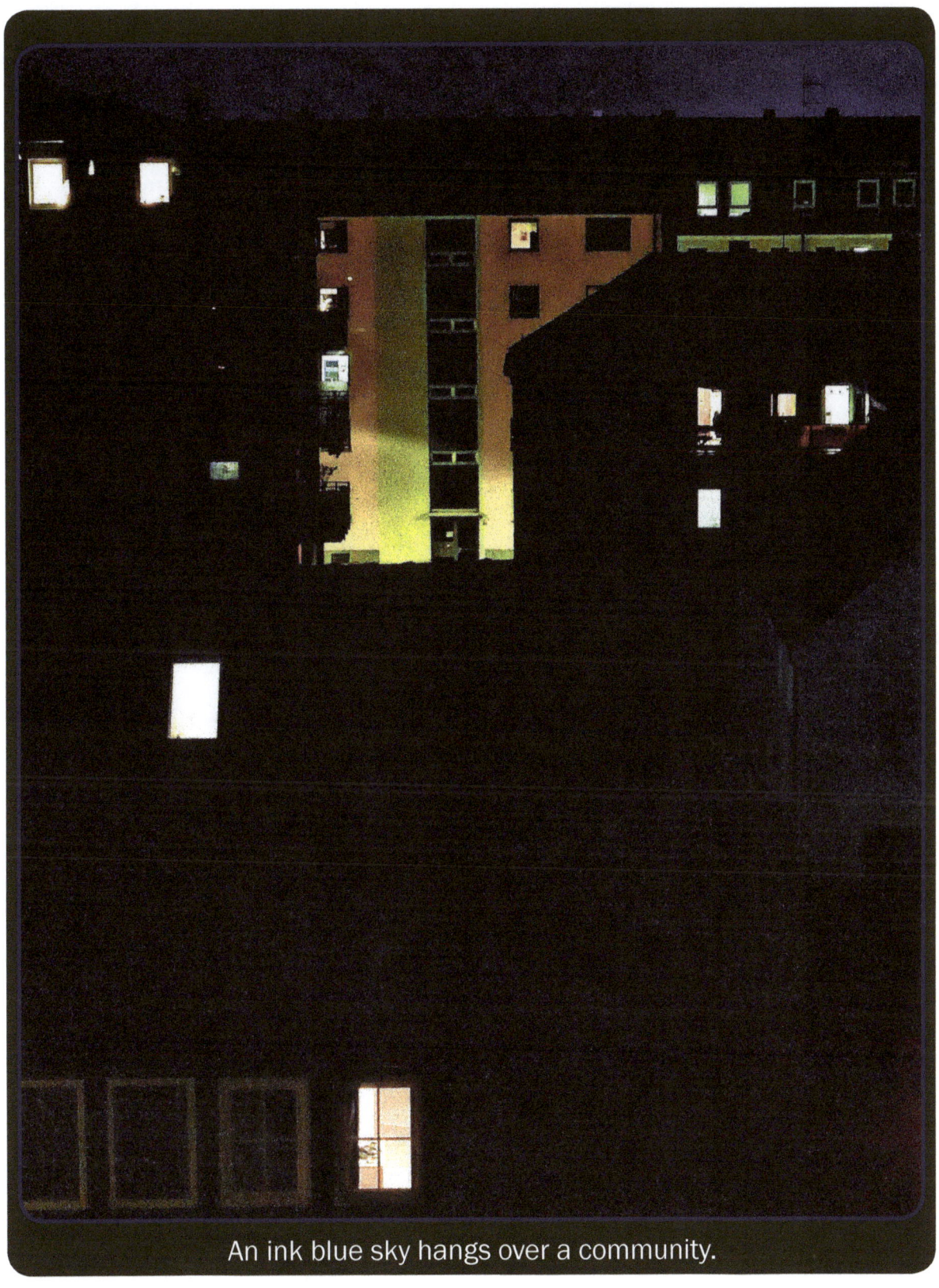

An ink blue sky hangs over a community.

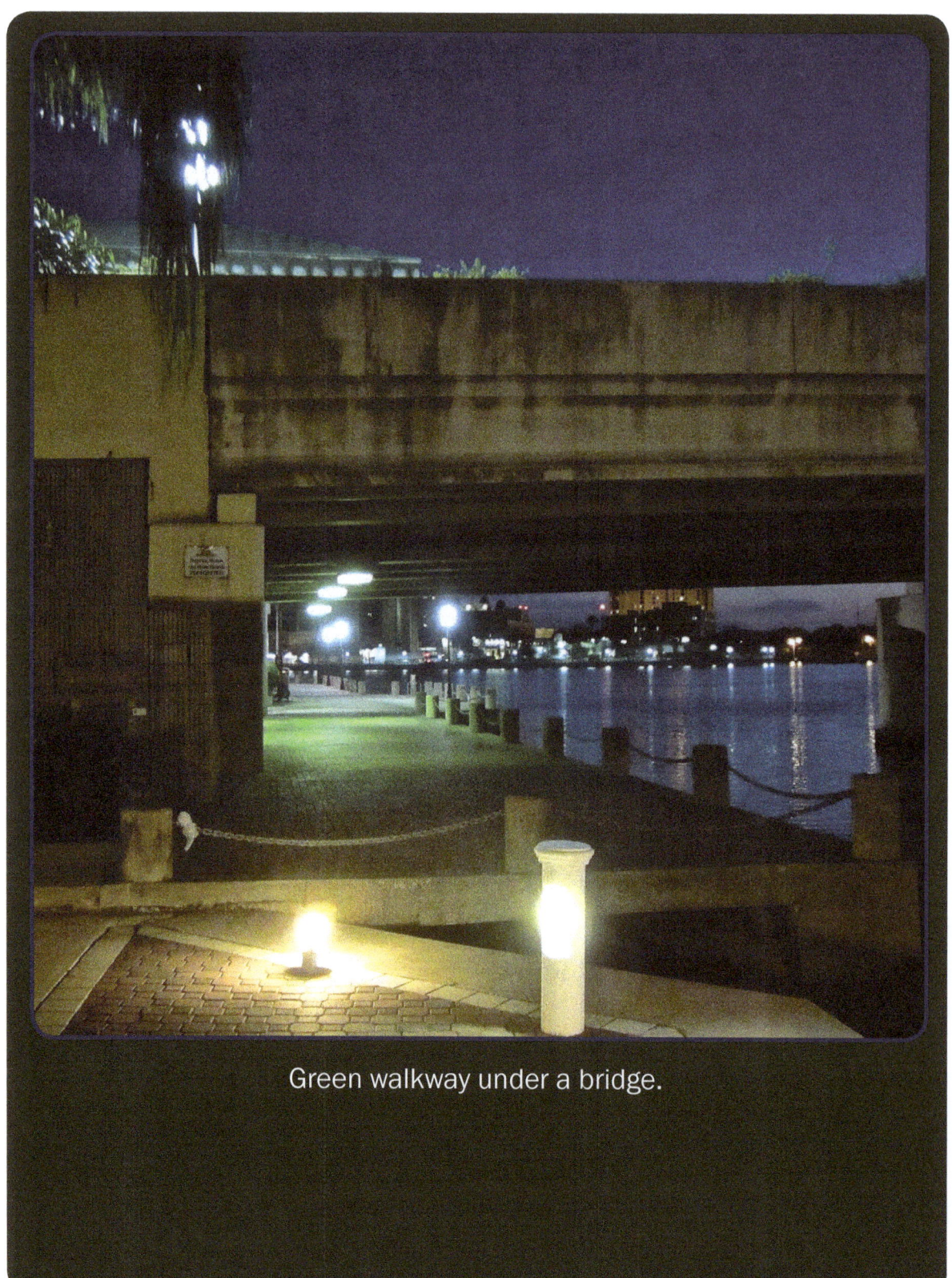
Green walkway under a bridge.

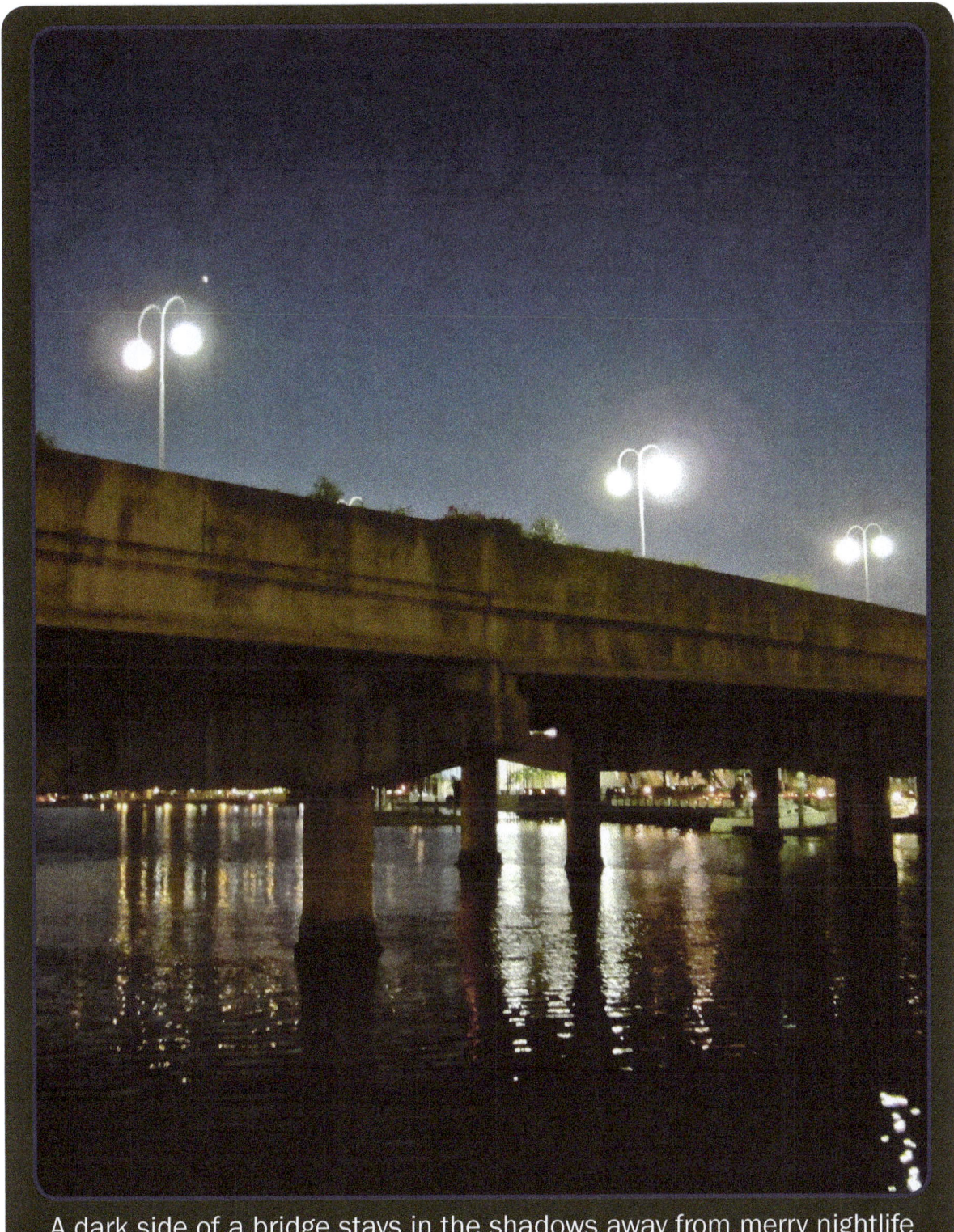
A dark side of a bridge stays in the shadows away from merry nightlife in the distance.

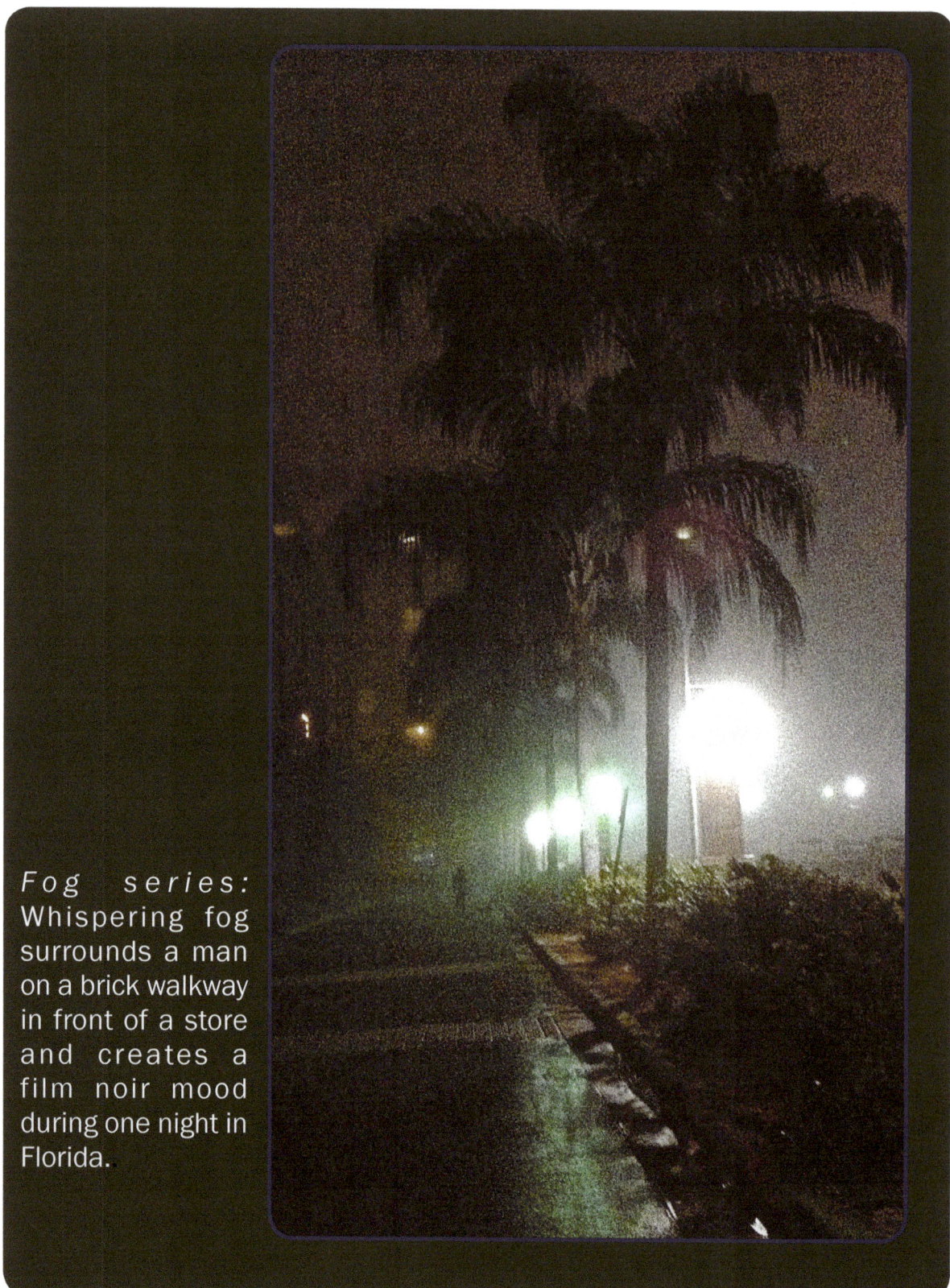

Fog series: Whispering fog surrounds a man on a brick walkway in front of a store and creates a film noir mood during one night in Florida.

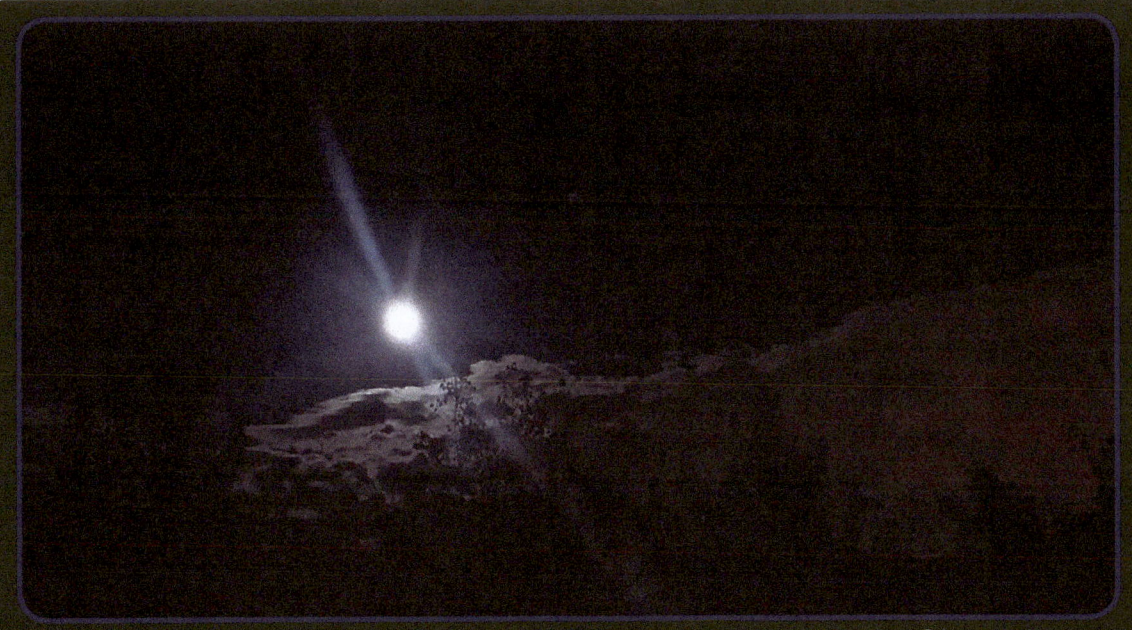

Moonbeams reach across the night sky to touch the tips of branches outside homes.

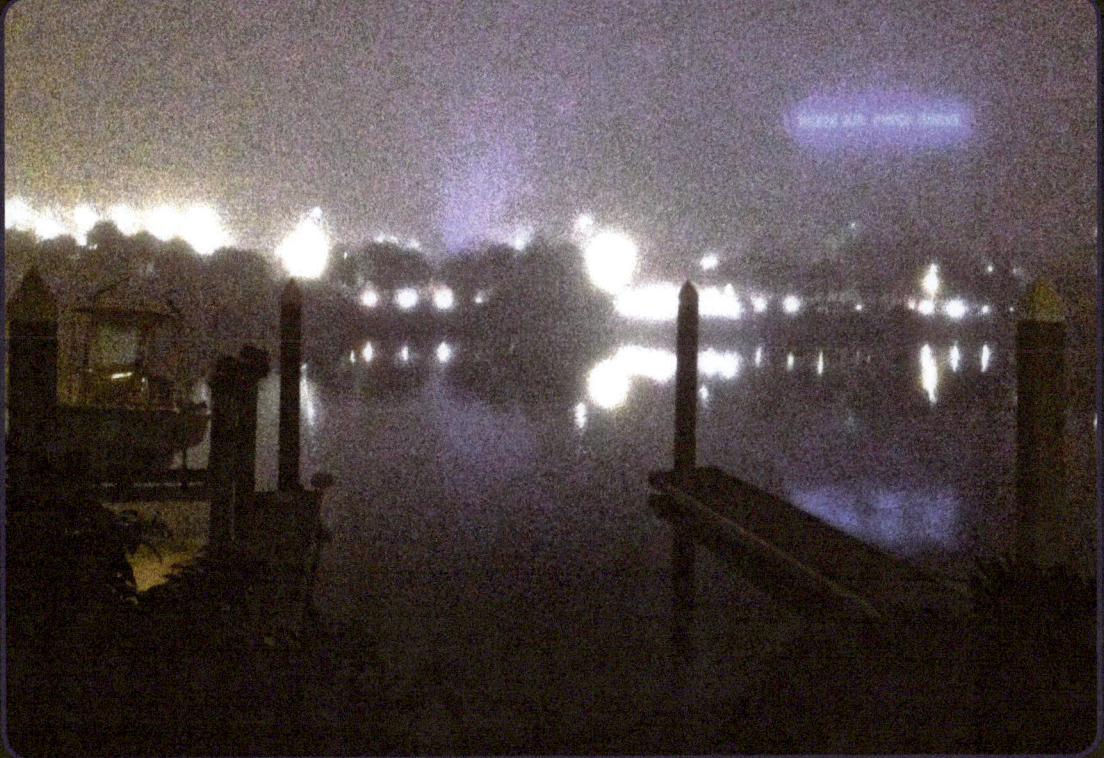

Fog series: Woolly city lights glow warmly behind a boat moored next to an empty jetty.

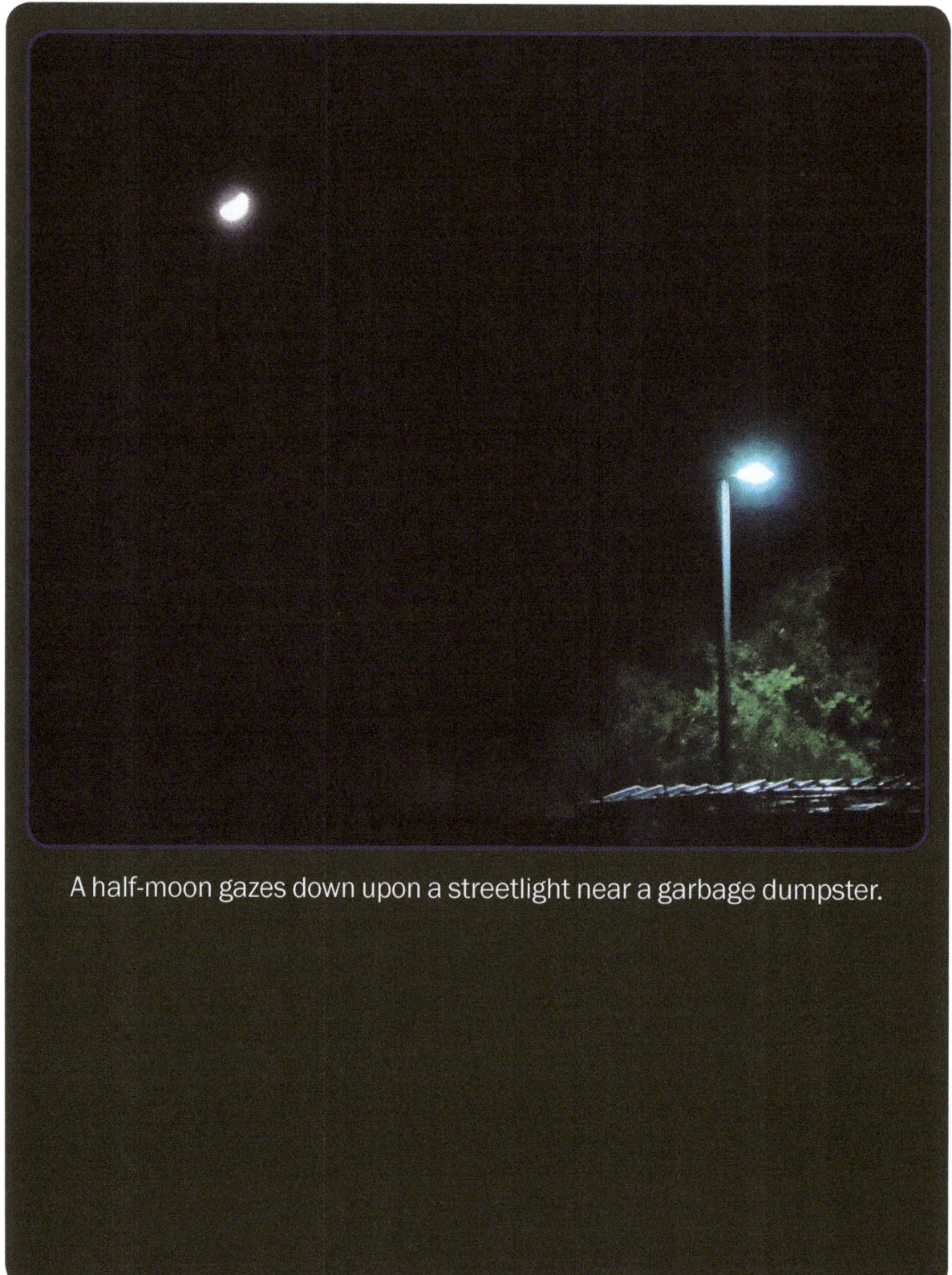
A half-moon gazes down upon a streetlight near a garbage dumpster.

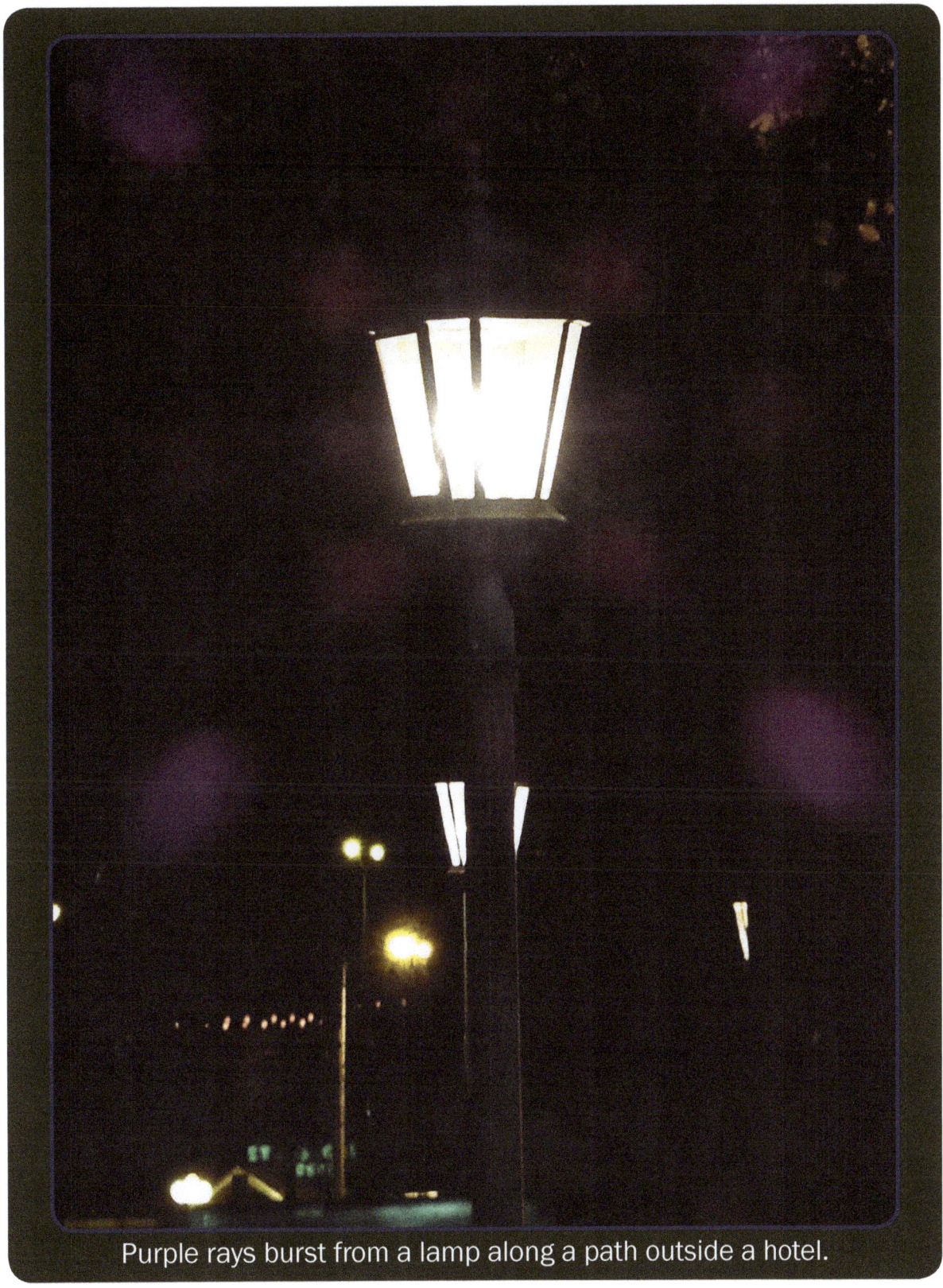

Purple rays burst from a lamp along a path outside a hotel.

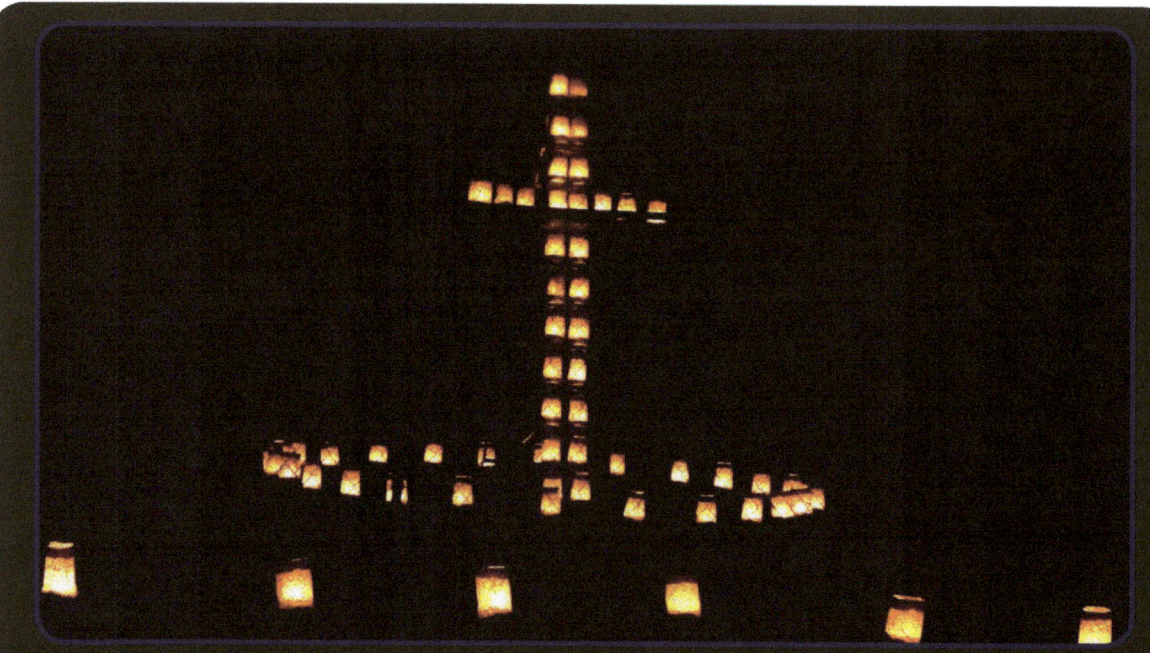

Christmas luminaria lights' series: A cross has been created in this yard in New Mexico on Christmas Eve using traditional Hispanic luminaria lights. Crosses are created by making arrangements on ladders that transform into images of beauty and wonder in the darkness.

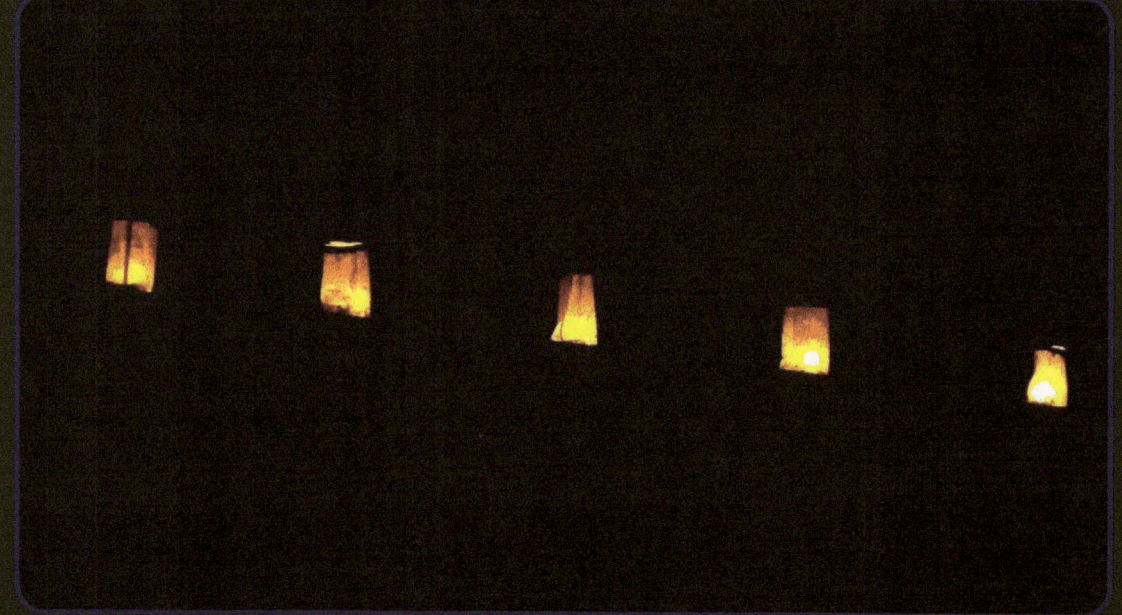

Christmas luminaria lights' series: Brown paper bags filled with sand become pathways for baby Jesus on Christmas Eve when the candles inside are lit.

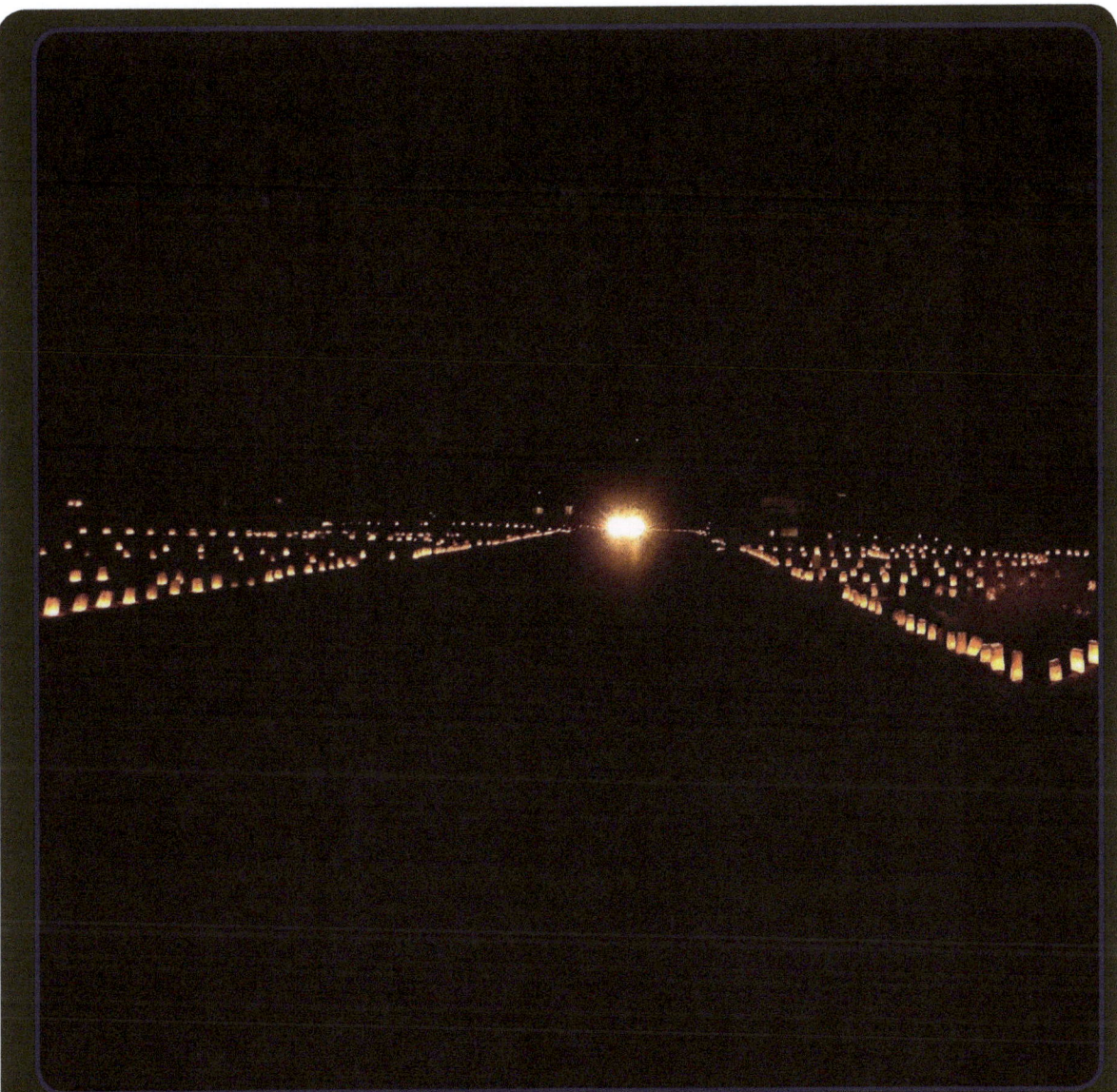

Christmas luminaria lights' series: Car lights outshine the luminarias in a neighborhood. In New Mexico, many people follow the Hispanic tradition of placing luminarias outside the edges of their homes on Christmas Eve. The lights are to illuminate a path in the night for baby Jesus to come into your home. Many neighborhoods, like the one above, join together to have a continuous display of luminarias along all streets and in all yards. Cars are supposed to turn off their lights on Christmas Eve when driving through luminaria areas to better experience the serenity amid the darkness.

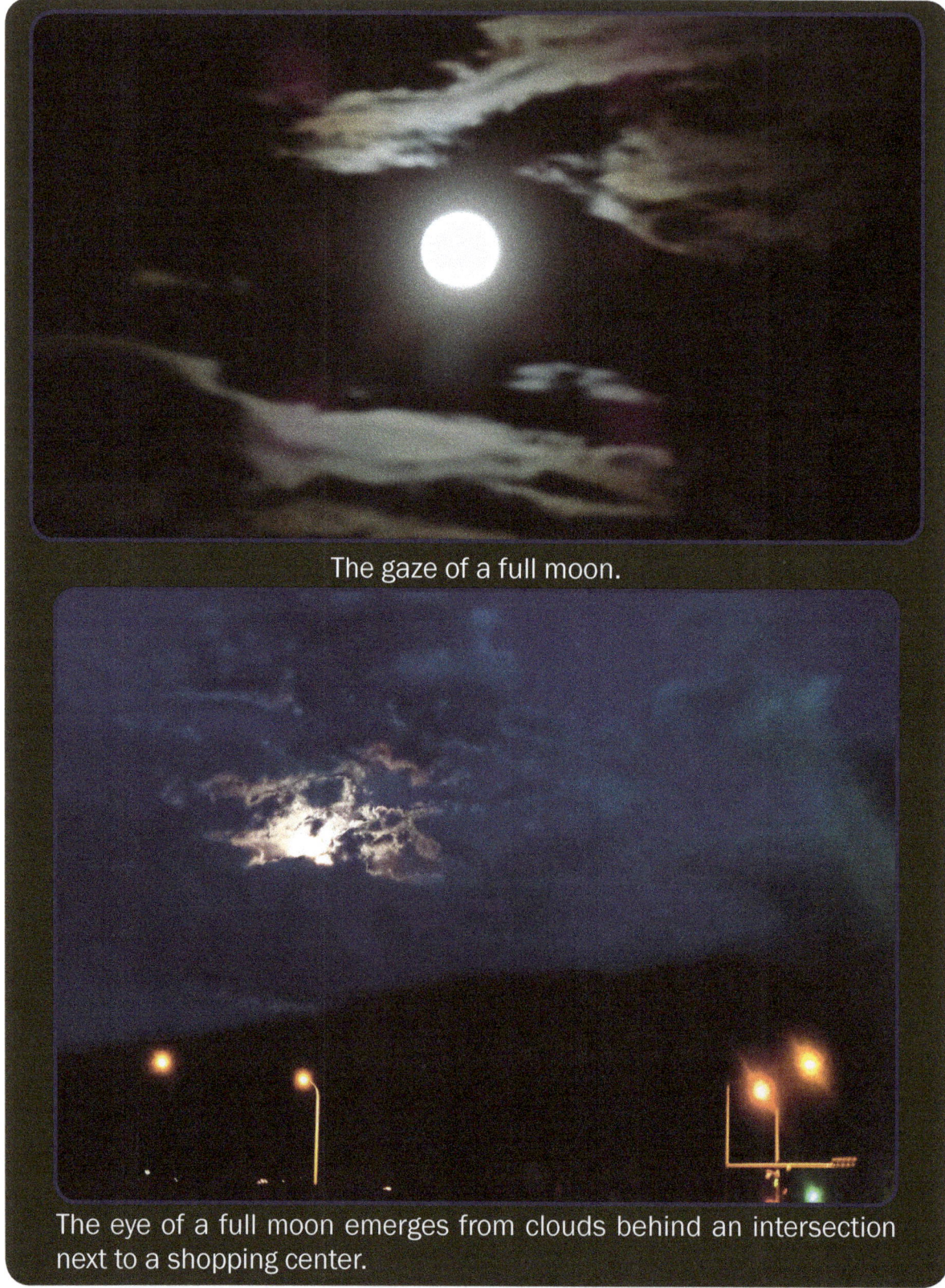

The gaze of a full moon.

The eye of a full moon emerges from clouds behind an intersection next to a shopping center.

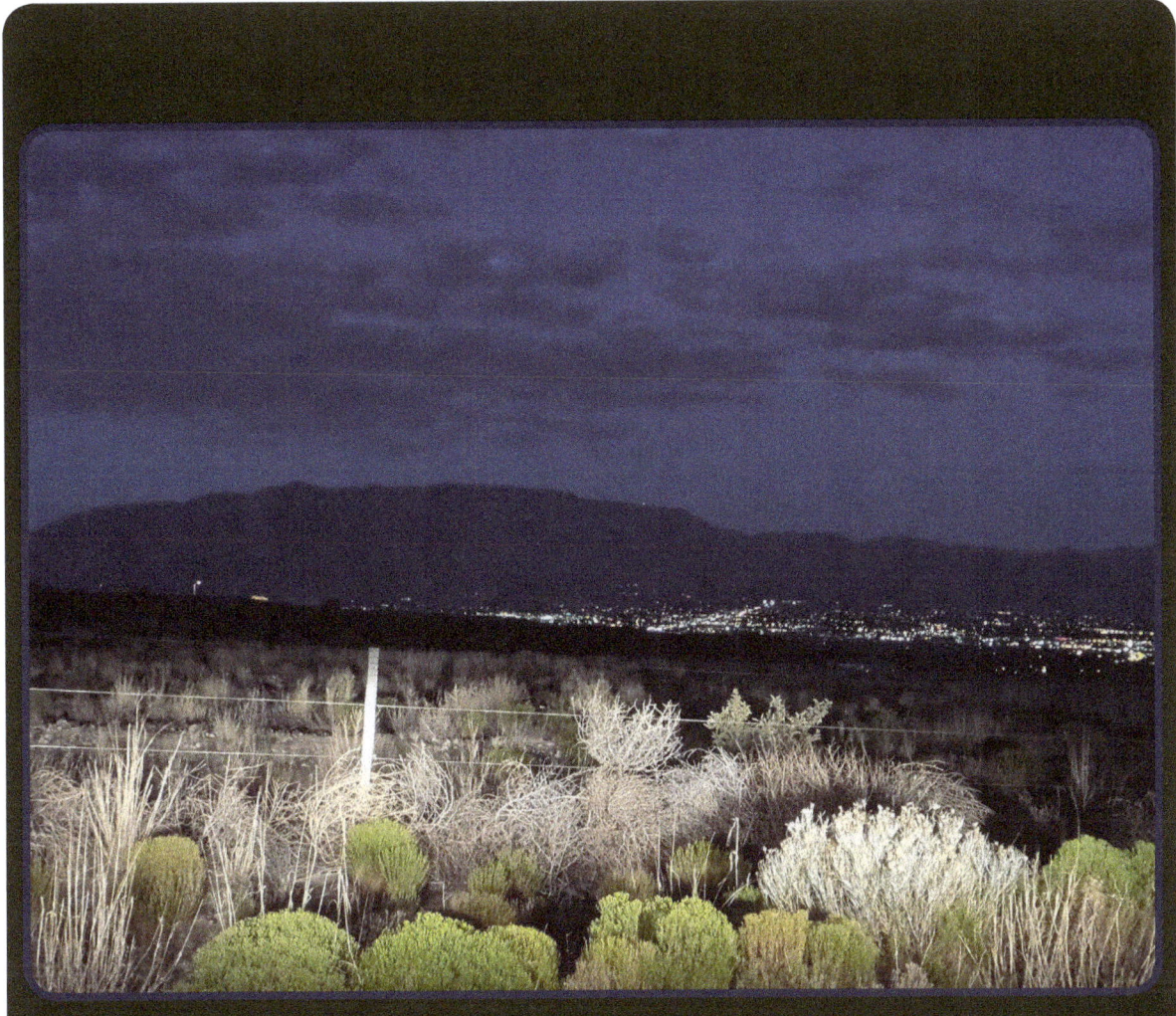

Sagebrush blankets the mesa as night falls over the high desert and Sandia Mountains in the distance.

Patterns

Chapter 10:

Fall leaves are sprinkled over a railway track at the Santa Fe train station in New Mexico, which is along the famous Atchison, Topeka and Santa Fe Railway.

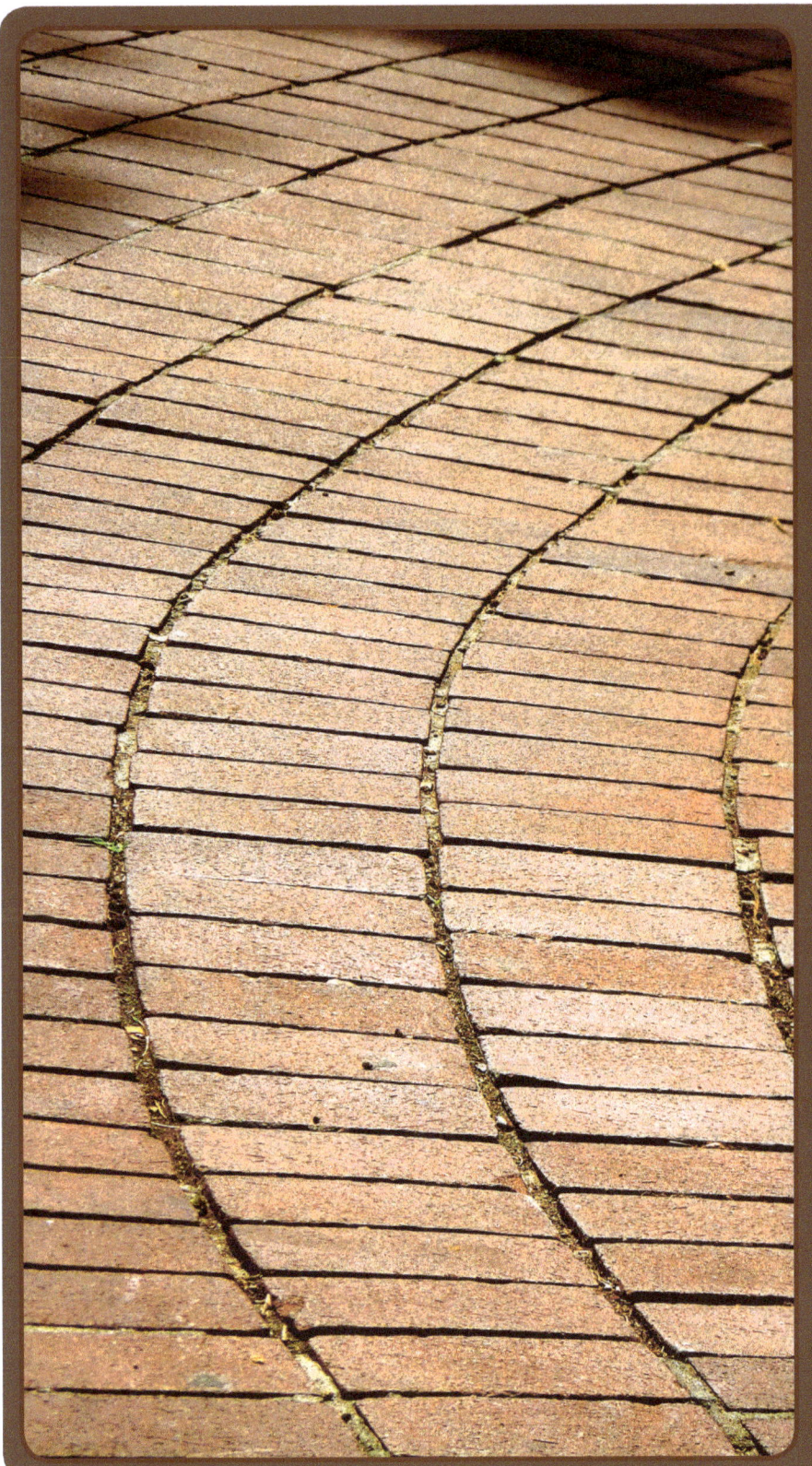

These bricks have been placed in a historic location in Albuquerque, N.M. The city was founded at this plaza in 1706 and named after a Spanish viceroy.

These bricks are said to cover the graves of hastily buried Confederate soldiers who died during a Civil War battle when the Rebel Army briefly held Albuquerque in 1862.

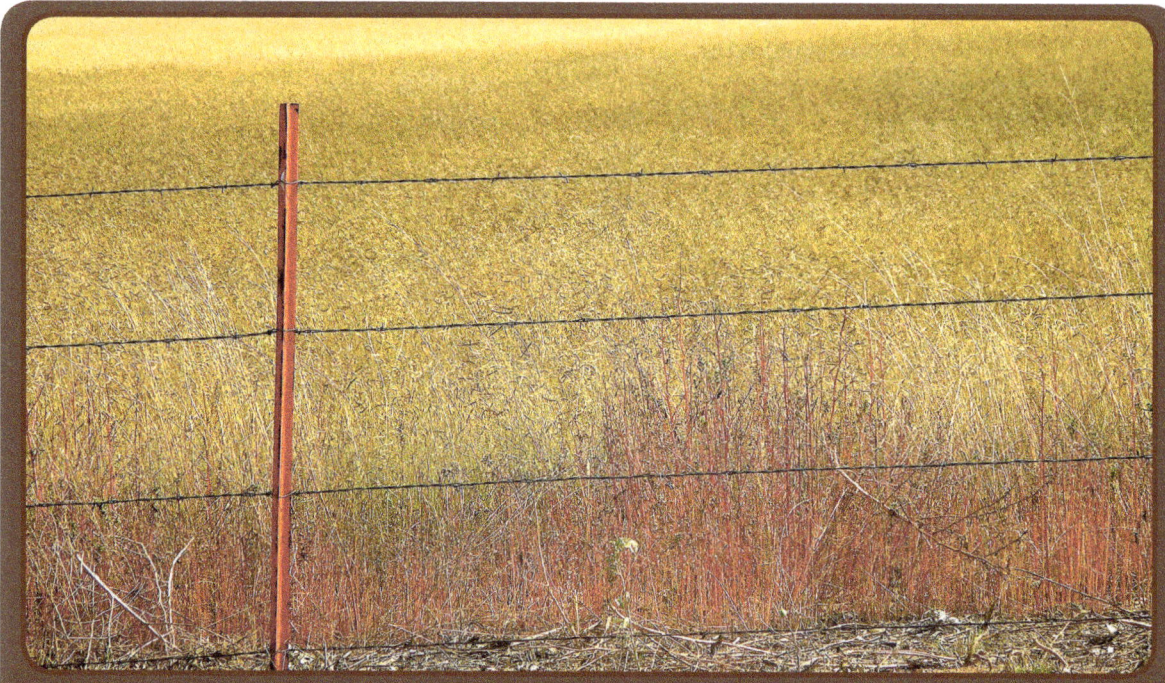
An orange iron fence post matches the color of wild grass in a field in eastern New Mexico near the *Llano Estacado* (Staked Plains).

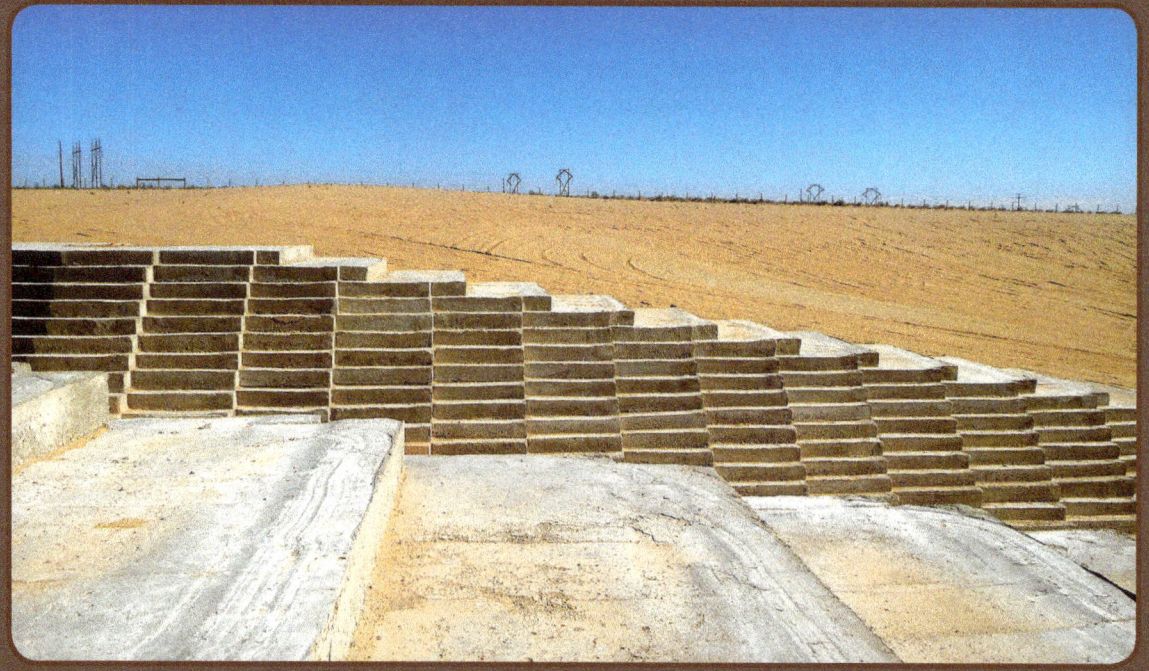
Concrete stepping structures form a barrier in open space against destructive summer flashfloods.

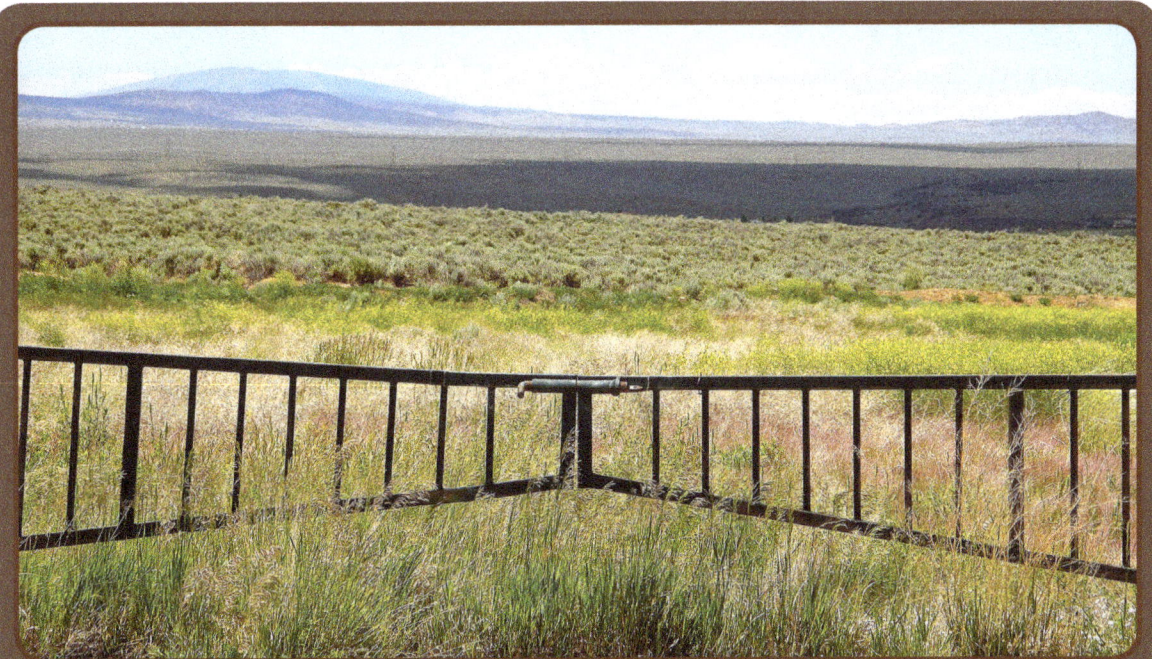

A cattle gate points to the Rio Grande Gorge (a rift in the Earth's crust), located in the ground below the enormous shadow of a thundercloud outside Taos, N.M.

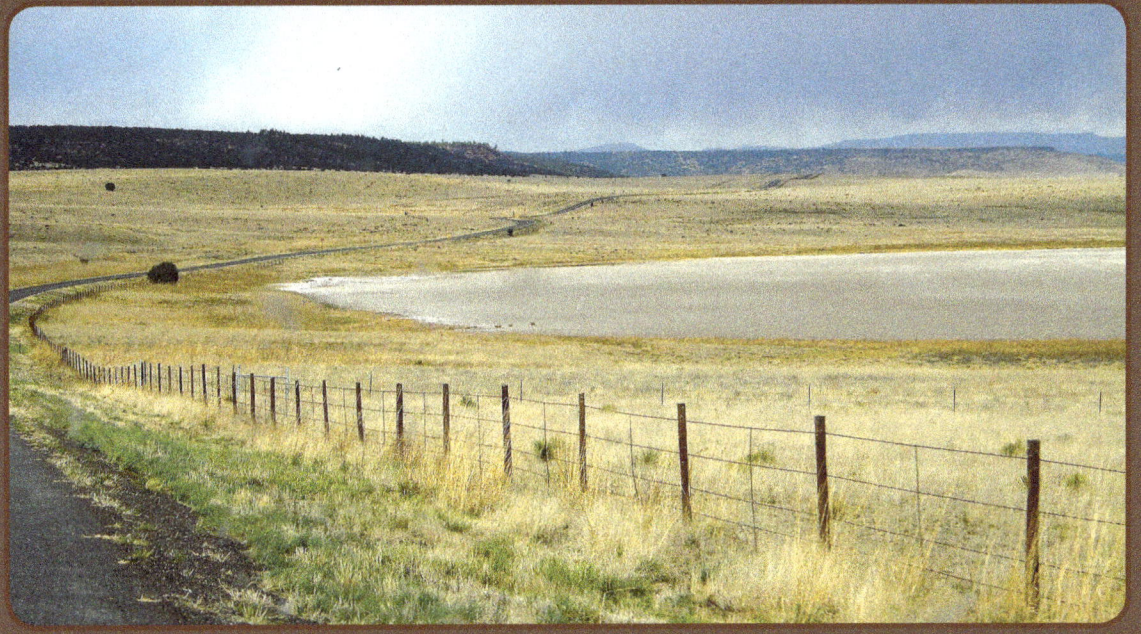

A fence winds along part of the Old Santa Fe Trail, which borders a highway to Fort Union. The fort was a major U.S. military hub in the Southwest from 1851 to 1891 and operational base for fighting various Indian wars as well as repulsing Confederates during the Civil War.

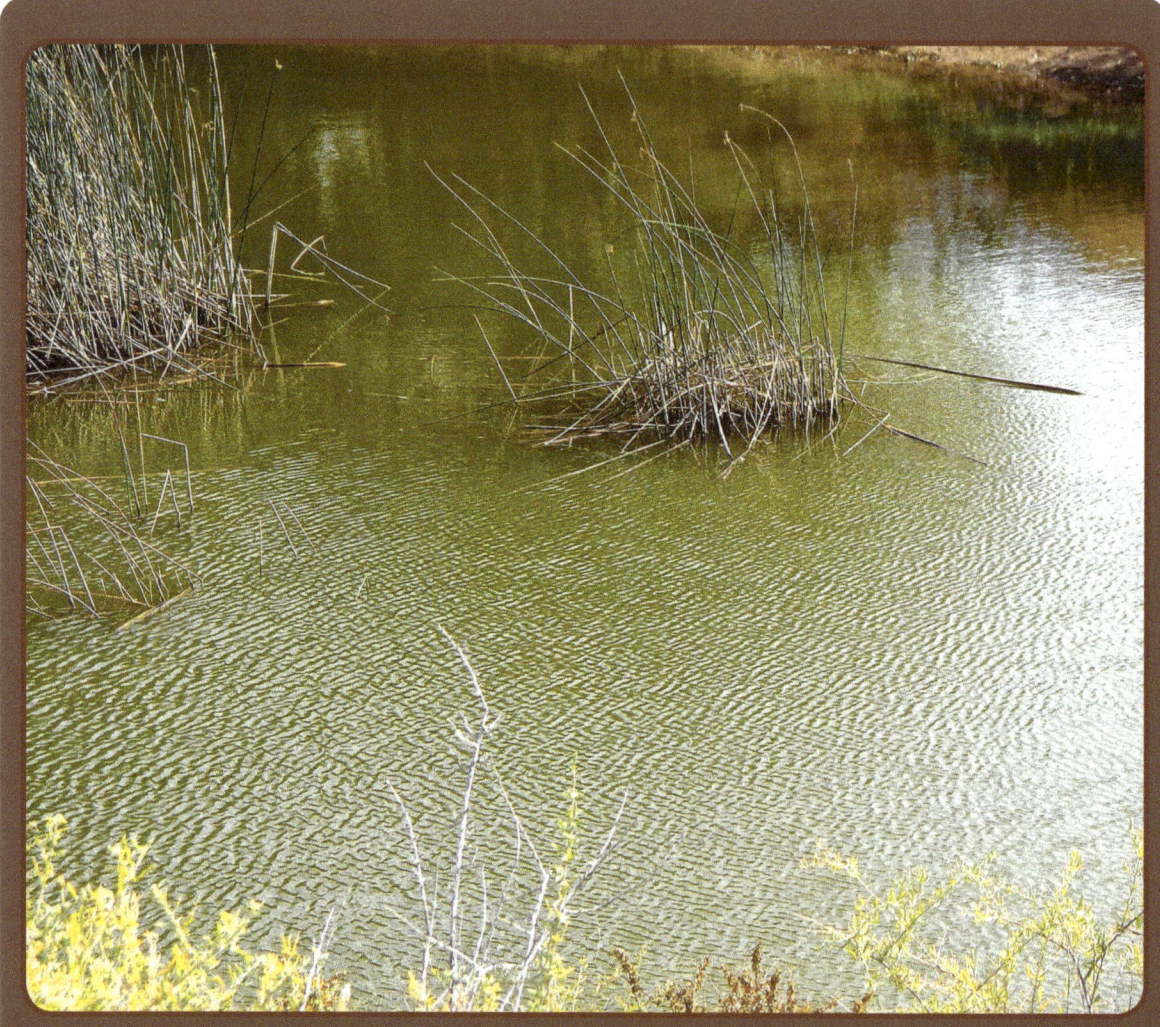
Wind causes checkerboard ripples in a pond outside a walking trail and baseball fields.

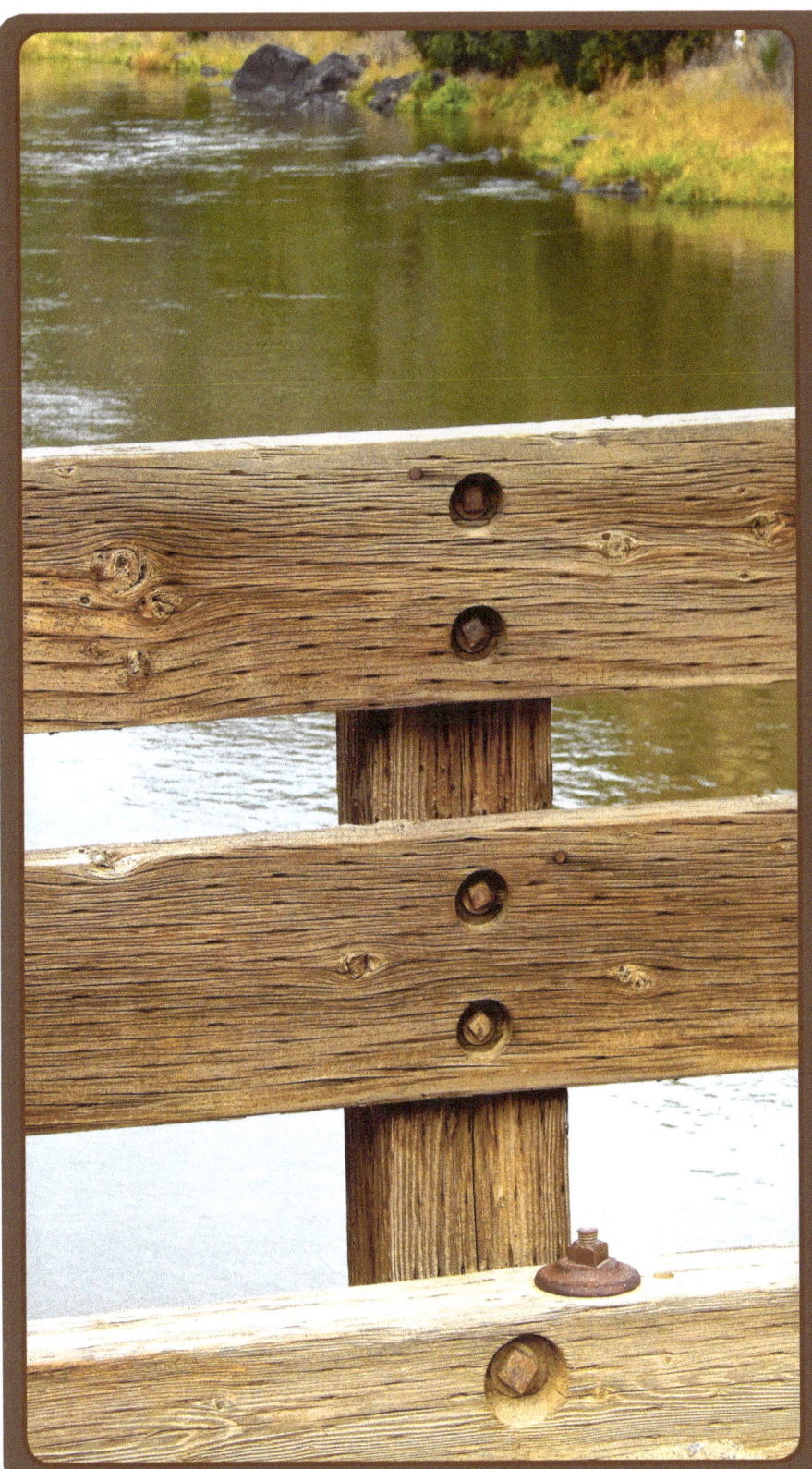

Rusted screws and bolts hold together a bridge over the Rio Grande.

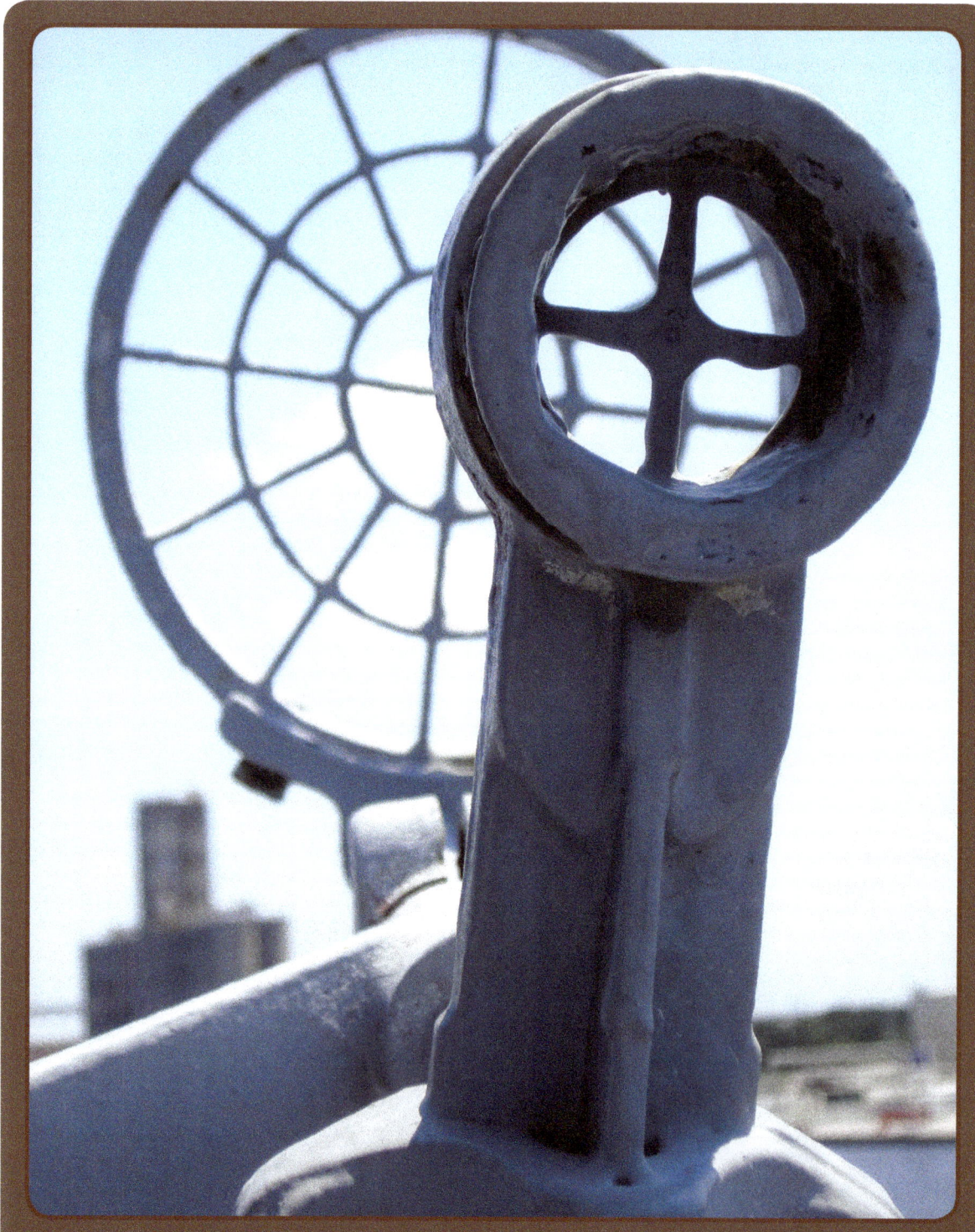

Peering into a gunsight on the one of only 4 operational World War II ships in the United States.

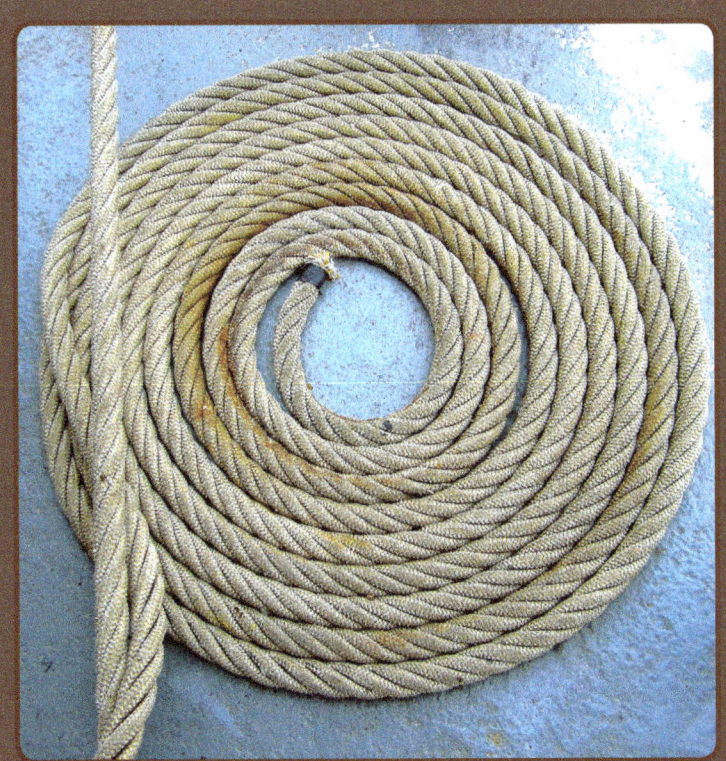

A rope swirl on a vessel.

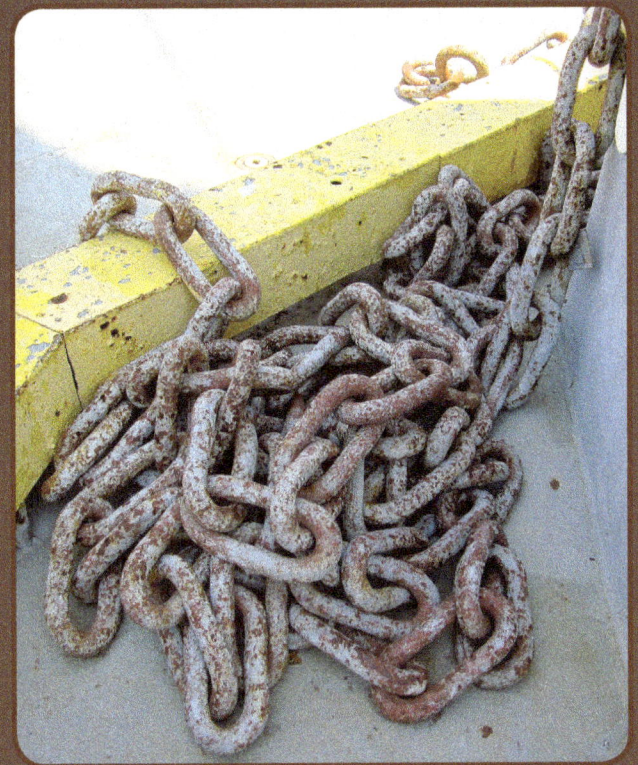

A crumpled rusty chain.

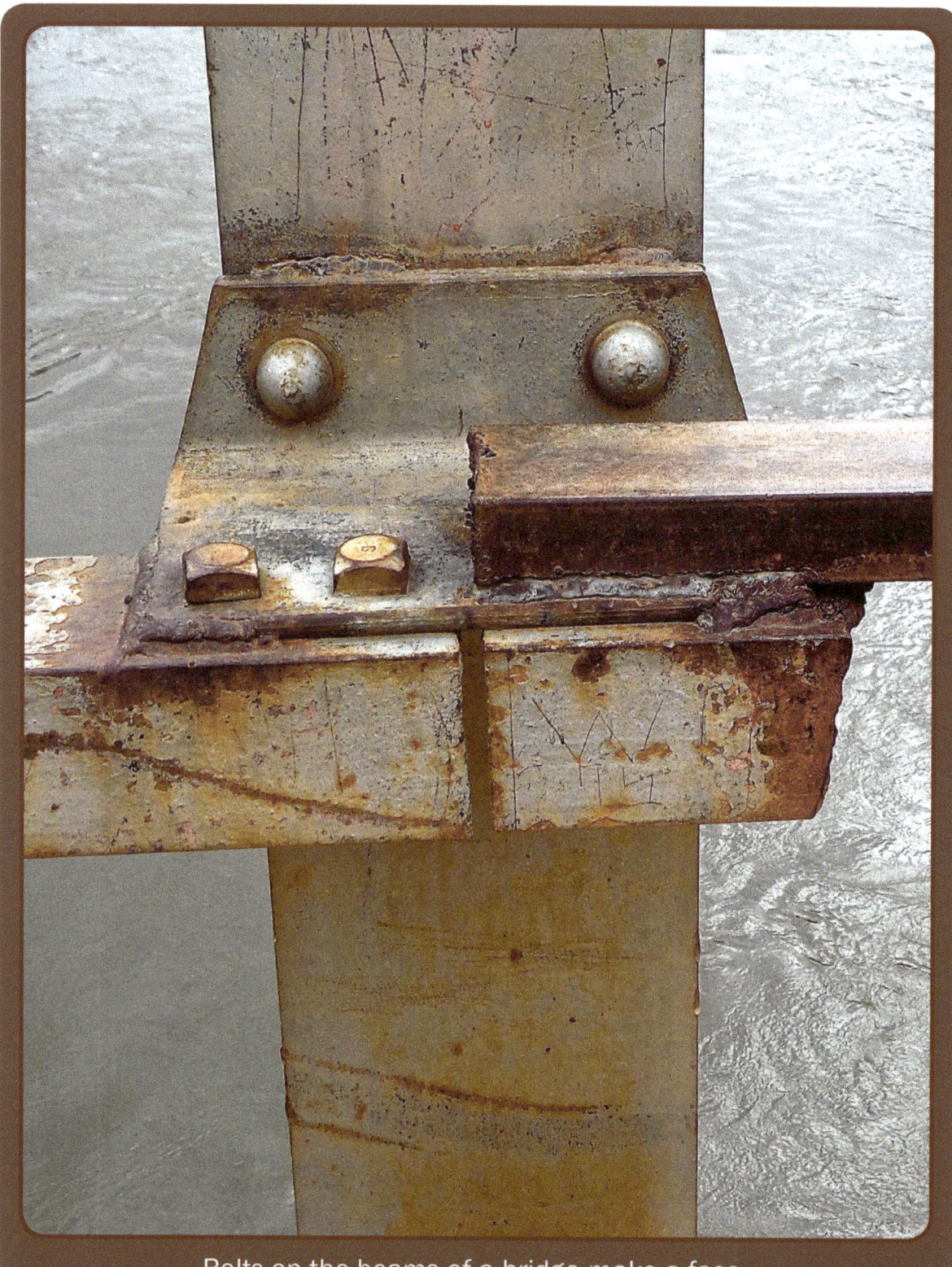
Bolts on the beams of a bridge make a face.

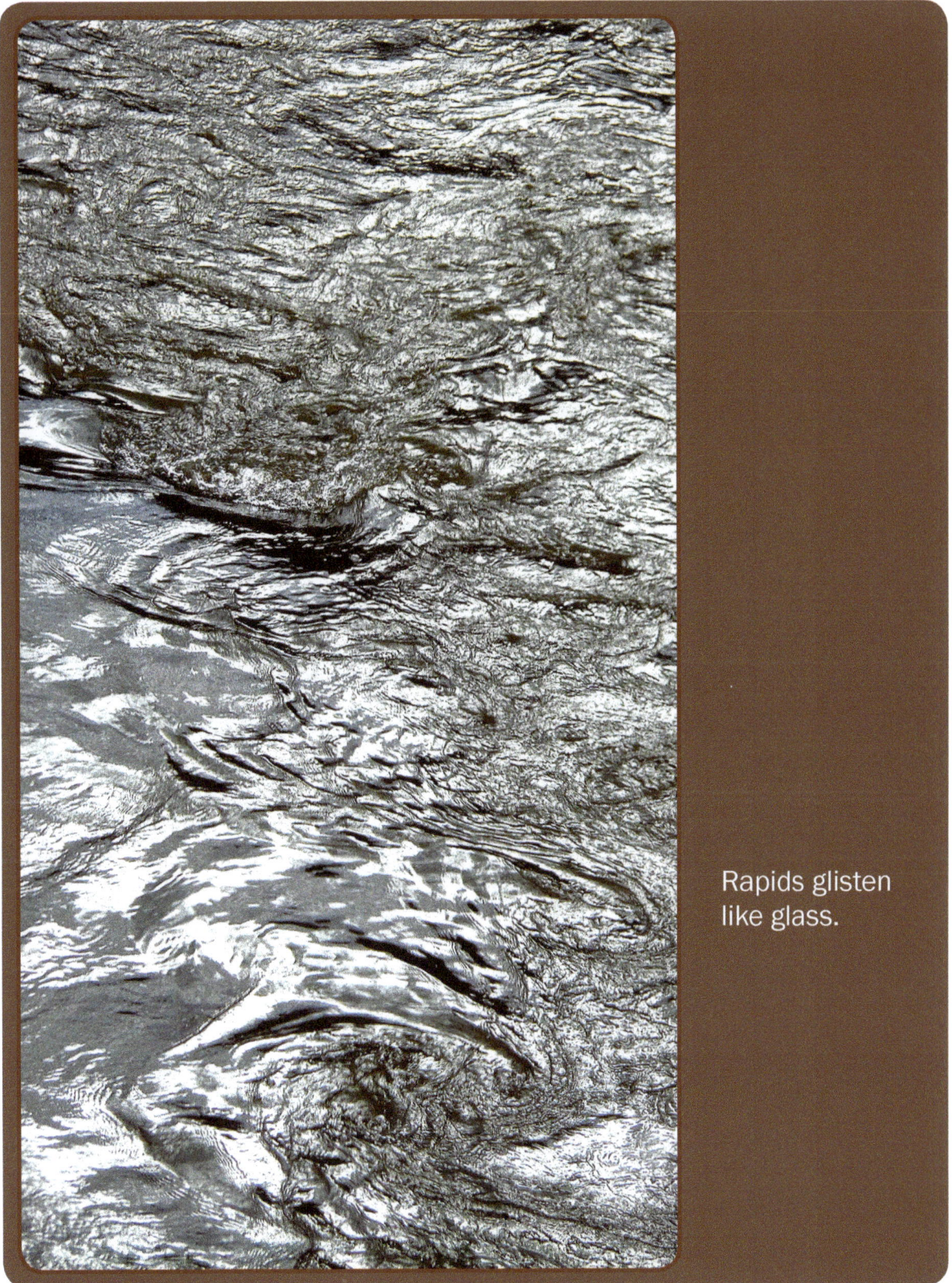

Rapids glisten like glass.

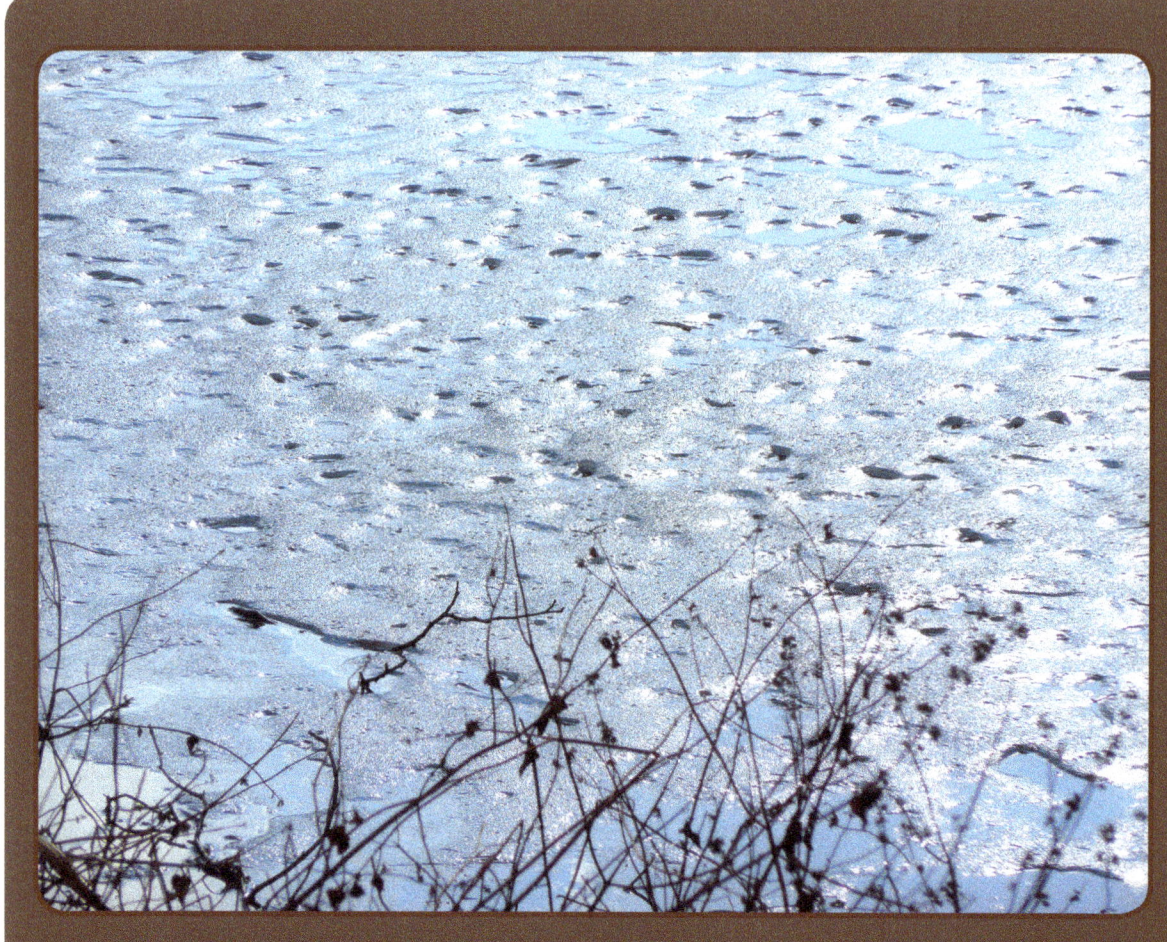
Bushes watch ice begin to disappear.

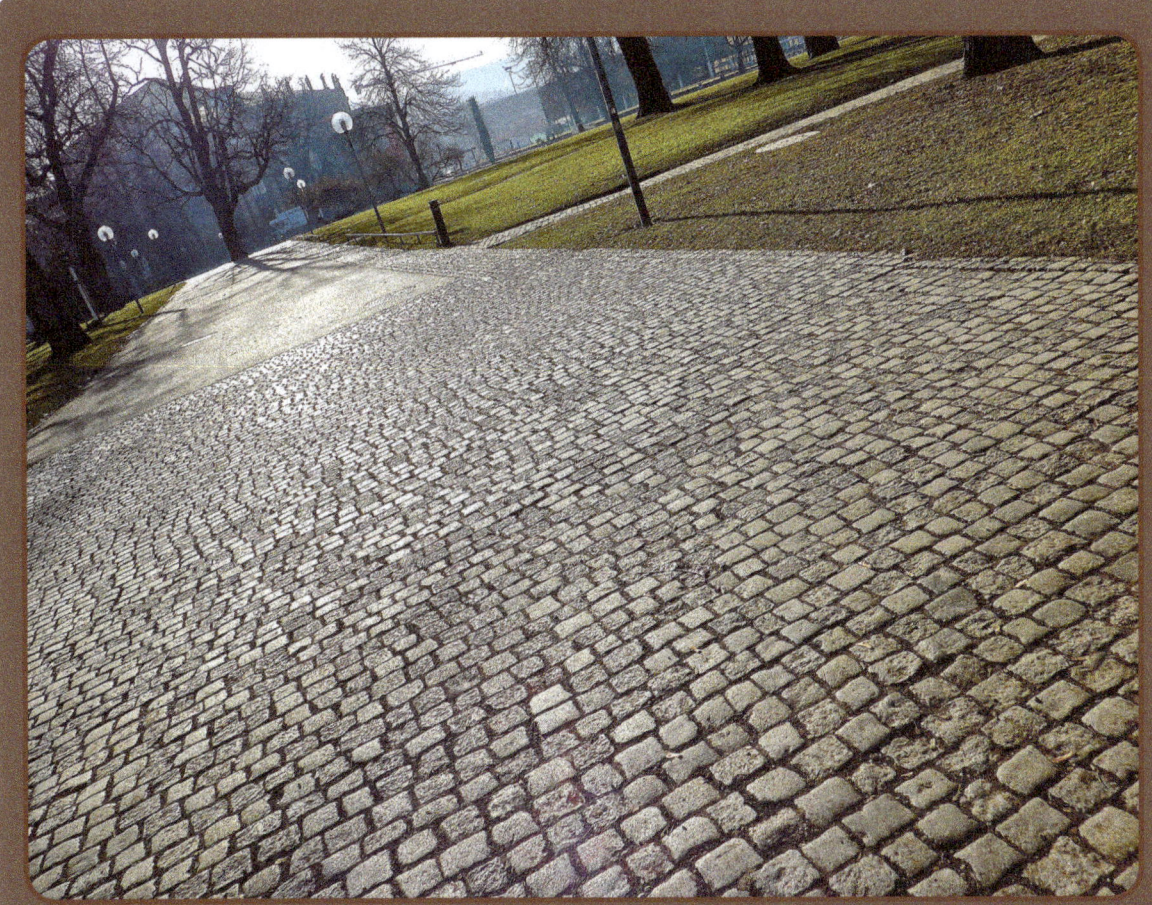

A brick walkway in Stuttgart glints under the warm morning sunshine.

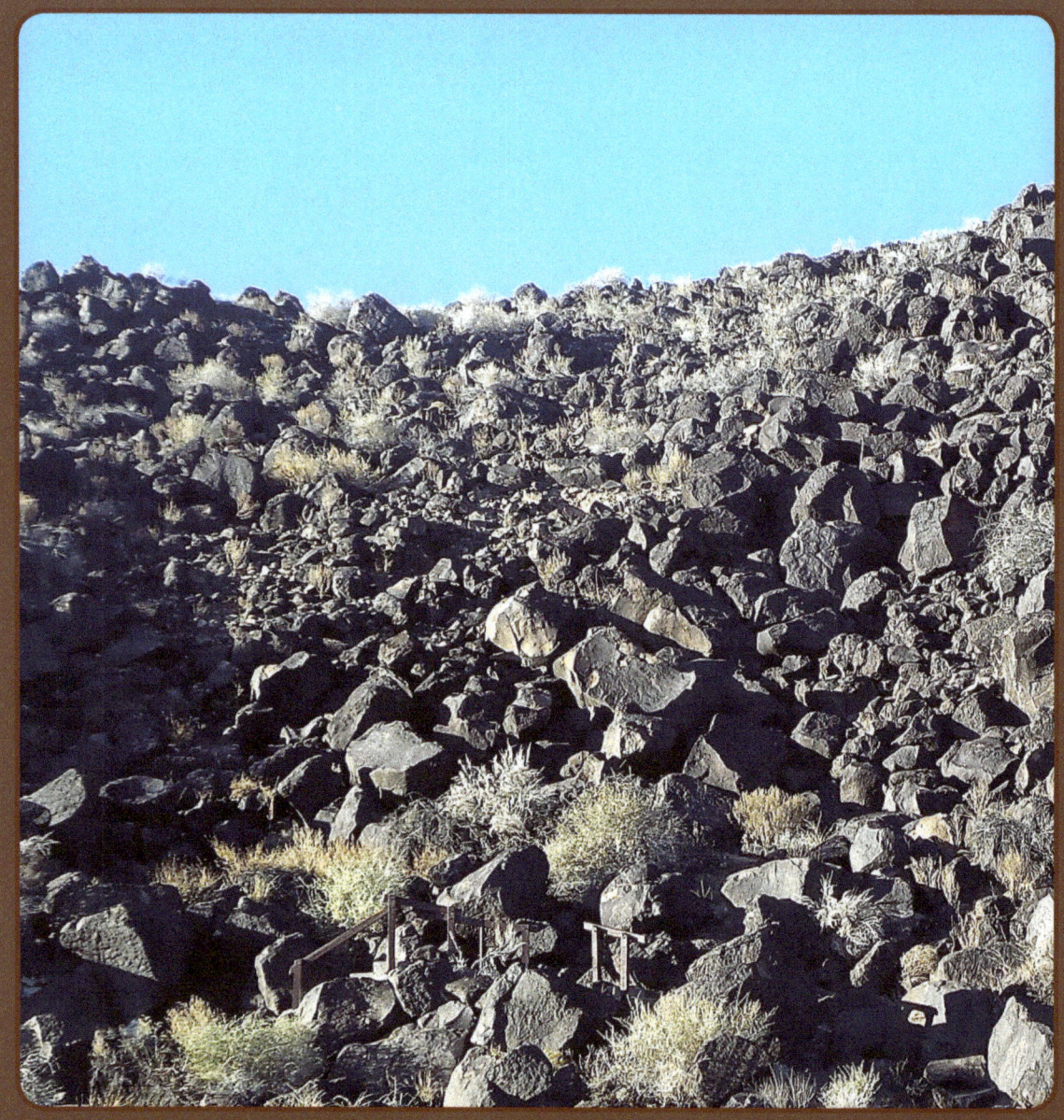
Wooden handrails appear as feeble structures against the overhead might of volcanic boulders in Albuquerque, N.M. at the Petroglyph National Monument, among the largest such sites in North America.

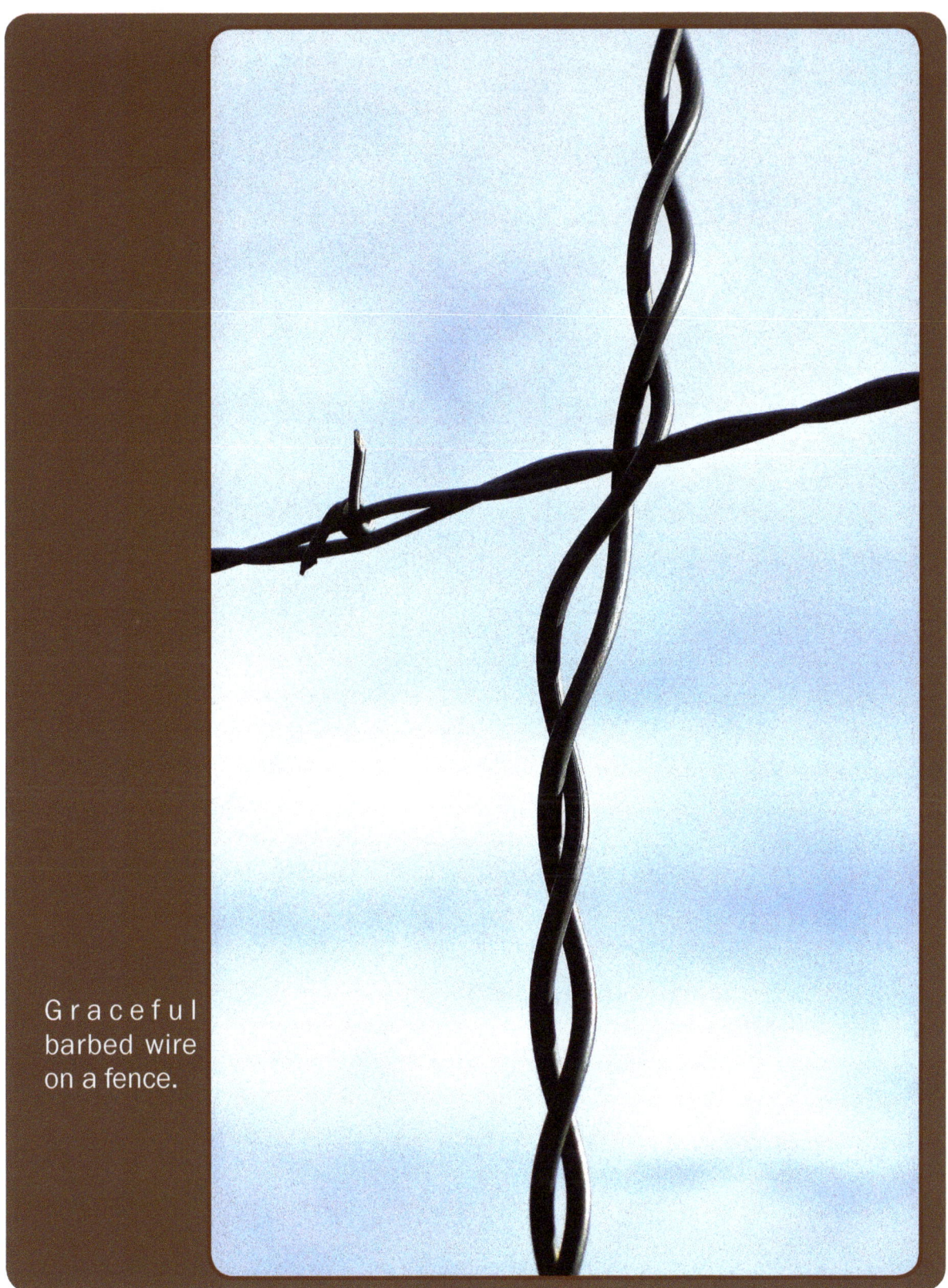

Graceful barbed wire on a fence.

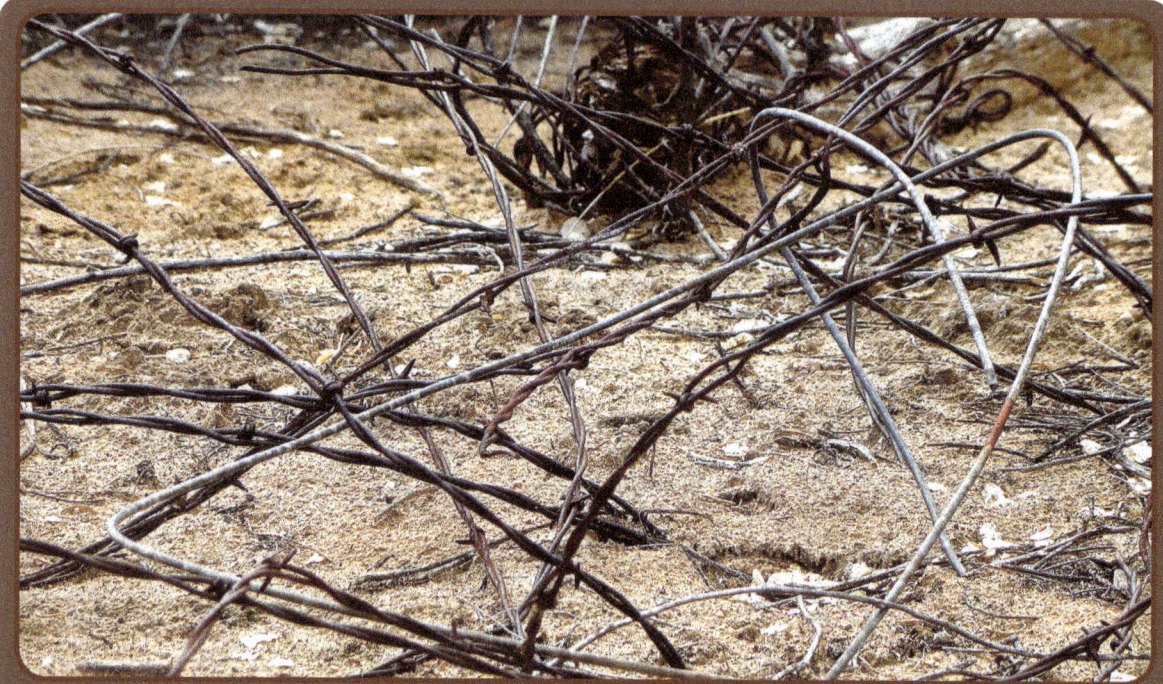
Discarded fence wire rusts in a tangled mess near an area rich with wildlife.

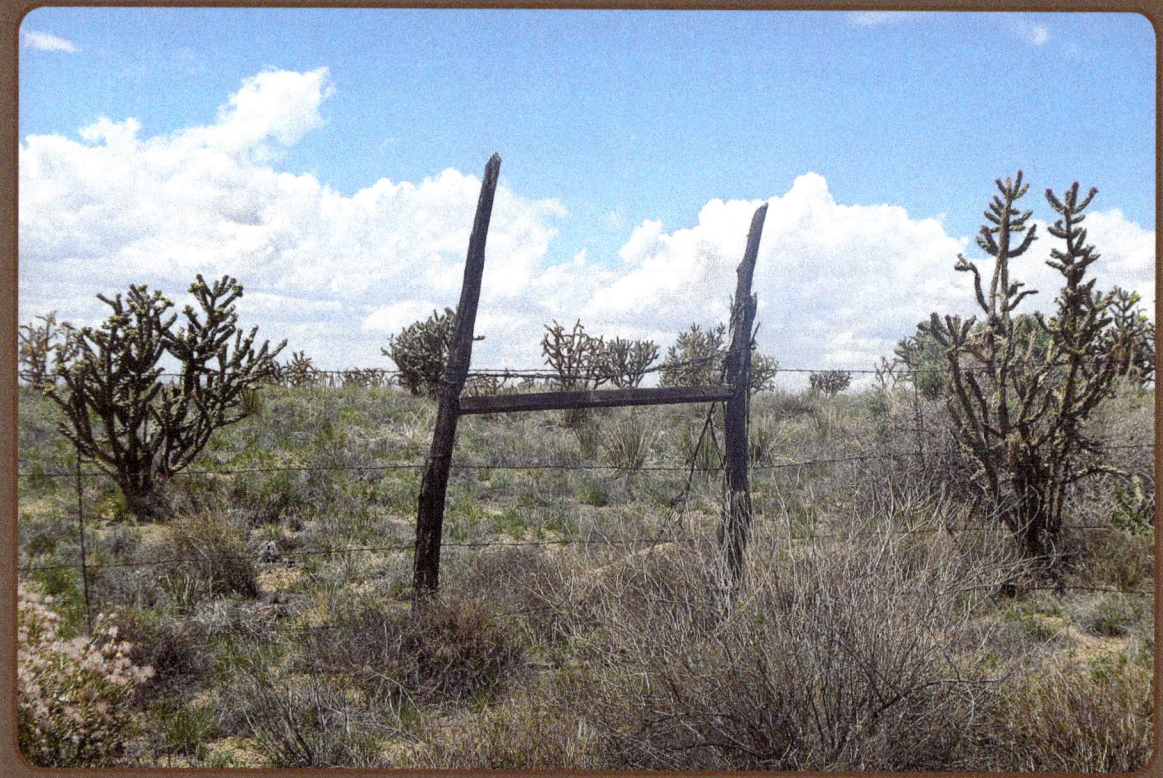
Faded gate posts made of tree branches form the shape of a letter "H" near a wilderness area at the foothills of the mountains.

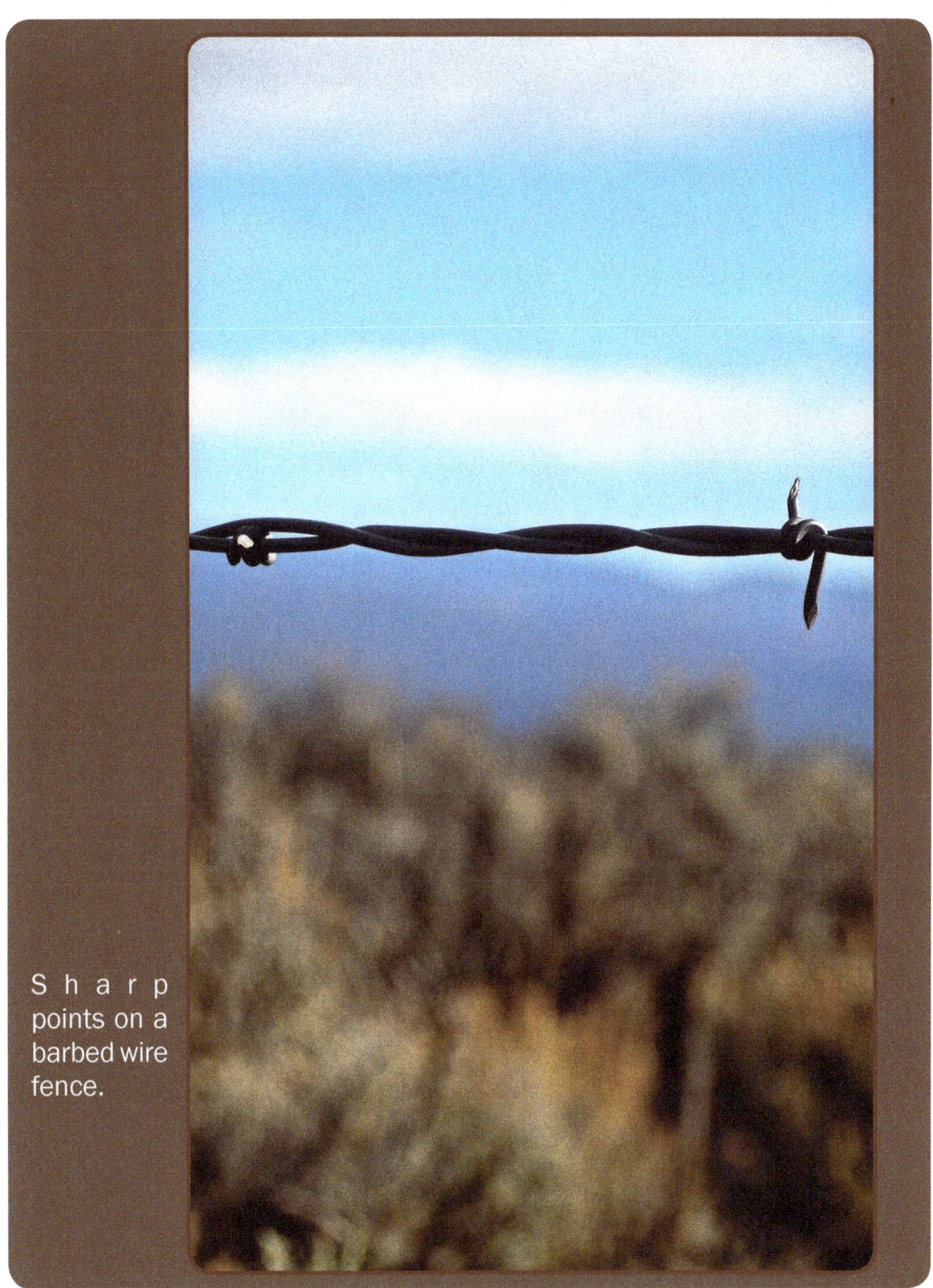

Sharp points on a barbed wire fence.

Rain

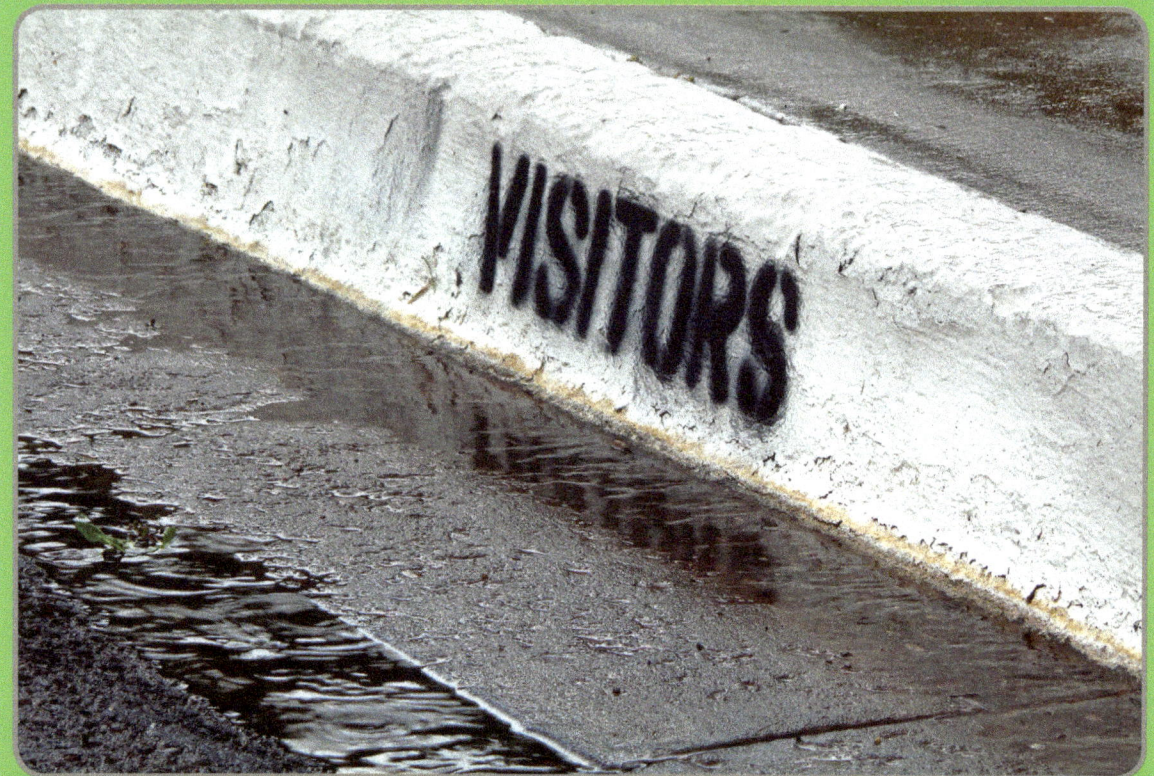

Lettering on a curb reflects on pavement after a rain shower.

Chapter 11:

Pathways in Time: Photo Journeys • 133

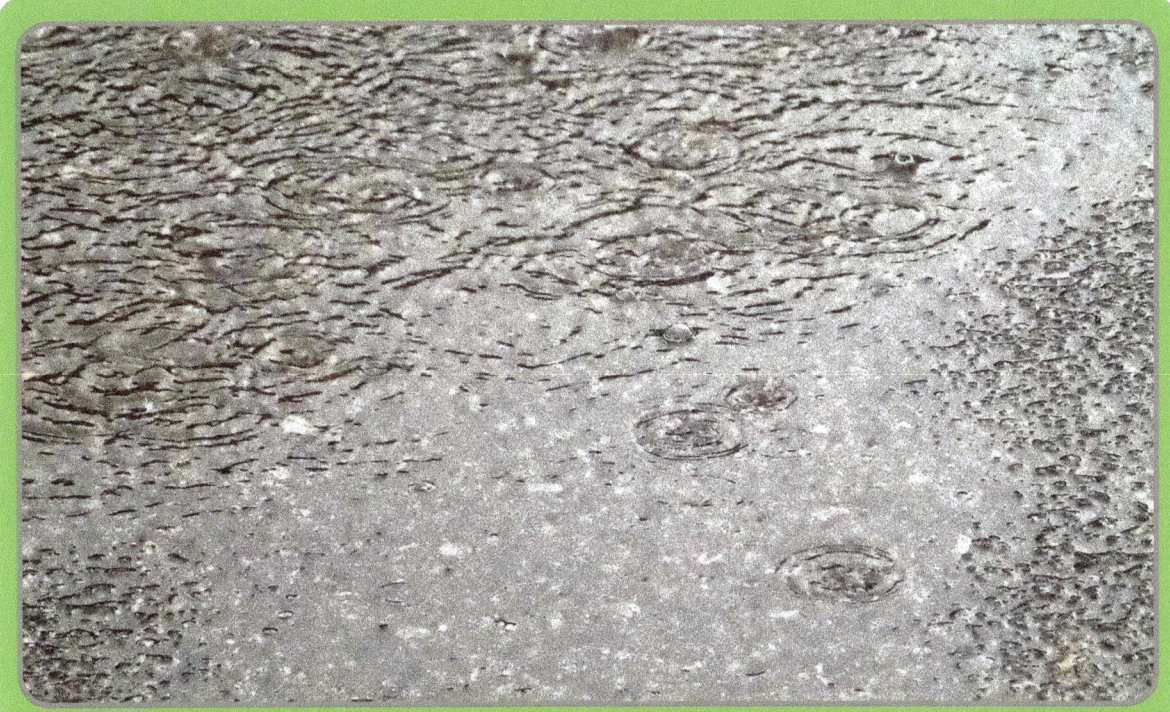

Rain pellets hit the bull's-eye.

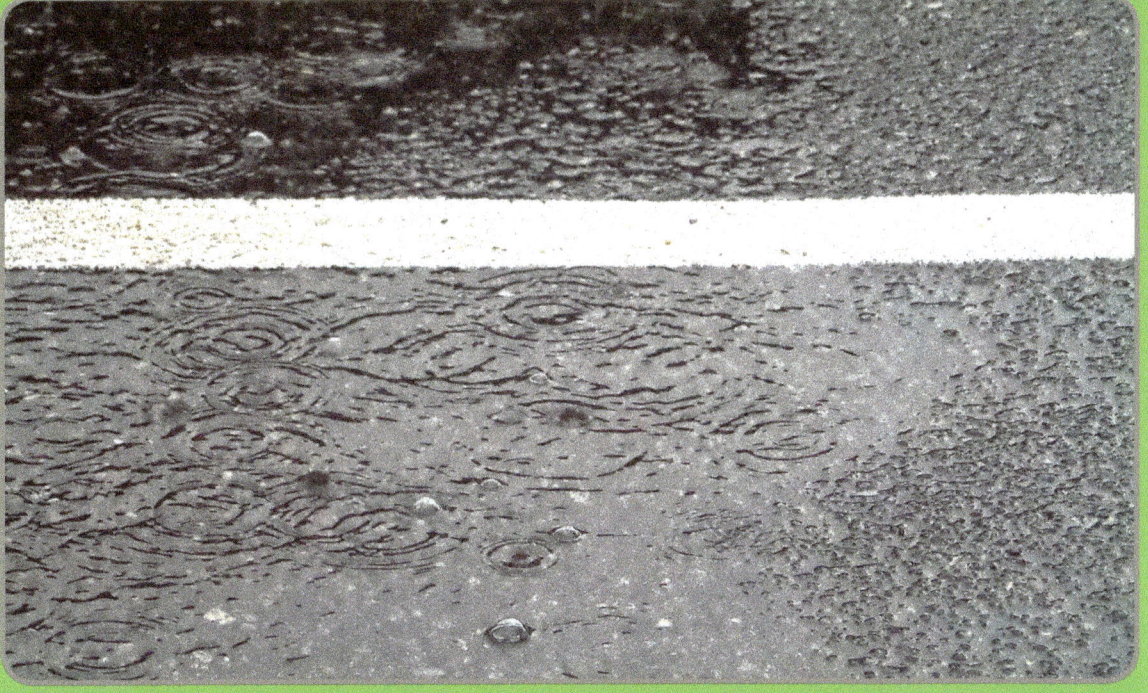

Raindrops send bubbles moving over a wet parking lot surface.

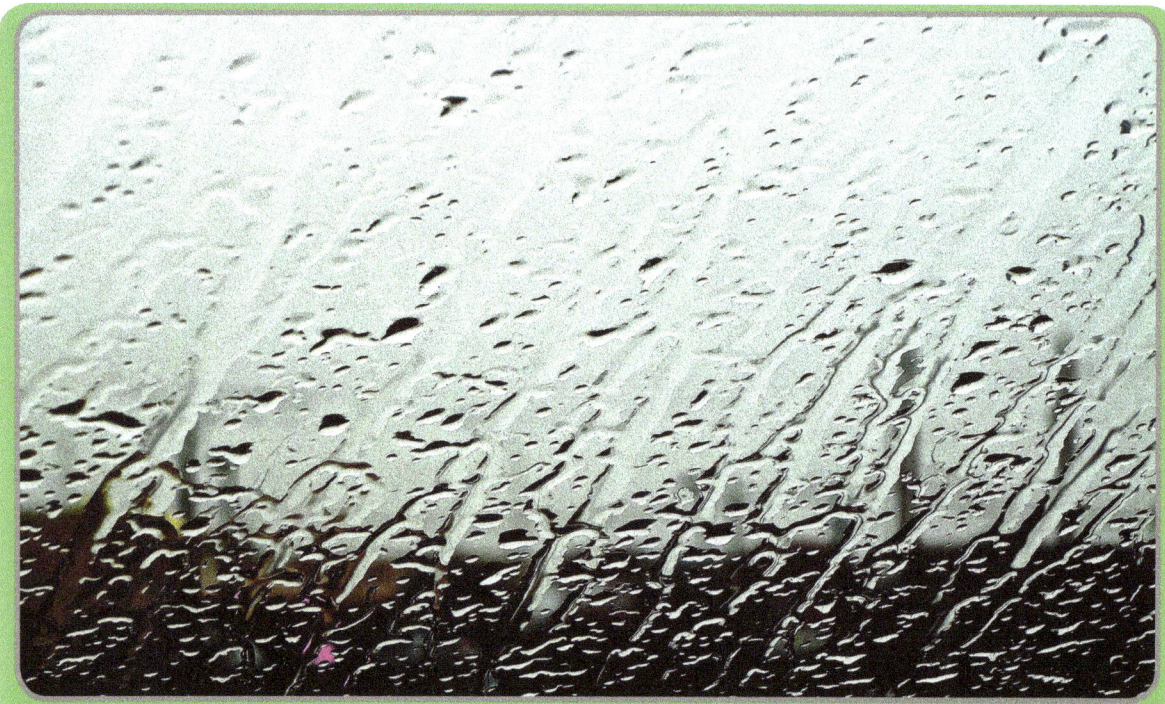
Car windows cry in the rain.

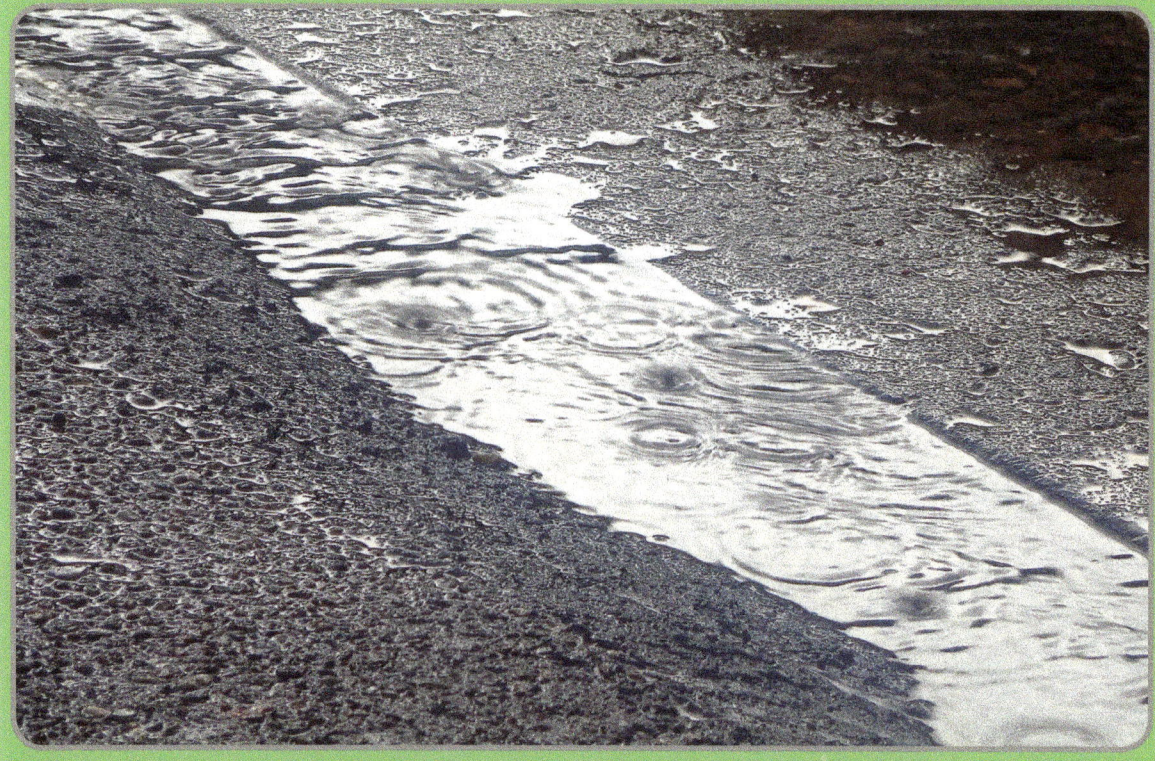
Rainfall makes a street glint like liquid metal.

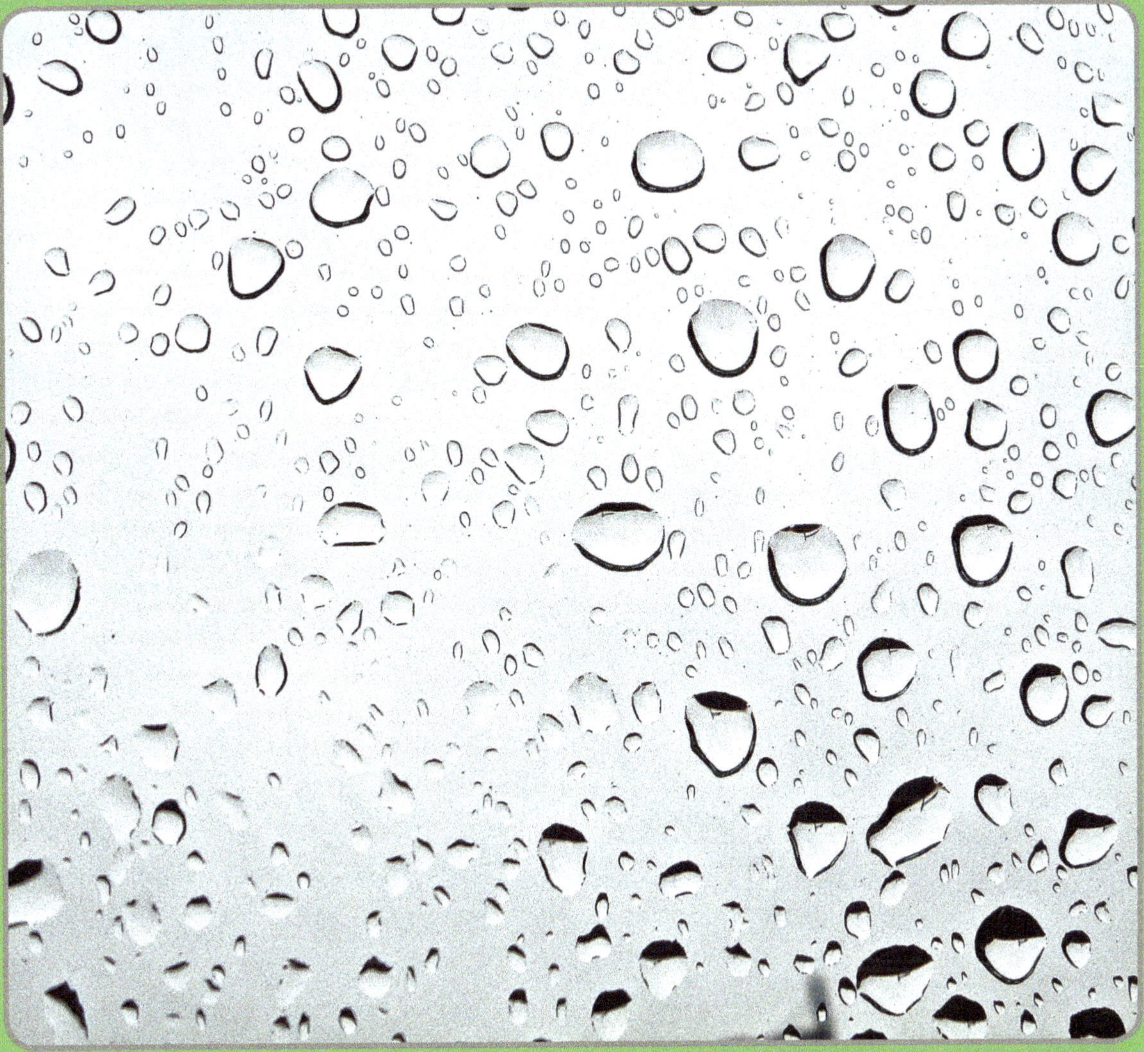

Raindrop families of babies, youths, parents and elders on a car window.

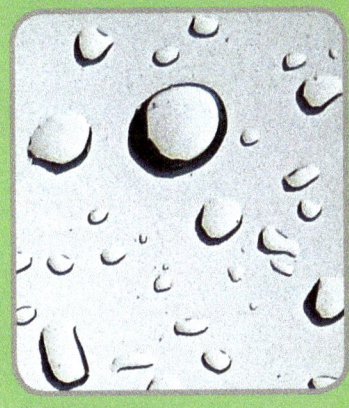

Up close raindrops look like liquid pebbles.

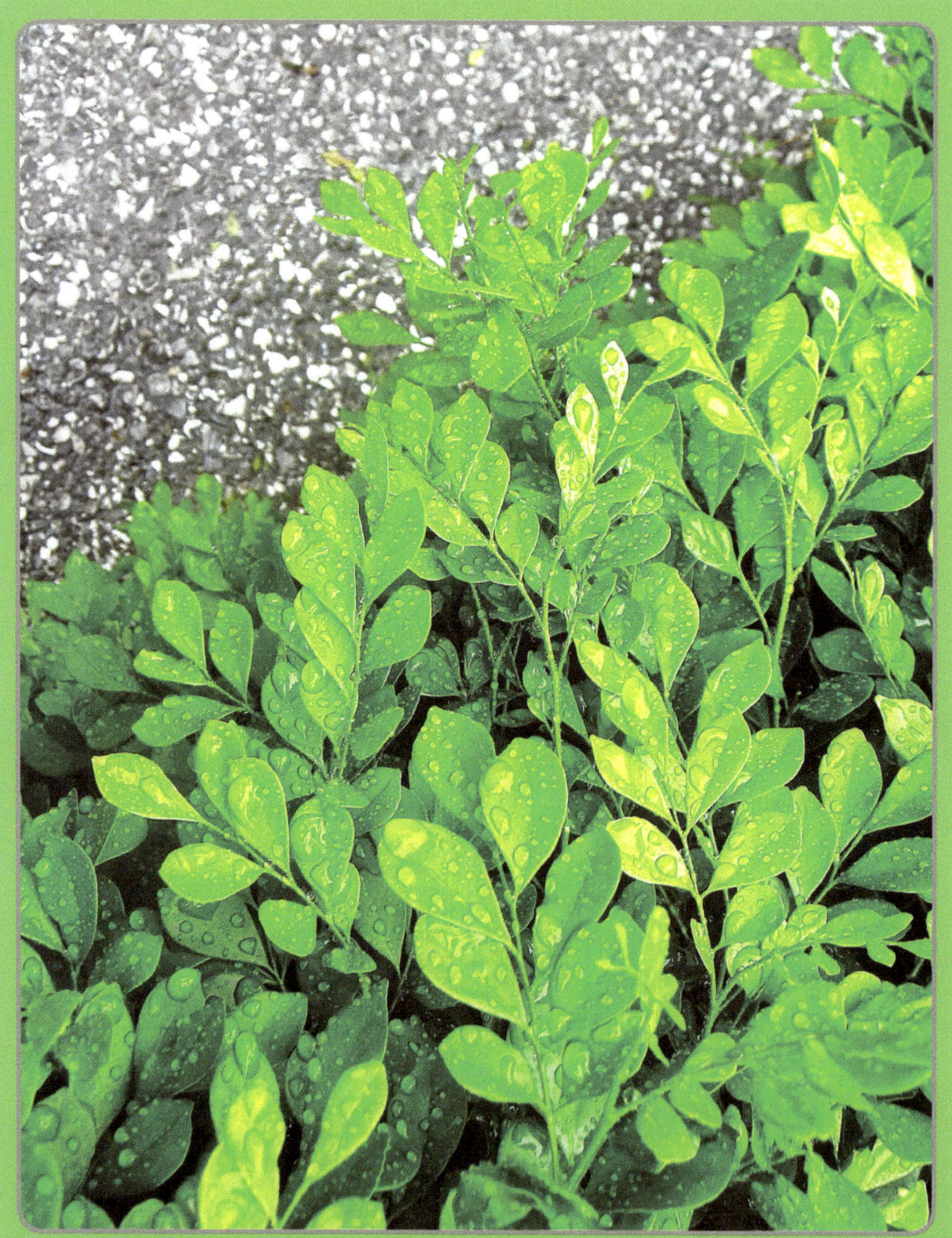
Rain droplets dance on leaves within a museum garden after a cloudburst.

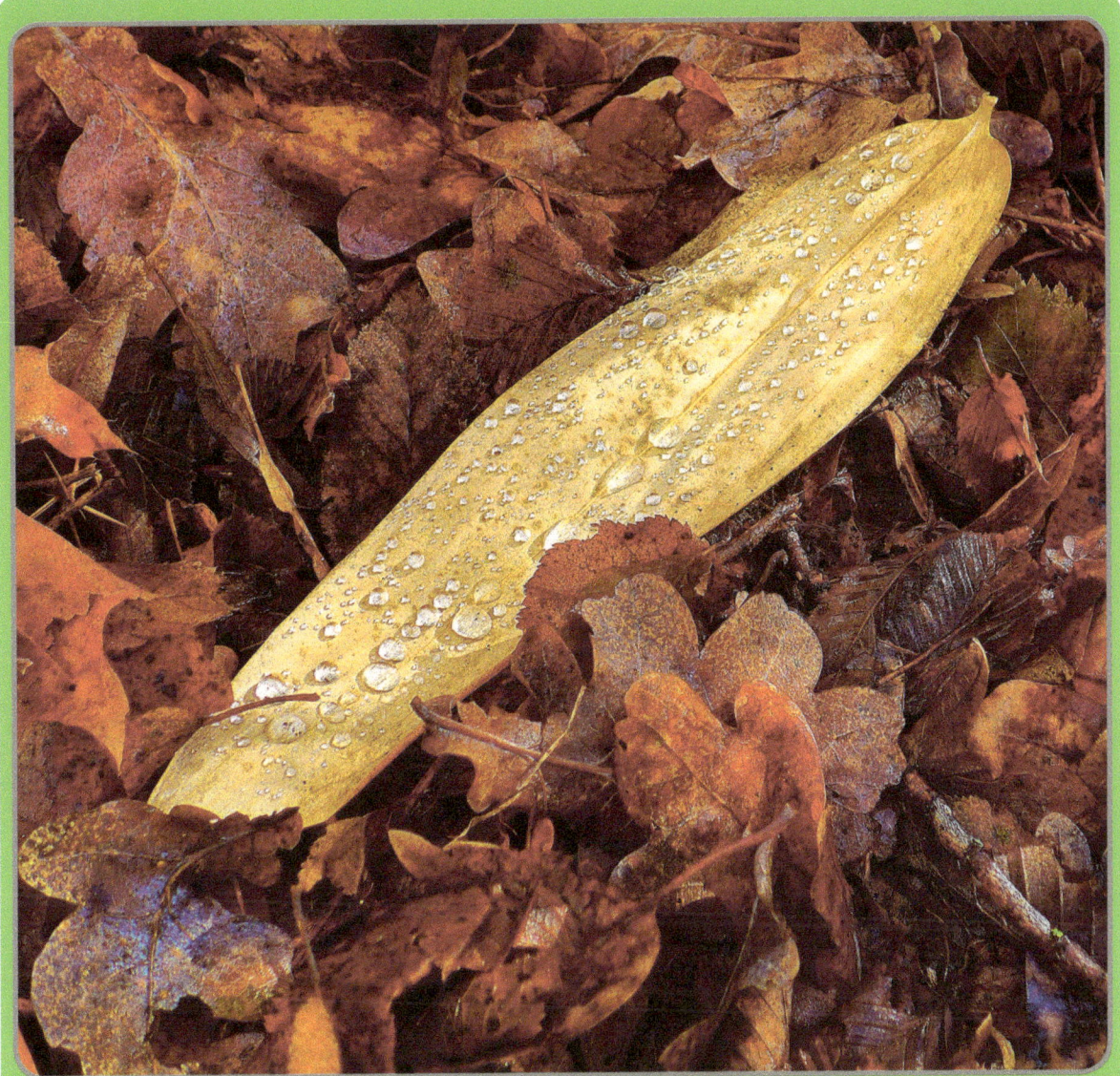

An overnight rain shower leaves behind glass jewels on a leaf next to a sidewalk.

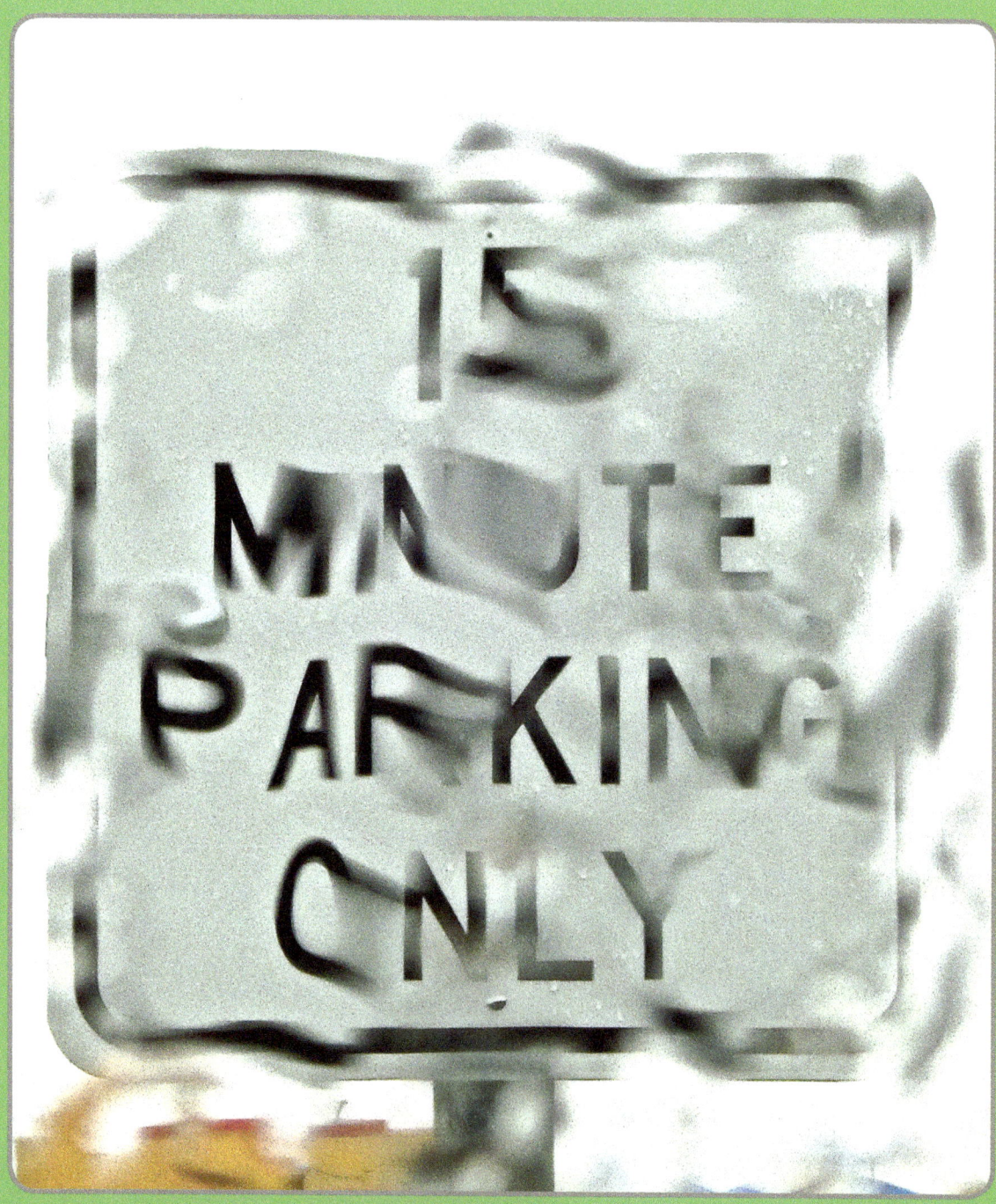

Rain streaks across the outside of a car windshield blur the view of a parking lot sign.

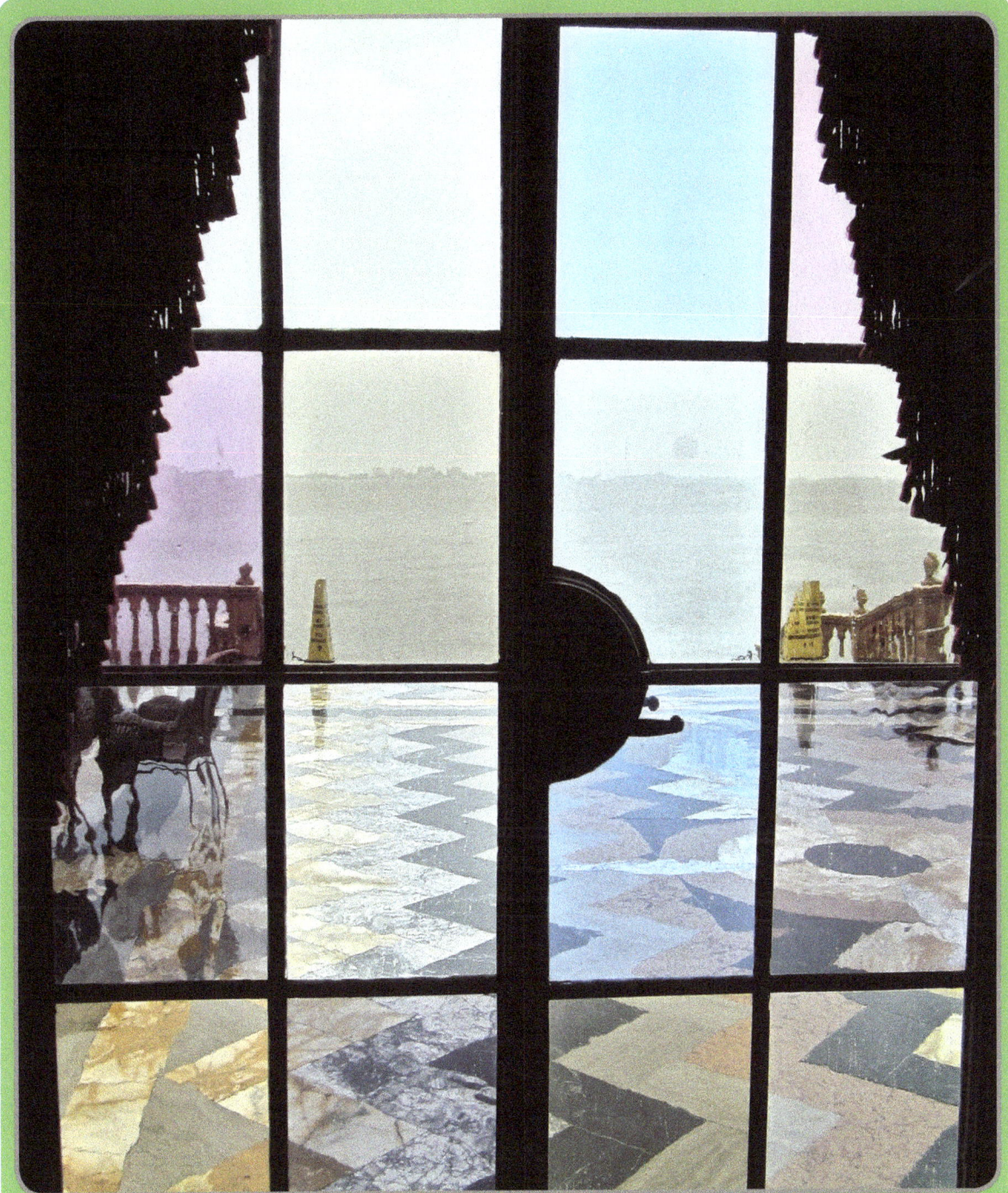

Rainwater reflections on a patio floor create a psychedelic image when viewed inside through a door's glass panes.

About: Me

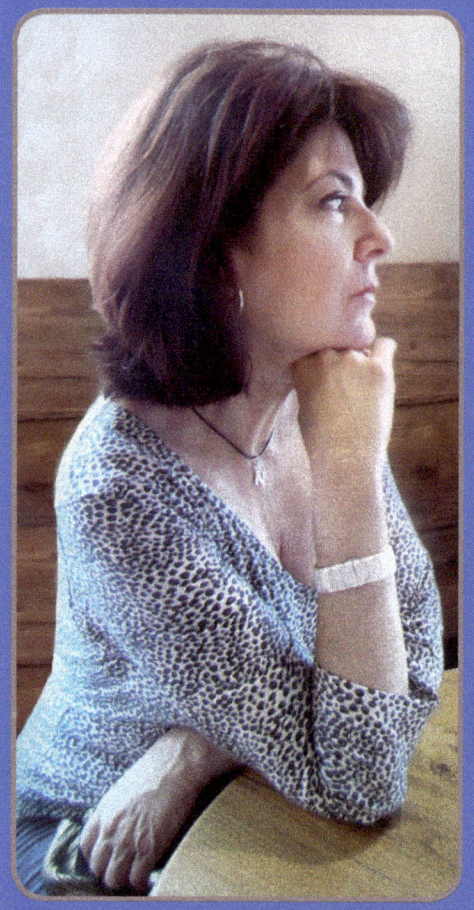

Noël Fletcher is a journalist, author and photographer of Hispanic and English descent. She is from New Mexico, a land rich in rugged beauty and the Southwestern cultural blend of Native Americans, Hispanics, and Anglos.

Her Hispanic ancestors came as Conquistadors to the Rio Grande valley and settled there. Among them were the Perea family of Spanish-Arab origin, who helped found the famed Santa Fe Trail and served in government roles under the Spanish crown, the Mexican era, and the American acquisition.

On her father's side, her Fletcher and Ballinger relatives were early East Coast settlers from England; some from Virginia served in a volunteer militia under the Continental Army during the Revolutionary War.

Early in her career as a journalist, Noël worked through the trenches of daily news coverage at the *Desert Sun* newspaper in Palm Springs, an interesting locale of intrigue and affluence.

A few years later, she left on a whim to Hong Kong—with one suitcase in hand, $200, and the names of four people she'd never met—to become a foreign correspondent in Asia. Within two weeks, she landed a job at the *Hongkong Standard* newspaper covering the Supreme Court, a.k.a. the "High Court." She learned the ropes of the British legal system by reporting on a world populated by red-coated High Court justices, wigged barristers, black-frocked solicitors, and prisoners in the dock. She covered white-collar crime and sensational murder trials as well as the Court of Appeals.

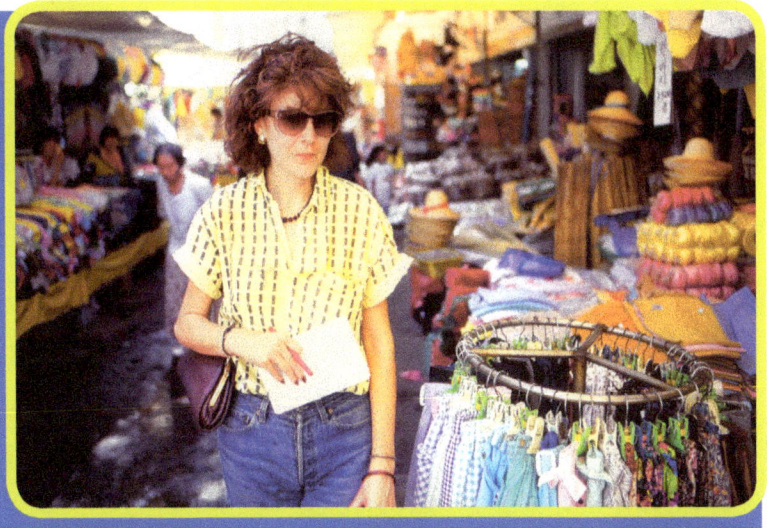

Noël with her reporter's notebook in Hong Kong.

Moving up the ranks as a foreign correspondent, Noël focused on business and financial news, thereby becoming part of an elite American press corps. Her beat was Asia.

She lived and worked in China, Hong Kong, and traveled through many other Asian countries including South Korea and Singapore. She was posted in Beijing as a prestigious "China correspondent" and became fluent in Mandarin. She delved deeper into the art, culture and history of Asia.

Noël experienced a poignant chapter in China's history during the events of the Tiananmen Square Massacre, which took place a few miles from the diplomatic compound where she lived. One of the few American women journalists there, she was on the last U.S. flight evacuated from Beijing and returned to China two weeks later to continue reporting.

Her work as an author, artist and book publisher reflects her interests in art, history, and diverse cultures. Her books often involve investigative research. She seeks to blend visual imagery with writing, including her own artwork and historical images.

Noël's other Books

Captives of the Southwest *by* NOËL FLETCHER

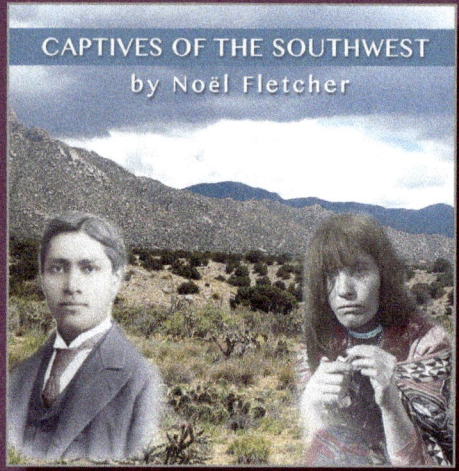

Take a journey into the lives of people who vanished in the Wild West. Explore true stories and eyewitness accounts of the kidnappings and experiences of Anglos, Hispanics, and Native Americans taken captive in New Mexico and the Southwest.

Each chapter takes the reader into a unique setting alongside new casts of characters—including lost settlers, greedy prospectors, elusive desert traders, vigilante lawmen, nomadic tribesmen, courageous women and resilient children. Stunning historical and modern photographs provide vivid glimpses into the life of each captive and the environments they experienced.

Author and researcher Noël Fletcher provides a local perspective and expert analysis for events and stories. Interesting historical details and rare images of key people and places are described.

A rare gem for readers of Wild West history containing gripping tales of adventure, hardship, courage and personal sacrifice. Included are rich illustrations including 115 historic photos, 14 maps, 35 news articles, 40+ modern photos and more.

River of My Ancestors: The Rio Grande in Pictures
by Noël Fletcher

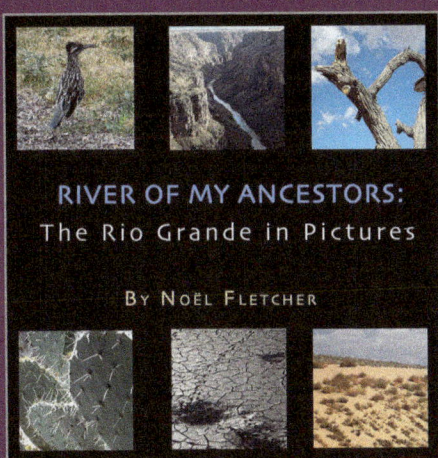

Take a journey along the wild and rugged Rio Grande. Beautiful pictures capture the essence of the famous river and its importance in the arid Southwest. Native New Mexican author and photographer Noël Fletcher provides family stories and insights about frontier life.

Follow the Rio Grande through deserts, wetlands, and rocky cliffs. Experience natural wonders, including volcanic lands and river rapids, and encounter wildlife such as snakes, wolves, cranes, and bighorn sheep. With 180+ striking color photos, the book features:

- Wild West history
- the world's largest cottonwood forest
- the legendary Rio Grande Gorge
- Spanish colonial irrigation systems
- Bosque del Apache National Wildlife Refuge
- Unique wildlife and plants
- Oral tradition from Spanish settlers and family stories
- Interesting facts about New Mexico, local culture, and life along the Rio Grande

This captivating book combines vivid photos and the written word to tell a living history of the famous Rio Grande and the beautiful desert land of New Mexico.

The Strange Side of War
by SARAH MACNAUGHTAN & NOËL FLETCHER

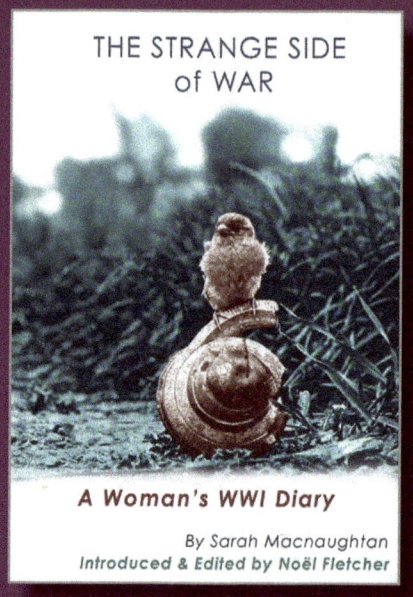

    Take a journey across the dangerous battlefields of a world at war. Accompany Scottish novelist Sarah Macnaughtan as she volunteers alongside British humanitarian groups to alleviate the suffering in war-torn lands. Her many adventures tell unique stories of tragedy and triumph, taking readers on an unforgettable journey from the trenches of Belgium to the distant frontiers of Persia and tsarist Russia.

    Author/editor Noël Fletcher provides new historical context that brings Sarah's story to life and helps readers to remember the bravery and sacrifice of those who died. Illustrated with 130+ rare photos and propaganda posters from World War I, this important work features historical insights about the people and places involved in the conflict.

Two Years in the Forbidden City

by PRINCESS DER LING

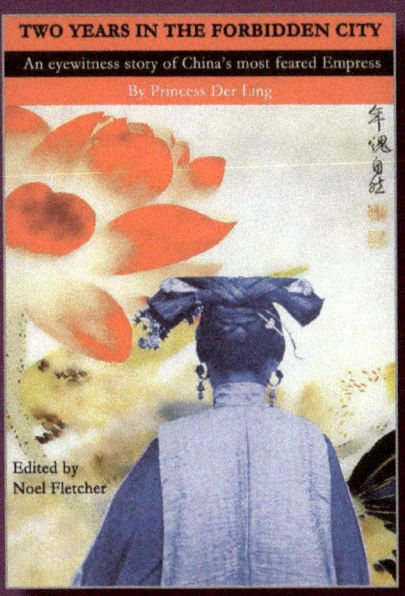

  This true story was the first eyewitness account of the Imperial Court written by a Chinese aristocrat for Western readers. It provides an up-close view of the notorious Dowager Empress Tzu-hsi in her final years. Enhanced with rich imagery and additional historical notes, it includes interesting historical details and photos about China's infamous Dowager Empress, the Boxer Rebellion and the Imperial Court. It is illustrated with 100+ historical photographs, illustrations, and paintings from the late 1800s to early 1900s.

  Author/editor Noël Fletcher that provides context for this book in modern Chinese history.

More Books
from
Fletcher & Co. Publishers

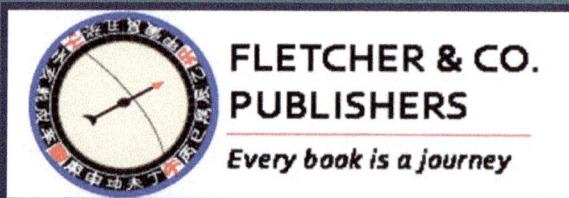

Every book is a journey. Fletcher & Co. Publishers is an independent, art-house publishing company. We use new media and graphic design techniques to transport you into the world of the novel.

Our books aren't just written words. They're experiences: international cultures, art, suspense, history, and adventure.

Watch our video trailers on YouTube and Vimeo to preview each book, see interesting images, and learn more about our newest releases.

Visit us our website to find out about our latest news.

Edge of Suspicion *by* ZITA STEELE

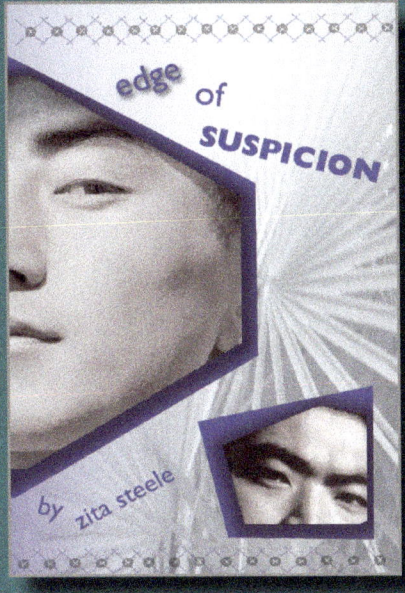

 Justin Moon of South Korea is the world's top private eye. He travels to Singapore to catch an elusive cybercriminal. The pay is lucrative. His client is an attractive blonde CEO. It should be the easiest job in his career. Things get complicated with the arrival of Okada, a mysterious drifter with a mission of revenge. As Moon tries to solve the mystery, he uncovers a tangled maze of deceit.

 Each new clue leads him in an unpredictable direction. A deadly game of cat-and-mouse begins.

 Featuring over 100 photos, *"Edge of Suspicion"* is both an exciting story and a work of art.

Envoy: Rule of Silence *by* Zita Steele

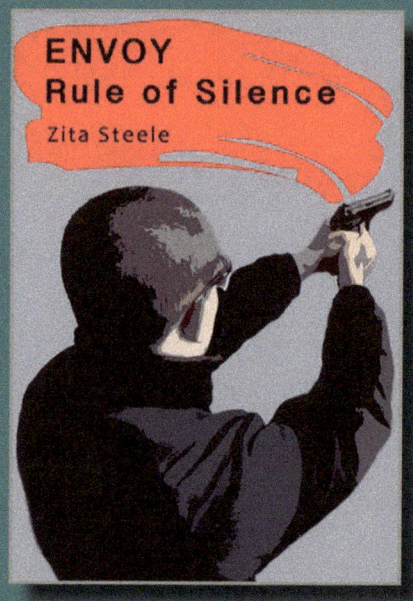

Take a journey into a thrilling world of secrets and lies in modern-day Europe. Polish ex-secret policeman Michal Krynski is tired of working as a double agent for France's security bureau.

His last mission — to track down a runaway DJ. As he travels to the strange island of Malta, Krynski plots revenge against the system that ruined his life. Will he catch the DJ or kill him?

Zita Steele is a novelist and artist. She writes with an expertise in criminology, cybercrime, and international relations. She creates her own illustrations.

Diné: A Tribute to the Navajo People *by* Zita Steele

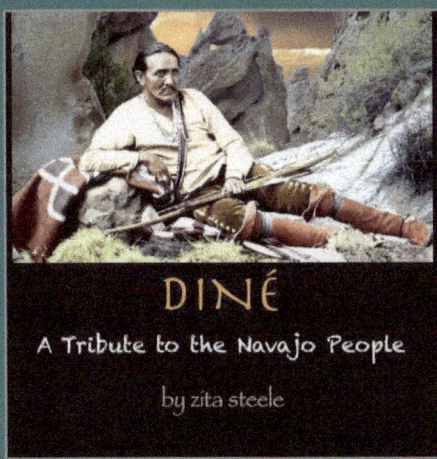

    Take a journey into natural freedom and beauty in this tribute to one of America's most vibrant nomadic tribes. Author/artist Zita Steele commemorates the Diné (Navajo) people of the Southwestern United States with a vivid collection of color images. Four chapters honor the Native American tribe's freedom, ingenuity, strength, and joy.

    The images create an experience of nomadic life without reservations or borders. The book provides insights into Diné culture and highlights the tribe's vast ancestral roaming territory.

    Features include: 40+ original photographs, 25+ photo montages and special introduction by the author and additional artwork

Erwin Rommel Photographer Vol. 1: A Survey
by ERWIN ROMMEL AND ZITA STEELE

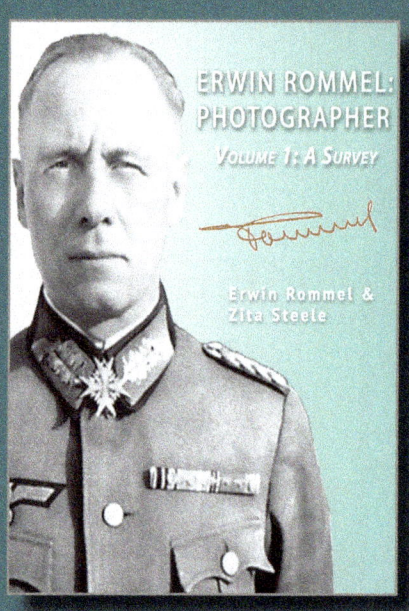

Take a journey behind the camera of a world-famous military commander. Experience WWII firsthand from Field Marshal Rommel's private photo collection, seized by U.S. forces in 1945. View 340+ images, including photos Rommel took during campaigns in France and North Africa and others he collected. Included are Rommel's personal photos of family and friends. The photos are digitally restored for detail. Some are accompanied by Rommel's own handwritten photo captions.

Author/artist Zita Steele uses her knowledge of German language and culture, with in-depth research about Rommel and his campaigns, to provide context for the photos. Zita also analyzes patterns in Rommel's photography to shed a light on the artistic personality of this notable military leader.

Erwin Rommel Photographer Vol. 2: Rommel & His Men
by ERWIN ROMMEL AND ZITA STEELE

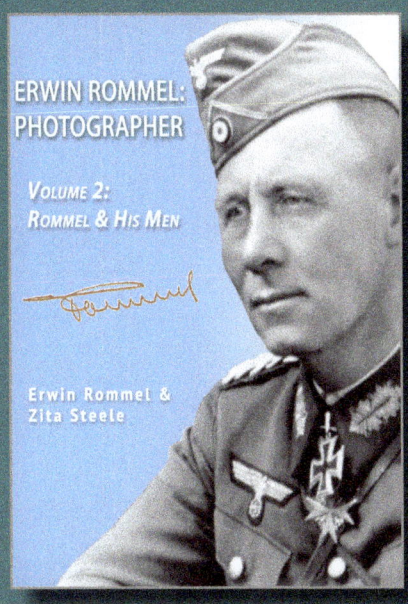

Experience life on the frontlines with Field Marshal Erwin Rommel. View 200+ images from Rommel's private photo collection, seized by U.S. forces in 1945.

Join Rommel as he interacts with his German and Italian troops. See him and his men at work, at rest, and on the move. View Rommel's mementos of his men and military leaders.

This book provides a candid view of Rommel as an ordinary soldier rather than a general. The photos are digitally restored and enhanced for detail. Some are accompanied by Rommel's own handwritten photo captions.

Erwin Rommel Photographer Vol. 3: Adventures in Color

by ERWIN ROMMEL AND ZITA STEELE

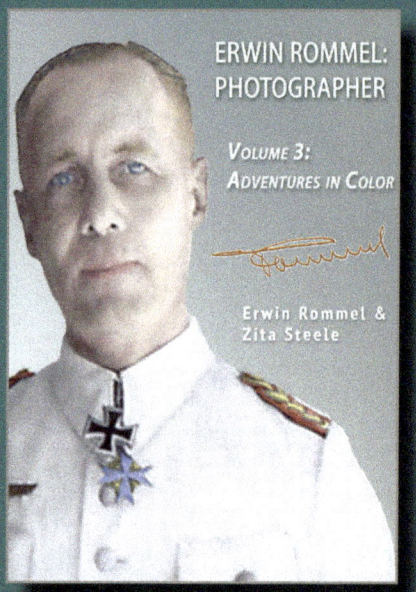

Join Field Marshal Erwin Rommel in WWII through his rare color photographs. View 130 color images from Rommel's private photo collection, seized by U.S. forces in 1945, and a selection of Rommel's hand-drawn sketches of his war experiences. Join Rommel as he travels across vast and colorful terrains, flies a dive bomber plane, drives across desert battlefields and explores North African villages. The photos and sketches are digitally restored and enhanced for detail.

Also included are 10 original sketches by Rommel as well as historical facts and analysis.

The Spy *by* JAMES FENIMORE COOPER

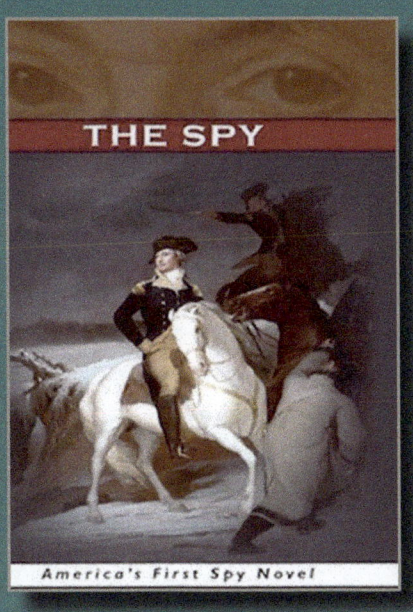

    During the dark days of the Revolutionary War, America struggles for nationhood. Meanwhile, in the shadows, a spy is trading secrets of vital importance to the cause — but for whose side? Colonials and loyalists play a game of cloak and daggers in America's first spy novel. Our edition features 30+ color photographs, chapter titles, and illuminating notations, designed to give you a front-seat experience.

    This was the first major fiction novel on espionage ever written and published in America and an important milestone for fiction writing.

Lantern of the Wicked *by* CHARLES CLEMENT

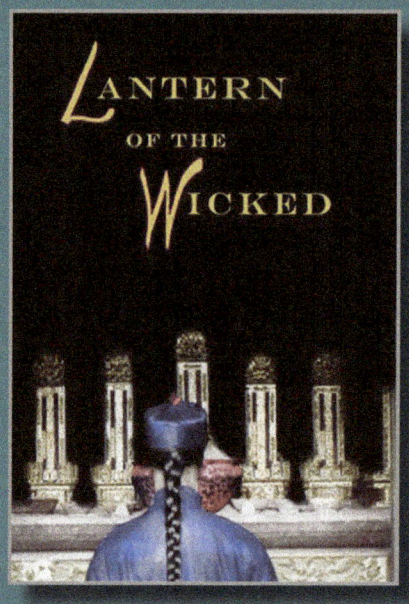

 In the decadent and dangerous Shanghai of 1929, someone is spying for the Japanese, and the International Settlement's British police are on the hunt. Now, in the midst of the Mid-Autumn Moon Festival, American aviator Jack "Ace" Jordan becomes the prime suspect.

 A thrilling narrative blending fact, fiction and rare photographs, *"Lantern of the Wicked"* creates an atmospheric window into the complexity and dark grandeur of the colonial Orient in this gripping historical mystery.

Mystery of the Yellow Room *by* GASTON LEROUX

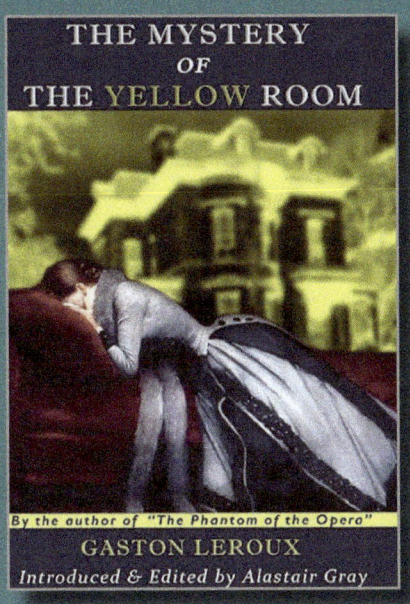

    News of a strange crime spreads like wildfire in Paris. Someone has attempted to murder the daughter of a brilliant scientist. But nobody can explain how the murderer got in and out of the locked room of her isolated country home. Only Joseph Rouletabille, an impatient young journalist, has the genius to solve this crime.

    Written by the author of *"The Phantom of the Opera,"* this novel was published in 1907 as France's reply to Sherlock Holmes. Our edition has adapted text from archaic Victorian to standard English. It also features updated maps and is illustrated with 30+ historical paintings and illustrations from 19th century France.

New Mexico Ghosts and Haunting Images
by Ariela Desolina

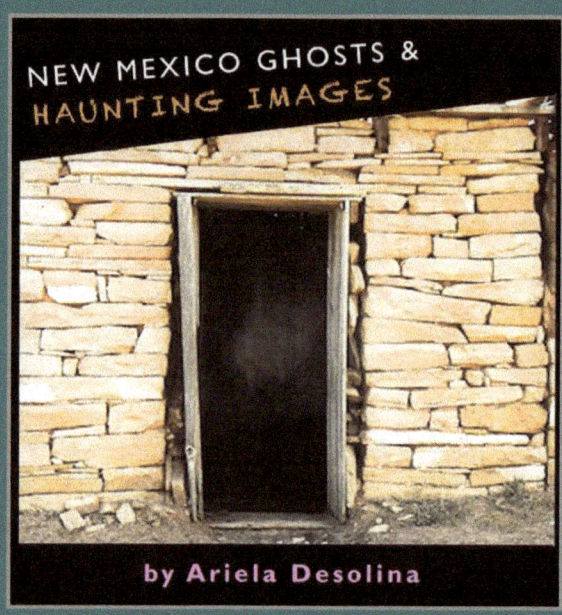

    Let explorer-photographer Ariela Desolina spirit you away to New Mexico, where haunting ruins — some with ghostly inhabitants — will capture your imagination.

    With photos from the St. James Hotel, a notorious hangout of Western outlaws and gamblers, and other mysterious locations.

    Mysterious shapes and ghostly forms (undetected when the pictures were taken) sometimes appear in her photos. Includes photos of the haunted ruins of the Kelly Mine, once among the richest old gold and silver mines in the Southwest.